AMERICA,
AS I KNOW IT

by
R. I. Mansfield

AUTHOR'S NOTE:
For a pretty good look at the foundation of 20th Century American character, look no further than the excellent work of my friends, H. L. Mencken, George Ade, and H. Allen Smith.

ESTUARY PUBLICATIONS
ISBN: 9781077247147
© 2021 estuarypublications.com

Give a man a fish, and you've fed him for a day. Give him a book, and you've given him a doorstop.

CONTENTS

"Ce que l'on conçoit bien s'énonce clairement."
Nicolas Boileau-Despréaux, 1674
That which is truly understood can be expressed clearly.

PREFACE [don't worry, nobody else reads this part either]

The title of this book is: America, as I know it. It is merely, solely, and nothing more than a collection of stories about my personal experiences regarding a variety of things that seem to be nagging some of us these days (race, drugs, guns, that sort of thing). The answer to those various concerns is not found in ideology or wishful thinking but in American character, with its limited capacity for injustice and the presumption of Liberty.

Americans are fiercely independent individuals, naturally resistant to authority, and particularly distrustful of government. They are willing to do what's necessary to protect their own. Those I've known always say what they mean and mean what they say. They live by two simple admonitions: Mind your own business, and Keep your thoughts to yourself. At once, Americans remain open to other points of view and are always willing to help one another. In general, I believe, we tend to look at each other and see ourselves.

Those traits imbue us with a form of humor which is—I have always somehow felt—naturally and particularly American.

When heroes are found here, their heroics may be of the quietest sort; small actions taken or words spoken which reveal an underlying morality that makes them both typically American and (for that very reason) well worth remembering.

There are also stories here that display regrettable weakness—usually on my part—thus establishing a dark background against which true American character sparkles all the more brightly.

This is America, as I know it; you can draw your own conclusions. I'm not selling anything.

R M

One final note: Those events told to me by my father can be taken as fact, pure and simple.

AMERICA,

AS I KNOW IT

HATRED in AMERICA,
as I know it

THE GRANDE DAME (1968)

I'd been in Richmond for eight months when one bright, sunny Sunday morning (around Easter), my very timid, truly lovely, Southern girlfriend Joanie and I were strolling arm-in-arm, down Monument Avenue.

She—as described by her closest friend—was as shy as can be, frail as a tea cup, very pretty, very very sweet, and had been, before we met—according to that same friend—simply dying inside for the want of meeting me. Joanie was very much like an angel. In truth, angels could have learned a thing or two from her about sweetness and composure. She was more timid than I and, honestly, though skinny, awkward and unsure, I was her champion. One could hardly find two more innocent or more harmless people.

It had just turned spring and we were softly, sweetly, deeply, purely in love. The birds were chirping away in the newly flowering trees, the sky above was blue, there was a gentle breeze; it could not have been more idyllic. Monument Avenue was exquisite! In those days (before the madness), huge bronze equestrian statues rose up on islands at the end of every block. All along that boulevard of white stone mansions, noble Confederate Generals on proudly prancing horse—sword drawn, eyes ablaze with assured victory, all defiance and indefatigable determination—stood as a reminder of the highly esteemed long-past Southern order.

So there we were, two innocents in love, strolling along in the spring, surrounded by trees, heroic statues, and large stately mansions with perfectly manicured lawns. On the sidewalk ahead, tottering slowly toward us, is a tiny (tiny) ancient (ancient) gentlewoman (a gentle woman).

She has on her white kid gloves, because it is Sunday; because it is spring, her broad brimmed flower bestrewn chapeau; because she is an aristocrat, a nice dress with lace at the collar and sleeves. Her suit is of a pink nubby material that we've all seen before on the cover of Vogue. She is unquestionably, immediately recognizable as precisely what she is: venerable, old Richmond, First Family Virginia, nobility. She's on her way home, fresh from church.

As we get close, Joanie—a true Southern belle and brought up properly—bows to this Grande Dame and says sweetly, "Why, good morning, Ma'am." Her words ooze a syrupy Southern charm.

This tiny, rheumy-eyed, frail old creature stops in front of us, smiles broadly at Joanie; there is a twinkle in her eye. She reaches out with one little nicely gloved hand and touches Joanie's wrist. In a kindly old voice with a slight quaver to it she says, "Why, good morning to you dear. How are you?"
It's as if they have known each other for years. These two Southern belles, though they've never met before, share an assumed gentility.

Joanie says, "It's a lovely day, Ma'am."
"Yes, dear," says the gentlewoman, "it most certainly IS a lovely day." She beams as she looks around to admire the day that the Lord has given us.

I'm smiling during this exchange, because; I'm an idiot and I'm in love and I'm watching something I've never witnessed before. This doesn't even seem real to me.

I've only seen such exemplary courtesy before in old movies.

Where I come from two women passing each other on the sidewalk seldom exchange words; they may grunt; occasionally one of them will spit—a sign at once of recognition and utter disregard—or mutter something under her breath. So, Southern charm is all new to me.

So, I'm smiling down at this kindly little old woman, this minuscule, fragile, gentle, distinguished, Southern aristocrat, and she looks up at me. She begins to quiver; she points a shaking gloved finger directly at my face, dead center, and she says, "I can remember a time when we didn't allow NIGGERS to walk on this street, let alone people like YOU!"

It is difficult for me to convey the viciousness behind that statement, but, that is precisely, word for word, what the grand old lady, remnant of the great and glorious South, said to me on that lovely spring day. She shook with rage as she said it.

This demands some explanation. In those halcyon days, due to some peculiar glitch in the American psyche, there was no greater crime on earth than for a male to have long hair. To have any hair touching your ears was a particularly vile, unforgivable, near criminal affront to every sniveling soul in the country. We were looked down upon by the lowest, and mocked by the most ignorant segments of our society. At home, previously loving, previously reasonable, parents struggled with the enormity of the problem; straining to see, underneath all that growth, the son they'd raised right and had once loved without confusion. (Apparently, we were a nation with a lot of time on its hands.)

So, yes, there I was, the epitome of all things vile, the physical embodiment of Evil itself. In the eyes of the respectable South, I am despicable; I am the enemy.
Here's the strange part: throughout all of this the old aristocrat still has Joanie by the hand.

She's clinging to my girlfriend as she stands there, shaking with an uncontrollable fury. While she's snapping and snarling and sputtering and throwing off saliva in all directions, she's leaning on Joanie. Her watery old yellowed eyes are locked in on mine, and the frail old bat is challenging me. She's got her chin up, her jaw set, while she awaits my response.

I'm an eighteen year old, six foot tall, 160 pound man.

After staring at me with revulsion long enough for me to get the point, she shakes her blue-grey head in disgust, forcefully pushes her way between us, and totters off, down Monument Avenue. (I'd like to say that she spit on the sidewalk, but she didn't. I'm pretty sure she could have, though. That would have been a nice touch, for my purposes here.)

When she first approached us, I smiled nicely and bowed a goofy little kind of bow. And while the ladies exchanged pleasantries, I stood in silence with my hands folded neatly, properly, in front of me—a fixed grin plastered idiot-like on my amiable, pale, pock-marked face. I was just as nice as can be. While these two examples of code-encrusted social order exchanged niceties, on that particular beautiful sunny Sunday morning, I was the perfect gentleman. I had no idea how it had come to this.

As a child I had been taught a special deference toward females and exceptional consideration for old ladies. At no time, however, did anyone ever tell me such creatures could be vicious. (And, I wouldn't have guessed it either.) So the fear that this particular old woman planted in my heart, at that moment, on that day, was near catastrophic. None of my upbringing had prepared me for meeting this tiny spuming Southern aristocrat on the sidewalk, on Monument Avenue, in Richmond, Virginia, on a lovely Sunday, in the spring.

Of course, to be fair, nothing in her time here on earth had prepared our grande dame for running into anything as shameful, as disgraceful, as foul and disgusting as me. She just wasn't ready for it; Sunday morning wasn't ready for it; Monument Avenue wasn't ready for it; Richmond wasn't ready for it. It must have only irritated her more to see that I had a lovely little Southern girl clinging lovingly to my arm.

In those days, real hippies were seen driving around Richmond, the sides of their bus painted with the slogan: "We've Come For Your Daughters!"—a sign that perfectly expressed the fears of an entire nation—but I wasn't a hippie.

I was a middle class college student. I had never smoked dope, had never taken a drink, and my intentions toward Joanie could not have been more honorable. On this Spring morn, my button-down shirt, cotton twill pants with cuffs, my respectable nicely polished shoes—all of which my mother had purchased for me at J. C. Penny—carried no weight in my defense. My white, middle class background, my solid SAT scores, the tears that filled my eyes when our astronauts were shot hurtling through the atmosphere; the increased rapidity of my pounding heart as the flag of our country waved bravely over a wide swath of chalk-lined green turf while the Star Spangled Banner blared from a plethora of searing horns; the thanks that I gave joyously to Heaven above when I heard birds welcoming the morning with their inalienable chirpiness, all held no value.
The length of my hair outweighed them all.

Admittedly, my hair was what they called long in those days—it touched my ears on the sides, my collar in the back. And, by going out in public like that I flaunted my indifference to common decency. It would have only taken a pair of scissors and an ounce of, if not self-respect, at least some consideration for others, to expunge my crime. But I didn't. I chose instead to walk around shocking and offending everybody.

Only let me put up a kind of defense here, if I may (and then we'll be done with it). My hair was not as long as the hair on the heads of most of the cold bronze Confederate heroes that lined Monument Avenue. My hair was not as long, for example, as the hair of the always reluctant Jefferson Davis. Nor was it, by the way, half as weird. (Take a good look at a picture of that guy sometime.) It was not as long as the bigamist, Stonewall Jackson; though I had more on top than that cowardly Indian killer. My hair was about the same length as J.E.B. "Jeb" (for those of us who can't spell) Stuart's, but, shorter in back than the great and noble Robert E. Lee's. In sum: my hair was shorter than 3/5 of the highly honorable and greatly honored confederate generals proudly on display that day on that Boulevard of Honor.

And, I believe I should have gotten some credit for this too: neither did I sport their unruly beards. I was more cleanly shaven than 5/5 of them. Also, I want no credit for it, but only wish to mention in passing, that I neither chewed tobacco, nor spat, nor used vulgar language. I should, at this point, rest my case.

But, childishness awakens in me one final thought. It occurred to me at the time that my hair was not near as long (as you've probably guessed already), as Jesus'. For proof, look to the picture which, more likely than not, hung in whatever church this flinty old woman was on her way home from. I'm sure you've heard that argument before. (Apparently it carries no weight.) At any rate, until we met this grande dame of the never dying Confederacy, on that sunny spring morning, I hadn't yet been officially welcomed to Richmond.

So, there we were standing there, both stunned. The sniping had been so unexpected, the shot so clean and decisive, that neither one of us knew what to do or say.

Joanie, bless her sweet heart, was almost in tears; she was gasping for breath as she put one hand on my arm to steady herself, and raised the other to cover her heart out of some purely feminine instinct. She began whispering an apology. "Oh, I am so sorry..." she said. To her, I was a guest in her homeland, and she felt responsible in some unexplainable way for this weird occurrence. Me—I was gasping too; caught so completely by surprise, wounded so neatly. And, naturally I was ashamed of myself for having brought this about, for having put poor Joanie through it. The idea that my presence might draw fire and that Joanie might find herself involved in it sickened me.
I was also scared.

It scared the hell out of me to discover that there was such hatred in the world. I'd lead such a sheltered life until that moment. We just stood there looking at each other for a while. Then I said, "I gotta get out of here." I remember it so clearly. I didn't know whether I meant Monument Avenue or Richmond or Virginia or the South, I just know it was a matter of serious urgency at that moment. "I gotta get out of here."

My fear, I think, was that that woman's offspring had probably been filled with her venom and, in turn, they probably had a batch of their own little venomous vipers. They were all out there somewhere at that very moment, filled with a seething, nagging discontent. But, I didn't feel that they were just out there *somewhere*, I felt like they were out there *everywhere*. I had the feeling that Richmond was full of 'em, and we were surrounded with generations of bitter, spiteful and (really, after all) just plain vicious, stupid people.

Was this the very best the South had to offer? Were these elegant houses, these mansions, filled with such people?

There was no forgiveness in the streets of Richmond in those days and I was (albeit self-marked) a target for hatred.

I wish I had responded differently, although I cannot say precisely how. I wish I would have said something; maybe something clever. Ideally, I would have simply laughed it off. Alas, that ability—to laugh things off (though I admire others who employ it)—has always been beyond me.

Here's a charming little tale entitled: **A Lovely Outing near Richmond, Virginia, Heart of the Confederacy** (1968)

SCENE: Springtime. Richmond, Virginia.
Two young lovers taking a little ride out into the country, in a nifty old car. What could be nicer? 'Nothing,' you say. Precisely. Your understanding makes my task so much easier.

So far we have spring, Love, a little ride out in the countryside.

Joanie snuggled in beside me; she had both arms entwined in my right arm; she had her lovely face pressed warmly, adoringly against my shoulder—we were filled and overflowing with the very goodness of Life; it moved like a rhythm within us.
We were happy. If we found ourselves giggling with delight from time to time, well, that's understandable, isn't it?

As we drove on, the pasture on either side of us rolled away smoothly, quietly, taking the cattle and trees along with it, without resistance. The road was a gentle roller coaster under the warm, softening tires of my old car.

Windows open. Gentle breeze. Clouds, birds, stream running along beside us for a bit before swerving off into the distance and disappearing between two lush green perky hills…that sort of thing. It's a pretty picture. We are the only ones on that road. It's me and her and everything in nature that counts as good.

A pickup truck passes by. I hardly notice it; I'm in love. She's a true southern belle, gentle, soft spoken and uncommon lovely— and, as a rule, such creatures don't notice pick-up trucks. They don't notice shotgun racks or leering rednecks.

The truck slides up over the top of a rise and around the curve, out of sight, ahead of us. They have no part in our little world.

However, when we round that curve, I see that same truck stopped up ahead, in the very middle of the road.

I slow down as we approach it. This is unusual, I think. What on earth would a pick-up truck be doing stopped in the middle—right smack dab in the middle—of a country road?
"Do you think they're OK?" she asks. "Maybe we should stop and ask if they need help," she says.
I slow down to a crawl. This ain't right and my instincts are telling me so. My instincts are screaming at me. This ain't right, this ain't right.

I notice that the driver of the truck is turned around in the seat, one arm thrown over the seatback, grinning at us. The guy in the passenger seat is doing the same. They look like unshaven leering jack-o-lanterns. Between these two is a baby seat with a child in it. She's squirming, craning to see what the men are looking at.

The driver continues to stare at us as we roll slowly toward them. He unconsciously reaches over and pats the little child on the head. By this time we are maybe a dozen feet from them, and I have come to a complete stop. Something is very seriously wrong here. I don't know what it is, but something is not right. Joanie is sitting bolt upright, "Do you think they need help?" I can tell by the break in her voice that she's hoping that's the case; she's hoping the matter is as simple as that.

The driver turns away for a second, and now his truck is coming at us in reverse. I can hear it whining as he accelerates. He's climbing on the accelerator. The truck is fishtailing wildly as it comes barreling toward us. Both of these men are grinning at us as the truck slams into the front of my car.
The impact has the truck bouncing.

"Oh my God," screams Joanie. She can't believe this is happening. The truck pulls forward, and suddenly he's coming at us again in reverse.

My trusty old Peugeot has conked out from the impact. I'm telling Joanie to brace herself for the next hit. Meanwhile I'm frantically trying to get the engine of my little car to turn over. Seconds before he hits us again, it starts. The collision takes place just as I throw it in reverse. Now, I'm driving as quickly as I can away from him in reverse. Joanie is in tears, crying, "Oh God. Oh God. Dear God."

We've managed to put about 30 feet between us and them, when the Peugeot conks out again. As I frantically get it started I'm keeping my eye on them. The driver of the truck ruffles the hair of the child, reaches up and takes a shotgun down from the rack that hangs above the child's head. The passenger and the driver both get out of the truck; they're laughing as they pick up parts of my car—pieces of grill and trim from the headlights. They hold them up jokingly, victorious, and toss them into the back of their truck. Then the driver points the shotgun at us, and peering down its barrel he begins slowly walking toward us.

I am praying as loudly and as quickly as any reprobate has ever prayed, "Dear God, help us. Dear God, help us. Dear God, please help us."

And God does help us. The vicious redneck moron bastard father lowers his shotgun, laughs, spits in my direction (this is a male dominance thing), goes back to the cab, replaces his shotgun on the rack. He gets in, his door closes—clunk. His buddy stares at us for a bit longer, then gets in the other side. His door closes— clunk. They drive off, with the child between them looking back at us. What could be nicer than a little ride in the country around Richmond, in the spring?

For several months I refused to leave my loft, except to go to school, and I sat up nights keeping an eye on my car from the window overlooking the park. I was convinced that anyone crazy enough to attack us like that, out there, was crazy enough to come into town looking for us—or might stumble across my car while driving through town, and new visions of glorious violence would open up before their eyes.

Here's irony or something... an historical note at any rate. A few weeks after this event took place, a movie called Easy Rider came out and EVERYONE who knew me went out of their way to caution me NOT to see that film. I took that advice. But, I'm guessing the friends of those guys in the pick-up truck probably urged them to go see it.
"YEW two GOTTA go see that flick, Beau! I think you'll relate pretty strongly to the antagonist."

I'll tell you what I honestly believe. I do not think God stepped in to save our lives that day. I think God stepped in to save the life of the lovely young woman beside me. I just happened to be in the right place to be saved along with her.

Ever since then I have made a point of seeking out, latching onto, and, if not always remaining strictly devoted, at least remaining in close proximity to the finest, purest and most wonderful women on earth. And, that has really worked out pretty well. I now have the best wife any man has ever had— perhaps in the entire history of marriage—and, I'm as happy as a man of my peculiar temperament can possibly be. So, for me, it's been a blessing.

Those idiots in that pick-up truck did me a favor.

BURGER STAND BAPTISM

After our redneck encounter in the Virginia countryside I'd pretty much barricaded myself inside my studio. I hadn't budged for months when my friends, Rick and Ginger, coaxed me outside and convinced me to go with them to a drive-in.

It would be a short jaunt, and we'd have a good time and, by this method, I would have broken the dark spell my shotgun totin' friends had cast upon poor little oversensitive me. The clouds, I was told, would be driven away by burgers and the sun would once again shine down upon me like golden fries.

So, with Rick driving and Ginger up front, I cowered like a coward in the back seat.

When we pulled into the gravel parking lot of this hamburger stand all my reasonable fears were overthrown by the spirit of the moment. Possessed completely by who knows what inspiration (I like malts), I boldly announced, "You guys just stay in the car, I'll be right back." While waiting in line at the stand, I was busy going over their orders in my head. Once the short fat girl in front of me had placed her order, she stepped over to the pick-up window and waited. I took a deep breath and stepped forward. This would be my first dealings with redneck society in months, and I was a little nervous.

I smiled and began rattling off the list of things we wanted to the girl behind the window. When I looked up I saw that she was not taking it down; she was not marking anything on her little pad; she was just staring at me, unblinking. And although this may sound like a highly innovative approach to expressing hatred, it is actually a long-established traditional approach in the South; I'd experienced it many times before during my short, pleasant stay in Richmond.

Quickly now, here's a list of some of the places in Richmond, where I'd received that same treatment: The Plantation Room, Morton's Tea Room, Ilene's, and that little restaurant directly across from the Village Tavern, the name of which I cannot recall (some guy's name). And here are a few cities where they practiced the art: Saint Louis, Mo., Salt Lake City, Flagstaff, AZ, and the entire State of Texas. Though in fairness I must say that the Plantation Room served me when I showed up one evening with a little black kid in tow (as I recall Federal law had recently been demonstratively reiterated); Morton's Tea Room surrendered and began serving the likes of us after a tall skinny homosexual named Terri shattered the long-hair barrier there (they didn't realize he was a male until they'd already served him), and the place across the street from the Village Tavern, the name of which I cannot recall, eventually discovered that our money could be deposited along with that of their bristle-headed regulars and no one would even have to know.

Meanwhile, back at the ol' drive-in, I told the girl behind the window, "I'd like to order…"

This time the lovely creature squinted at me, pursed her lips as a sign of disgust, and slammed the pencil down on the countertop. She refused to hold any implement which might aid in feeding the likes of me. She leaned on the counter and stared at me through the glass in some kind of peculiarly porcine challenge. Frankly, I didn't expect it; even less did I know how to respond.

She broke her stare long enough to deliver food to the pick-up window and say cheerily, to another customer, "Thank you kindly. Y'all come on back again." Meanwhile, someone had come up behind me and the cook came charging out from behind the grill. He leaned toward the window and snapped, "Will you step aside so people can order?"

I was confused momentarily—mainly because for a very long time I had been convinced that I *was* people.

"YOU," he said pointing at me, "Step aside so PEOPLE can order."

I went back to the car and crawled in back, defeated, and by that I mean, thoroughly shaken. After being prompted, I stammered, "They won't take our order."

"What? Why?"

"I don't know. They refused to take our order."

"What happened?"

"The girl just stared at me. Then some big redneck chef-guy told me to step aside so that 'people' can order. They're not going to serve us. OK? Let's just go."

For me the social experiment was over; I was frightened and anxious to get out of there.

"This is ridiculous!" declared Rick boldly. He got out of the car and strode across the parking lot and got in line. He'd been raised in the striving/thriving middle-class of Maryland and since early childhood had been convinced that he was people too.

While waiting in line, he kept turning around and miming various things to us with broad joyous gestures. It was all a joke; he'd take care of it. I always admired how comfortable Rick felt moving around in the world.

"Don't worry," Ginger told me, throwing one arm over the seatback to comfort me, "we'll be chompin' on cheeseburgers in no time."

When Rick stepped up to the window, we could see that something was happening, though we could not tell quite what. It didn't appear normal though. Then suddenly the girl behind the window lunged forward like a vicious dog, and Rick jumped back. She was immediately joined by the cook. He was bent over the counter so far that his head was lodged in the slot where customers passed their money through. Red-faced, from that weird position, he was yelling at Rick.

Rick came running back to the car, got in, and was beginning to explain what had happened, while we rolled up the windows and locked the doors. Soon, we were surrounded with rednecks and the car began to rock from side to side. While the males were rocking the car, the females were standing around behind them, picking their noses, chewing gum, and looking appropriately vacant. Ginger, who'd been born and raised in the mountains of Ol' Virginie, expressed serious concerns when one of these gentlemen started pissing on her side of the car. When she told us that, Rick found it so unbelievable that, for scientific reasons I suppose, he crawled across the seat to confirm it for himself. At the moment I didn't have time to think about it, but later I wondered about anyone so full of venom that he could piss at will. At the moment, *fear* was having that same effect on me.

By the time Rick got the engine started our new friends had achieved synchronization and the car was rocking pretty seriously. Ginger was bracing herself for the moment it rolled over completely. I was shouting at Rick to drive the goddamned car and get us out of there. Rick put it in gear and we started moving slowly through the crowd.
'Run 'em over! Get us out of here!" I was yelling.
They were pounding on the hood and the roof, and there was a lot of shouting (nothing memorable, nothing clever, nothing either pithy or Shakespearian), and, as we drove off, random handy items were thrown at us; small rocks, beer cans (empty), paper milk shake containers (half full). I didn't look back.

As we drove along in complete silence I was, once again, cowering in the back.

All in all it had been a pleasant little outing, and it drove home the fact, once again, that not all of us were entirely and perfectly welcome guests in the still smoldering Capitol of the convulsing, not-yet-dead Confederacy.

From that point on I never left the Fan District except to go very far away, and as quickly as possible.

JUST US SAVIORS (1970)

Rick and I were up very late one night in his second floor apartment on Grove Avenue. It was always quiet in that part of town at night, except for the rare passing car. We were laughing hysterically, actually literally rolling around on the floor laughing over who-knows-what idiocy, when we heard a commotion outside. There was some shouting and what sounded like threats. Rick went to the window on his knees, peered out cautiously, and saw, in the distance, a guy running down Grove Avenue in our direction. He turned, motioned to me, and I crawled over and had a look.

In the distance, through the tree tops, we could see two guys, following slowly, on the other poor fella's heels. Rick got up, went over and turned off the light. Then we both ducked down and sat in silence with our backs against the wall. We wanted nothing to do with this, whatever it was.

I suppose the guy chose our building because he'd seen Rick's light blink out. We heard the sound of him bounding up onto the old wooden front porch; the downstairs door creaking open and slamming shut; footsteps coming quickly up the stairs. Next, there was a quiet tapping on the door, and a moral debate began, mimed in urgent silence: Should we let this poor guy in or not?

When the tapping became louder and more frantic, our debate escalated and we broke into whispers. The final convincing argument went something like this: "I don't know whether or not we are all brothers, but I do know we can't just sit here and listen to some poor guy being disemboweled in the hallway right outside your door... can we?"

Apparently, we couldn't.

24

Rick got up, went over to open the door, and a nervous, skinny, older black fellow slipped inside. He quickly threw his back against the door and put a bony finger to his lips. He stood there breathing heavily for a while before slumping to the floor. Meanwhile we carefully monitored the approach of the hunters by their shouts, on the street below. Apparently they'd lost him.

I scooted across the floor to the opposite wall and sat there taking it all in. Rick took a few steps backward and lowered himself quietly to the floor beside me. When the stranger locked the door, Rick and I looked at each other. "Great, now we're *locked in* with some desperate black guy!' I whispered.

Things got suddenly worse when our guest grabbed the bottle of wine we'd been drinking and, in one frighteningly skillful motion, shattered it against the leg of the iron bed—scattering glass shards and wine all over the floor. He then sat on that bed with that vicious looking weapon clenched in his fist. Rick and I were numb with fear. What had we gotten ourselves into? Lambs at slaughter, we looked at each other. "Great," I muttered, "NOW we're locked in with an ARMED desperate black guy!"

Outside, his pursuers had slowed their pace. They were making their way down the street methodically, like hounds, sniffing at every door and calling out threats. Rick and I were frozen, helpless. Neither one of us was sure what was going to happen. I was wondering if this black guy understood that we were on his side; that we had just helped him escape. At the same time, I was also wondering what this man, whom we were sheltering, had done to inspire such dedication to his capture.

We all listened intently as his hunters drifted past us and continued on down the street. We sat in silence, ears cocked for a very long time after that.

I don't know about Rick, but I was convinced that this guy was going to cut us up and leave us in bloody chunks amidst the glass and wine on the apartment floorboards.

When it was clear that the hunters were not returning—after long minutes of silence—our guest got up and cautiously slipped out the door, taking the broken bottle with him.

Rick and I crawled over quickly to the window on our knees to watch as he emerged and ran down the sidewalk in the direction from which he'd originally come.

This entire event lasted half of an hour maybe, if that, and at no time during that time was I convinced that either Rick or I would live to see the next day's glorious breaking dawn. After our guest left we stayed up talking about what had happened until we both fell asleep exhausted.

I don't know whether that guy owes us his life or Rick and I should be thankful he didn't take ours. I don't know who among us had the most fear, or was the most grateful, or had faced the greatest danger or had been shown the greatest kindness. I'd like to think that we're all brothers and blah blah blah, of course.

Oh, and another thing occurs to me; the guy was barefoot.

MODERATE HATRED (maybe 1969)

After a weird little windfall—payment for doing something I'd never done before and haven't done since—I had a pocketful of cash and a little time to think about things. So, I went over to a little redneck diner where they were known to actually serve people of my particularly repulsive, unacceptable sort.

As was her way, the woman who ran the place fixed me with icy eyes and did not blink and never uttered a single word while she took my order. Nor did she nod, or give any indication that she had heard me. She listened to my order and did her thing and placed the bill in front of me, and took my money, and slapped my change down on the counter with only mild disgust, and put the two dogs and the carton of milk I'd ordered into a bag, all in silence. By this time-tested method she made it clear she didn't like me, but she had no objection to my money.

In those days, that had become an acceptable arrangement, for everyone involved. Though mimes could have learned a great deal in that joint, I don't think I learned anything from the experience. Oh wait, actually I have.

These days, I don't do business with anyone I don't want to support or see prosper; I don't care what they offer, or how badly I might want it. So, naturally, it's just a bit awkward for me, looking back, to admit that today I am not as open minded as that redneck woman was 50 years ago.

MS. SWEETE (2009)

As Fate would have it this woman's name was Sweete. She had checked in to the hotel, in the afternoon, with her cowering little female companion and they had been in their room until sometime in the evening when I got a phone call.

The cowering companion told me that Ms. Sweete wanted something which we do not have—I forget the specifics, and by the time I finish telling you this, you will too. Whatever it was, I explained that we did not generally provide that and, knowing me, I suggested a place where they might go out to obtain it. Ms. Sweete took the phone from her friend to make the demand herself but, despite the blunt-forcefulness of her demand, we still did not have what we did not have ten seconds earlier. She said a few foul words to me before hanging up.

So far, everything was normal.

About twenty minutes later Ms. Sweete's meek little companion showed up in the office door and apologized to me for the way Ms. Sweete had treated me. I told her that was OK, there was no reason why she should apologize for her friend's behavior, and when I said this, the poor woman began to sob and shake all over. She turned pale and I had the feeling she was going to pass out, so I asked her to please have a seat.

"I can't," she said. "If I'm gone too long she's going to come looking for me and that won't be good. You don't know how she gets."

"Oh," I said, "how does she get?"

"She gets really angry and... believe me, you don't want to know. I really... I really... I have to get back."

The woman sounded completely frightened.

"Are you going to be OK?" I asked.

"Oh, sure, she uh... she just gets really angry and it can get out of control for a while, but uh..."

The woman's lip began to tremble and then she said this, "I'm scared to go back, but I'm even more scared not to."
"You're frightened of her?"
"Oh yes. I have good reason. You don't know her temper."
"Why are you traveling with someone you're afraid of?" I asked, and the poor woman broke down in tears.

I comforted her as best I could within the parameters of my employment, but probably went a step beyond, saying, "You don't have to stay with someone you're afraid of..."
She looked at me somewhat startled and left in a hurry.

About twenty minutes later Ms. Sweete called down and asked once again for the same thing that she'd asked for before—which we still could not provide—and, once again I told her that perhaps she could get it at Walgreen's or at a corner store. She showed up at my desk less than a minute later—a short, fat, red-faced woman with tiny little eyes—with her trembling companion in tow.

Ms. Sweete stood in the doorway with her hands on her hips, shook her head, and said, "I shoulda known. I shoulda known. Just as I expected, some old white asshole with a tie."
I said nothing to that.
"You don't have anything to say?"
"What would you have me say, Madame?" I said.
"What would you have me say, MADAME?" she mimicked me.
"I'd have you say anything instead of that."
I remained in enforced silence.
She said, "Are you just going to sit there staring at me, you flaccid old prick, or are you going to say something?"

She sat down heavily across from me. "If *you* can't think of anything to say, I want to speak to somebody who can. Is there a manager around here?"

"I am the manager at the moment."

"There's no one else around? No REAL manager?"

"I am the manager."

"I want to speak to a REAL manager. A REAL manager. Is that phrased simply enough for you to understand?"

"There's no one else... I'm it."

"OH, so suddenly you're the only one around? I want to speak to your manager!" she demanded.

"I am the manager, you can speak to me."

"Well, then I want to speak to the owner."

"The owner is not here."

"Oh, suddenly there is *no* manager, there is *no* owner, all I have to speak to is this useless old white asshole who can't think of anything to say but, I AM THE MANAGER, I AM THE MANAGER... Is that it?... everybody's gone home and left you in charge?"

"What may I do for you?"

"You can get someone in here with some balls, that's what you can do for me. I want to speak to somebody who can get something done around here." I said nothing. "Oh, so now you can't think of anything to say to that either? Is there ANYONE around here other than you—ANYONE with some brains, with some balls, who isn't going to just sit there blinking at me like a fucking idiot?"

"I'm it."

"You're it alright. You are the most useless piece of crap I have ever had to deal with. You can't answer a single fucking question; the manager and the owner have both mysteriously disappeared, leaving some old white asshole in charge; and HE can't even respond to a simple question."

I couldn't believe any of this was real. I just sat there looking at this disgraceful human being.

Meanwhile, Ms. Sweete's skinny little companion stood cowering behind her, in the doorway. She was in tears.

Ms. Sweete turned and snapped at her, "Is this the guy?"
The companion nodded. "You," she said, pointing at me, "better learn to stay the fuck out of other people's business." She instructed her companion to go back to the room and the woman fled. "I should call the cops, that's what I should do," she said running her hands over her jaw. "I should just call the cops."
"I'm not entirely sure what the problem is, but if you want me to call the police, I'll do that for you."
"I should," she said, "I should call the fuckin' cops."
"Would you like me to call them?"
"Yes. Yes, call the cops. Call the fuckin' cops and let me speak to them. It'll certainly be better than sitting here and watching you stare at me. DO IT! Call 'em!"
So, with the hope of bringing this to an end, I called the police.

Naturally I suppose, they wanted to know why I had called. It was a good question. I wasn't quite sure myself.
"Well, I'm a desk clerk at a hotel and we have a guest here and she asked me to call you."
"The guest is there with you?"
"Yes."
"What is the nature of the problem?"
"I'm not sure."
"You're not sure."
"No, she asked me to call you."
"Can I speak to the guest?'
"Sure." I handed the phone across to the woman.

Her side of the conversation went like this: (sweetly) "Yes? I have no idea, Officer. We were just sitting here talking and he said, 'I'm gonna call the cops.' I really have no idea, Officer. There's no problem that I'm aware of. As I said, we were just sitting here and he suddenly decided he needed to call you. No,

no problem at all. I could not possibly even guess." Then she extended the phone to me and said, "They want to speak to you."
"Yes."
"Do you need police assistance?"
"No."
"Then I want to advise you. Do not call here if you are not in need of police assistance. OK?"
"Sure."
"You sure?"
"Yes."
"Don't do it ever again."
"So. Asshole," she says to me after I hang up, "I hope you're happy." And she gets up, and she walks out.

And even as she goes, I know that it is only a matter of time before I'm called into the owner's office. Why did I not try to make this guest feel more welcome? Why did I not do whatever I could to accommodate her needs?

When the letter arrives, a few days later, it will say that I was rude—and I guess perhaps I was.

As for calling the police, I can offer no explanation; I'm still confused about that myself.

THE DANGERS of MAILING THINGS AT NIGHT in SF
(2019)

My habit is to pay bills the day I receive them and to drop return
DVDs in the mailbox immediately after viewing; luckily, there's
a mailbox on the corner about 90 feet from our front door.

So, my dear wife and I had finished with whatever it was that we
had watched (I don't remember a damned thing about any movie
once FIN comes upon the screen), and I sealed it up in the return
envelope, and I went outside to put it in the mailbox. It's about
1:30 or 2 AM on a Saturday night in San Francisco, during the
madness.

As I turn toward the corner, where the mailbox sits just in front
of a The Family Club—where lately it has become acceptable,
due to public policy, for junkies to squat and shoot up—there is a
limousine. The doors in back of that thing are open and three
chicks have just popped out. They each look like the Venus of
Willendorf, though less modest; they're each wearing sequin
encrusted miniskirts, so short as to be indecent by anyone's
standards... but their own, apparently.

As I head toward the mailbox, they start walking, 3 abreast,
toward me. They are staring directly at me and saying something
amongst themselves. As we are about to cross paths, one of these
lovely creatures says something, directed at me, which I don't
hear—so I do not respond.
"Oh, you better not say it!" warns one of them loudly to me.
"You better just keep walking, old man."
I think this is good advice—though I don't need it—and I do; I
just keep walking. I get to the mailbox, drop my envelope in, and
when I turn to go back home, I see that they have stopped, and
they have turned, and they are looking right at me.

One, or maybe two of them have their hands on their hips, and they are all glaring at me. Even in the street light, at night, I can see nothing more than hatred in their eyes.

"You better not say anything..." one of them warns.

Again, I think that's an excellent idea, and I take it. Neither do I utter a word, nor do I take a single step toward them.

This standoff demands some explanation. At about that time, a small (we hope) segment of our 'society' had acquired a taste for something they called 'the knockout game'—where cowards approach unsuspecting innocents, typically from behind, and, without warning or provocation, hit them so hard in the head that they're rendered unconscious. Then, while the victim of this senseless crime is left on the sidewalk, the cowardly assailant just walks away.

So, although these three had the decency to warn me, in their somewhat oblique but perfectly clear way, I knew they were in the mood, and possibly looking for the opportunity, to take down an old white heterosexual male (that's the big prize—the universal oppressor). At very least they wanted to put a little fear into me. So, I said nothing and I did not move.

After a while of staring me down, they laughed raucously, gave one another a congratulatory hand-slap, turned and, laughing so hard they could not walk straight, went on their way.

These days, during the madness in America, it has become acceptable to hate someone merely for the color of their skin.

RACE in AMERICA,
as I know it

BROTHERHOOD (2019)

Late one night, my wife asked me to go down to Walgreens to pick something up for her; I forget what exactly… iron or vitamin D or something like that. So, I slipped down the street and made my way into Walgreens and over to the vitamin section, only to discover that I could have anything in that store—anything at all—except the single item for which I had come. They had every vitamin and mineral on earth, and several different brands of each; they were all lined up nicely, neatly on display, surrounding the gaping emptiness where the one I was after should have been.

But, I know how these things work, so I stood there for a while and looked things over carefully, deliberately, systematically, just to be sure. And then I looked again.

As I was standing there, a man—maybe a little younger than me, maybe a little heavier, but every bit as weary—passed by. He was wearing a Walgreens badge, so I collared him.
"I'm looking for (iron or vitamin D or whatever it was)," I told him, "I don't see any on the shelf…"

"If it's not on the shelf we don't have it," he replied, with blunt-force indifference, and turned his back on me. He began moving things around on the shelf directly in front of him.
"Do you think you might have some in the back, in stock?" I asked.

He sighed, straightened up, turned to study me coldly.
"If it's **not on the shelf**, we **don't** have it," he said, with maybe a bit more emphasis than was really necessary.

We both shook our heads and stood there evaluating each other for a while.

"Are you a married man?" I asked.

His face softened. He smiled a crumpled little smile and nodded his head. Without another word, he went past me and through the double doors, into the back.

He emerged a couple moments later carrying a bottle of the stuff I was after, and placed it in my hand.
"There y' go," he said.
"Thank you," I said.
"You're welcome, brother," he said.

Richmond, Virginia (1968, that's my best guess)

One summer evening, my friend Calvin and I found ourselves tinkering with race matters in our own way, when we found ourselves on the wrong side of Broad Street… the wrong side of Broad Street for me that is. Calvin turned to me and said "You better turn back, man." He looked pretty serious.
I laughed. "You think I'm afraid to be in this district at night?"
"If you were as smart as you think you are, you would be."
I laughed again.
"I ain' jokin' with you, Richard. This is another part of town and there are people who will not be pleased by your presence here."
"But, Calvin, you'd protect your friend, Richard, wouldn't you?"
"Yeah but I'm just one man, an' I ain't that big. And, when the goin' gets tough I have a tendency to run."
We continued walking.

We were about three blocks into what Calvin called "the nigger district" when he stopped me and said, "OK, listen to me, this is serious now. If I say run, you better run; and you better run in that direction." He pointed in the direction of the college where we both went to school. "You better RUN to the other side of Broad Street; the white side; the right side; the safe side. And don't stop until you get in-side and lock the door. Are we in agreement?"
"Calvin," I said, "I am no more welcome over there than I am over here, maybe less."
"Yeah, well you don't want to find out how welcome you are over here, believe me."
The sun had since gone down and I was beginning to get spooked by all this talk, but tried not to show it. I was young and had been told that I was supposed to feel invulnerable.

"You want to break down some racial barriers?" he asked turning to me with a smile. "OK then, we can do that, Skippy."

38

"Look, Calvin…" I said, "I just want to see where you live. You've been to my place, I thought I'd like to see where you live, meet your grandmother…"

Calvin laughed sarcastically. "Oh yeah, my grandmother. She would for sure love to walk in and find herself a white boy sitting in her living room. You got to be out your mind; my granny would cut you herself; slice you up. She find you in her house, first thang she do is grab a knife. She don't want no white boy in her house. What would the neighbors think?"

"You can't have me in your own house?"

"Forget that, OK? The answer is 'No', but do you want to shoot some pool?"

"I'd love to shoot a little pool."

"Good, 'cause there's the place for it."

Across the street was a small, dark, corner bar with a long neon sign hanging down from the roof saying "JUBI" in flickering pinkish neon.

"No, man, I'm just kidding with you, Richard. Two of us go in Jubi, we'd be lucky if one of us comes back out alive. And," he said, "that one WILL be me."

In those days, I was crazy. I wasn't heroic. I wasn't brave, I may have been stupid, I don't know. But for sure, when it came to certain things, I was crazy. (I was born in Gary, Indiana for god's sake!) I grabbed a fistful of Calvin's jacket and started dragging him across the street toward Jubi. He dug his heels in and put up a struggle until, out of breath and laughing so hard neither of us could breathe, we stood on the shattered sidewalk in front of the place, bent over in laughter, two young idiots teetering on the precipice.

He studied me for a bit. "OK, Mr. Big Man, White Boy, College Death-wish Fool, follow me."

The next thing I knew, Calvin and I were standing inside the bar and every head in the place was turning to look at us. Oh, and we were no longer laughing, I should make that clear. It didn't seem like the wise thing to do.

"Don't look at 'em," whispered Calvin as he took the bar stool closest to the door. I climbed up on the one next to him. He was between me and any hope of escape, so I envisioned myself plowing right through him on my desperate way out of there.

In those days Hollywood movies had not yet started promoting the idea that a white man can put himself in almost any situation and end up loved—when not worshipped outright—by the locals. So, wisely I believe, I lowered my head and began staring at the bar top in front of me. Calvin was pretending to be just a neighborhood kid who'd strolled in for a beer... which was pretty much what he was. Calvin was, in fact, in deed, and in every way possible, a neighborhood kid who'd just strolled in for a beer. Me? I was his invisible friend.

That became obvious when the barkeep came over, tossed a coaster on the bar in front of Calvin, and raised his chin.
I detected a quiver in Calvin's voice when he asked, "What kind of beer do you have?"
"We got one kind of beer," said the bartender coldly, and slammed a bottle down in front of Calvin. Calvin looked at me and snickered. "We in it now," he whispered, as the other customers started commenting on the matter openly and loudly. "We don't allow no college kids in here." and "Can't he get his beer over there with the white folk now?"
I was sitting there, with my head hung very low, thinking, "Man, they are as prejudiced as 'we' are."
I was watching Calvin from under my brow. He was trying not to laugh. I was trying not to cry. The barkeep snorted and started to walk away.

"Man, we are IN it," hissed Calvin. Then he cleared his throat and demanded, "How 'bout one for my friend?"

I leaned over and reminded him, "I don't drink, Calvin, you know that." (In those days I didn't drink.)

"You got a friend comin'?" asked the barkeep.

"It's OK, Calvin," I said quickly, "I don't drink."

The bartender, overhearing that, reached down below the counter, pulled out three cold beers and clunked them on the counter in front of us. "Two drink minimum!" he declared.

Apparently, from the uproarious response behind us, this was one of the funniest and most righteous statements ever made.

"Boy says he don't drink." I heard someone say.

"D' hell's he doin' in a bar then?"

"D' fuck's he doin' in DIS bar?"

"Jesus," I said, and leaning toward Calvin I whispered, "Let's just get out of here."

"Just stay there," said Calvin with some urgency.

"But, I…"

"I'll drink the beer," he whispered, "don't worry; just stay where you are. It's cool."

"It don't feel cool."

"Shhhhhh."

The barkeep went down to the far end of the bar and started talking to a skinny, pitch-black woman in a flowery housedress. She was smoking long skinny cigarettes and staring fixedly at me. I didn't have the nerve to turn around and face the rest of the customers, but I imagined that there were hundreds of them. It sure felt like there were hundreds of them. I imagined that they too had their eyes on me.

And I imagined that they weren't really pleased to have me in there. Well, perhaps I didn't imagine that part.

The idea that I would be forced to consume my first alcoholic beverage—first TWO alcoholic beverages—as the unwelcome guest in a black bar, in a black district, surrounded with people I couldn't see, under the hostile eye of the barkeep and that skinny woman in a housedress, was a little unnerving. On the other hand I felt like a beer might be precisely what I needed at that moment.

"Try it," Calvin urged quietly.

"I don't drink," I hissed back.

"Hey," shouted the barkeep suddenly, "This is a drinking establishment. If you ain't gonna drink, get out!"

God bless that man. Drink or get out. It was an excellent suggestion. I started to get up and Calvin put a heavy hand on my thigh, "Stay right there."

"Why?"

"Learnin' experience." He laughed almost inaudibly. "You wanted it, now you got it."

"This isn't funny to me anymore, Calvin."

"It's OK. Prove a point," he said.

We were sitting there like that, Calvin holding me down, the barkeep and his skinny girlfriend with their cold eyes locked on us, when the door swung open and in ambled one of the largest human beings I'd ever seen in my life. I didn't see him directly —Calvin was sitting between me and the front door—but his massive presence completely blocked out the mirror behind the bar as he squeezed by behind us. I went quickly back to staring fixedly at the countertop in front of me. My nose sank closer to the bar when I heard the scraping of barstools and the wheezing sound of the huge man taking up the stool beside me. I could actually feel the heat of his presence. I could smell his sweat; I could hear him breathing.

In the mirror, I watched in terror as the man's enormous head swiveled slowly in my direction and his eyes locked on me. Calvin said nothing, just sat there, hoisted his beer and sipped. I kept my head down as far as I could while keeping both eyes on the mirror. I was dazzled by my predicament; fascinated by the situation at hand. I felt like I was observing myself from outside.

The barkeep came down, stood directly in front of me, blocking the mirror and my view of my gargantuan neighbor, slapped a napkin on the bar and said, "Mike?"
"Bucket," said Mike.
And, this I swear to you, the barkeep took an aluminum bucket from off the counter behind the bar, and stood in front of me filling it with draft beer.
It was, as far as I could tell, about a four hour process.

Meanwhile Mike and the barkeeper were both fixed on me.
"And?" asked the barkeep.
"Turkey," said Mike.
He had turned to face me while he said this, and, for some reason, this got a big laugh from everybody behind me. When I looked at Calvin, he was laughing too. The barkeep took down a bottle of Wild Turkey whiskey, poured out a healthy shot and put it in front of Mike.

When he left, returning to the woman at the end of the counter, I got a clear view of the big man beside me again. He was slugging the beer from the bucket, had it up to his mouth with both hands... a BUCKET! Where I came from they filled buckets with ice and stuck three or four bottles of beer in there to keep chilled. After setting the bucket down, he slowly turned and looked at me with hooded eyes. I could feel his beery breath on my face. Was he purposefully breathing on me?

In the mirror I watched Calvin grimacing in exaggerated fear.

Meanwhile, the big man beside me continued to stare at me in silence. Calvin was mouthing something to me repeatedly, but I could not tell what. By this time Calvin had finished his two beers and reached over to take one of mine. The barkeep saw his hand reaching for it and ran the length of the bar to grab the beer from Calvin. While staring at him, he said, "Nuh. You can't come in here and drink other people's beer, now." He pushed the bottle back in front of me.

Calvin was smiling and nodding and, god help us all, he actually leaned in across the bar and gave a goofy little wave to the monster beside me. Thankfully, the big guy had his whole face in the bucket, and didn't see. When he finished the tub of beer he quickly slammed down the shot of Wild Turkey and leaned onto the bar with his huge, monumental, forearms. He entwined his meaty fingers and started nodding his huge head while staring, in the mirror, directly into my eyes.

I tried to concentrate on the beer in front of me, but couldn't help but look up from time to time. Each time I stole a glance, he was still staring at me.

Neither Calvin nor I knew what to do. The barkeep yelled, "More, Mountain?" The big man turned to me and said quietly, "What do you think?" My eyes moved toward the man who had addressed me, but my head stayed facing the counter directly in front of me. I scratched the side of my face nervously.
"Me?" I asked weakly.
"Yeah. You think I should have another bucket," he said, moving his big head closer to my ear, "Snowflake?"

Though he'd whispered it, all the folks in the bar laughed and made comments. Calvin covered up his own laughter. I kept my eyes to myself. The big man was in no hurry though, immobile, his face next to my ear, waiting for my answer.

There had been a lot of chatter going on behind me up to this point; that had all disappeared. Everybody in the place was waiting to hear what I would say. The barkeep was now leaning with both elbows on the bar; he seemed entertained by my situation. It was like some kind of badly staged play.

"Well..?" the big man whispered.
I shrugged. "Well…" I began pseudo-casually, "you're a pretty big guy. Why not?" I said very softly. I did not smile, nor did I look at the man, and my voice cracked as I spoke, but I said what I had to say. I had to clear my throat a couple times before getting all eight, finely crafted words out, but I said it.
He leaned away from me and shouted, "Willie!"
"Mountain?" said the barkeep from the far end of the bar.
"Bucket and a shot."

"You want another?" the barkeep asked me while filling the bucket and looking down at my two full, warm, putrefying bottles.
"I'll take another," said Calvin suddenly.
"No, you will not. You," he said widening his eyes, "definitely will not."

After downing half the bucket of beer, the big man said, "You shoot, Snowflake?"
"Shoot?"
"Use a stick?"
"Stick?" I was frightened and disoriented; I had no idea what he could possibly be saying.
"Pool," whispered Calvin. "He's talkin' about pool."
I cleared my throat. "Uh, yeah, I shoot a little."
"Let's shoot, Snowflake," said the big man as he put two huge hands flat on the bar top and raised his bulk off both flattened stools that he'd been sitting on. I got up and followed the huge man to the tiny, ill-lit pool table.

"Don't forget your beer," shouted someone from the dark, and there was raucous laughter.

"Bofe ob 'em," someone added, and that got more laughter.

At the pool table, Mountain put out one huge palm and stood looking at me. I looked to Calvin for guidance, and he started fishing around desperately for the quarter that was needed to get the game underway.

"Eight Ball," said the big man and put out his other hand.

From the darkened side of the bar someone stepped forward and placed a pool cue in the man's hand. It looked like a toothpick in that huge fist. I started to look around for a cue. This was a process that seemed to demand the advice of several people who advised me loudly. "Take a heavy one; you gonna need it." "Don't use Jerome's, he don't like no one to touch his stick." "Ain't got y' own custom stick?"

As is my habit, I just took the first thing that fell to hand. I looked at the tip briefly and went back and stood nervously beside the table. "Solid ebony," said the big man holding his cue out for me to admire, "hard as a rock, made of the same stuff white cops use to bloody the black man's skull." He turned it so I could appreciate the butt end. "Cue like this," he said, slapping the thing in the palm of his hand, "you can beat any man... and I mean beat."

I nodded... I may have whimpered, I certainly gulped.

"You don't want t' sight down that stick, check it for flaws?" he asked. There was laughter.

"Naw," I said.

"You sure? You sure that's the stick for you, now?" He licked his big lips and grinned.

"Uh, you want to break or you want me to break?" I said with more than the slightest trace of nervousness.

What the Mountain didn't know, Calvin didn't know, no one in that bar knew, is that we had a pool table when we were kids and rarely in life did I feel more comfortable than with a pool cue in my hand. When I was shooting pool, I was at ease.

"Guest breaks," said the big man, "Loser drinks a bucket and a shot."

"He don't drink," said Calvin quickly.

"He lose, he drink," said the big man, while looking at me.

This was the funniest thing anyone in that bar had heard all night. He lose, he drink. They'd win no matter who won the game. If he won I was force-fed beer and a shot of whiskey; if I won I guess tradition dictated that I buy him his next round. It didn't seem fair, but it did galvanize my conviction to beat the guy, if I could. I moved to the side of the table, inserted the quarter, released the balls, listened to them drop. Calvin racked them. I moved to the end of the table while the big man repositioned himself on the two bar stools he'd previously punished.

I broke without hesitation, got a pretty good scatter and dropped a couple low balls. I didn't know what anyone's reaction was, because when I shoot pool nothing else exists for me beyond the table.

"You want?" asked the big man from his throne.

"Huh?"

"Balls you want?"

"I have to sink a called shot first," I said.

"What?"

There was loud complaining coming from throughout the bar.

"You have to sink a called shot before you can choose," I said.

"What you talkin' 'bout. I been shootin' eightball all my big fat BLACK-assed life and you just sunk two balls, so choose."

Sitting near me, Calvin was urging me to choose and choose quickly. Martyred, I winced, hung my head and sighed deeply. Should I attempt to explain the rules of this game to this man, in this situation?

"OK," I sighed. I studied the table. "I'll take the high ones."

"You sunk solids and you takin' the stripes?"

"Yes." I said.

"You sunk SOLIDs and you takin' the STRIPES?" He was shaking his big head from side to side, and there was laughter throughout the place... and plenty of free advice.

"Yes." I said.

"Go ahead then."

I shrugged, called and took my first shot. It was a nice clean shot, nothing special, but there was a rumbling in the crowd. I called the next shot and it dropped softly. The atmosphere was infused with drama. Calvin was sitting on a stool behind me, as I lined up the next shot, chanting, "Don't do this, Richard, don't do this, Richard, don't do this, Richard." It was like a bad Hollywood movie: whiteboy comes to Harlem and teaches the locals how to shoot pool.

I looked at the table; it was tempting; nicely set up for an easy victory, but I didn't want this mountainous black man angry at me; I started taking riskier shots, but they continued to drop like in a dream. Calvin, who'd been raised in that neighborhood and who knew these people better than anyone, was pleading with me, quietly, desperately, to throw the game. He jumped off of his stool and threw himself on my shoulders saying, "What are you doing?"

I looked at my opponent and, in his way, he was smiling at me. Now, all my doubts were gone. The table was set for me to sink the last two balls with my next shot. With either luck or skill or any combination of the two, they'd both disappear. In my mind, it was a rock-solid certainty; this game was being orchestrated in heaven. Apparently Calvin thought so too; he was sitting with his eyes closed and seemed to be pleading directly with the powers above.

The big guy was leaning back with his elbows on the counter behind him, waiting. He didn't seem concerned. The barkeep had abandoned his post with his lady friend and he was standing behind Mike, supposedly cleaning glasses. He didn't appear to be either for me or against me. I called the most obvious shot, and (the phrase, cock-sure comes to mind for some reason here) I pointed. Recognizing what I was about to do somebody in that darkened barroom stood up and shouted, "OK, Slick! When the magic's workin', work the magic!" (Who said, nobody likes a showoff? That was 53 years ago and I can still hear that guy's encouragement. I also remember what happened next.)

I took the shot and—maybe it was better for everyone—one of those balls went nowhere, and the other came to rest on the lip of the pocket. If I had whistled a sharp note that ball would have dropped. When I looked up to surrender the table, things in that place had changed. An undeniable chill had blown in through the open front door. Suddenly, there was only silence in that place.

I turned to see what was happening, and there stood a skinny black kid in a full-length black leather coat and a black beret. He was leaning on Mountain's shoulder, as if he owned him. Mountain was sitting with his hands folded in his lap, like a schoolboy on good behavior, hoping not to be called on by the teacher. The skinny kid was grinning and actively picking his teeth with a toothpick. His front teeth were both gold.
He was nodding knowingly, grinning at me.
"You a cop?" he asked me.
"Me? No."
"You better hope you are a mother-fuckin' cop. Or you better hope I think you might be, 'cause much as we don't 'llow cops

in here, we even mo' don't 'llow white boys without the full
weight an' authority of the law behin' em."
I didn't know what to say to that. What could anyone say to that?
I was feeling pretty defenseless. In the barroom mirror, my own
image looked tiny and pale and very far away.

He raised his eyebrows in mock surprise. "You got no response
to my proper interrogatory?"
"I'm not a cop," I said, "if that's what you mean."
"Well, some of us have decided we don't want you in here,
whatever you are," he said, taking a step toward me. "Some of
the rest of us resent your presence in one of the only places we
might be allowed, by your indulgence, to call home."
I didn't know what to say to that either.

He was a skinny little bastard, and I imagined just walking over,
picking him up and breaking him in half over my knee. Not that
I've ever done such a thing; I've never in my life even thrown a
punch. Also, I was fairly certain that this would be the wrong
place to throw my first.
"You got no response to this which I have said either?"
I said nothing.
"You stupid, is that it?"
I didn't say anything. I didn't move. I just stood there looking at
this kid with the toothpick.
"You got nothing to say?" he demanded.

Someone said, "Rashid, whyn't you just let him go ahead and get
out of here?"
"The people want me to overlook your mis-step," he said and
laughed. "You want me to overlook his misstep, Midget?" He
leaned on Mountain's shoulder as he addressed him.
Mountain said, "He's just a college kid, Mr. X."

The skinny evil bastard came over toward me and stopped about two feet away, picking his teeth and looking me in the eye. "You just a college kid?"

"I'm a student, yes."

"They don't teach you nothin' bout not going into certain neighborhoods and struttin' your cleverness and educational superiority? They don't teach you nothin' bout how some of us lesser folk might find your superiority ranklin'?" With each question he was moving in closer to me and jutting his chin up further. "You think you can jus' waltz in here with us niggers, shoot a little sloppy pool with the Midget here, and stroll on out again after tramplin' on our pride? We s'posed to thank you for the honor of your presence? You a hero? That it? You some kind of white knight pool shootin' mother-fuckin' hero?"

There was a booming voice from nowhere, "Jerome!", and everything stopped.

"Rashid!" corrected the young punk bitterly, without turning to face the source of that commanding voice.

The barkeep was standing there, on our side of the bar, with a baseball bat held threateningly in one hand. "I ain't havin' it. Not in my place, Jerome."

The hoodlum turned his head. "Rashid! An', whyn't you keep to your own business, old man?"

"This *is* my business, Jerome. You want to cut up some of these college boys, that's your business—business of you and your friends—but you do it outside the Jubi."

Jerome turned and started for the door. "I'll be waitin' for you outside," he said, and pointed a finger at me like a gun.

"Better drink up," someone said, "I understand it hurts less if you're drunk."

I turned to Calvin, "What am I supposed to do?"

Calvin said nothing. He looked at me, he looked around at the bar keep. He looked into the depths of the bar room.

There was no solution offered by anyone. The bar keep came up to me and I thought he was offering me the baseball bat. "I suggest you head straight for Broad Street and don't look back." I looked at Mountain and he just turned around toward the bar without any hint of involvement.

(Thanks for that by the way, Mike.)

What none of these good people could know was that there were people who hated me, every bit as much as Rashid did, on the other side of Broad Street. The only difference was, they wore my same skin color. What these good people didn't know was that among these haters were some cops. For me, in a peculiar way, I felt more at ease, more accepted, in their neighborhood than I did in some of the neighborhoods around school.

Two guys in a pickup truck had threatened my girlfriend and me with a shotgun; some kids outside a fast food joint had surrounded our car and, rocking it back and forth, tried to turn it over with us in it; an old woman once said to me, "In my time we didn't even allow niggers on this street let alone people like you." Those people were all white. The people who refused to take my order, give me service, or accept my money, were all white. I didn't have time to explain this to the people in that bar. And I was fairly certain they wouldn't believe me if I told them, but I genuinely felt less nervous in their bar that night than I did walking down Floyd Avenue in broad daylight, where a guy once took a pot shot at me from his front porch, and winked at me when I turned around to see where the shot had come from.

No, the other side of Broad Street was no comfort to me.

Calvin once suggested, jokingly, that if I ever got into trouble in *his* neighborhood, I should proclaim loudly that I'm a descendant of Warren G. Harding. I was pretty sure that advice wouldn't help me on *our* side of Broad.

Once outside, Calvin wished me luck, headed off toward his grandmother's house, and I took off toward Broad Street. I'd never felt so ridiculous, nor so scared, in all my life.

I'd gone about half a block, nervous and very very very alone, when a dog came bounding out of an alley and paced himself beside me. I stopped. The dog stopped. He looked up at me wagging his tail. Then another dog appeared—they were both wagging their tails. Suddenly I was engulfed in milling dogs. Dogs were all over the place, leaping and snorting and greeting me. I knew what that meant. Down the alley, under the streetlight, I saw Amos ambling slowly toward me with his walking stick—all quiet dignity and gentle good-nature.

"Chou doin' down in here, Charles, down in the quagmire?"
"Visitin' a friend," I said nervously. (Amos was one of those who called me Charlie, for reasons unknown.)
"Well now, he cain't be much of a friend to lead you all down into this here. You better stick with me and the hoid."
(Amos called his hounds 'the herd'.)
"I'm truly glad to see you Amos," I said eagerly.
"Yeah, well, you should be. Was Speckles who sniffed you out. Thanks goes to that nose of his. Smell a bitch through three-inch cold-rolled steel…"
Amos suddenly took my arm and started leading me.
"Don't look. Just keep walkin'," he said quietly, urgently.

I looked around and startled. We were being followed. An old low-slung Chevy was behind us, rolling so slowly we could hear the grit being crushed under its tires. When we arrived at Broad Street, the car took a left turn, swerving so closely in front of us that I could have reached in the open window. The four young toughs inside were all looking directly at me, as they drifted slowly by.

Don't look at 'em," Amos instructed, "they tryin' to give you the stank-eye."
But I couldn't help myself. I was riveted.

The big block-headed guy at the wheel was staring regally at the street ahead. Next to him was Jerome, leaning his weasel face back over the top of the seat to fix me with his cold yellow eyes. In back, two skinny looking kids, dressed in black with black rags wrapped around their heads, stared at me menacingly.

"Welcome to my neighborhood," said Amos quietly.

SWIMPS

When we finally arrived safely at the park (near my place), five blocks away, Amos sat down wearily. "We come a long way just now together," he said and shooed the dogs off. They disappeared like ships into a fog bank, except for a little wire-haired white one, which stayed around, laying at Amos' feet with his head on his paws.

We sat there for a bit, quietly. Then Amos said, "Tell you a little story." I waited while he shifted around on the bench for a long time, and then cleared his throat a dozen times or more, and then rubbed his face with both hands for a bit. I waited, because I knew this was sometimes his way. He cleared his throat again. "I was a jazz musician. For a long time, I was a jazz musician; but you didn't know that did you?" He smiled revealing his own gold front teeth. I thought it strange that suddenly so many people in my life had gold front teeth—those who meant me harm and those who arrived like angels out of the darkest alley to comfort and protect me.
"You played jazz?"
"The disciplinarian's blues is what they sometimes referred to it as."
"Blues?"
"Yeah, it's blues! You don't know jazz is blues? It's all blues, man!"

Though blues would play a big part in my life somewhere down the road, at that point in time I knew nothing about blues. It spoke to me, but I didn't know it was blues speaking. It called me repeatedly, but I didn't pick up the phone.
"What instrument did you play?"
"I'd like to lie and say sax, but that ain't true. Be more cool, but not a bit more true. I'll save that for the womens. Even guitar would be better," he sighed, "but no, I played the drums."

"Nothin' wrong with drums," I said.

"No, nothin' wrong with the drums, but you know what they say…" Amos said, and then got lost in thought.

I didn't know what they say. But, I wanted to. So, I waited. I waited until it began to look like I was never gonna know what they say. "What do they say?" I finally asked.

"Oh, well, you know, they say a good drummer is hard to find and a bad drummer is hard to get rid of." I nodded as if I understood. I mean, I nodded as if I'd heard him.

"I must of been a pretty good drummer though, cause they seldom found me. Far as I can tell, I'm still lost." He laughed a dry little laugh, coughed a little, and then he drifted off in thought again. Eventually he sighed. "Still I made my living that way. Some can't say as much."

"It sounds like a good way to make a living."

"Yeah, it does-must look good from the outside. Hard work though, luggin' them pots an' pans around. Still, I had my good times. I had my share. Yes, yes, livin' the life."

"What did you do?"

"Spotin' mostly."

"Spo-tin?"

"Ballin', you know, carryin' on, jackass behavior…gettin' with the womens."

Later, I understood that he'd said sportin'; women and minor drugs, with a little gamblin' thrown in… occasional fights.

"I believe I had me my share. Yes indeed I did. You know I did." He started nodding his head to a beat that I could not hear. "But anyway," he sighed, "I wanted to tell you this little incident, when I was playin' with Coon Collins—you prolly never heard of him; real jazz musician; black jazz, hot jazz, real Southern jazz. Played with him all over this never-mind. Coon Collins and his get-up-if-you-still-can quartet. Coon and me were old army buddies, and that devil, Coon, he knew that I could not say… uh… you know," he paused, gulped, "swimps."

"SWIMPS?"

"Shimp. Swimps, you know them curly thangs."

"Curly things. What..? Is it a musical term? I mean what is it?"

"A thang you eat. It's a kind of fishy thang that crawls along the bottom I think. You know, like a crawdad, but not one" He shook his head. "Now I hesitate to even try… SWIMPS. Surely you mus' know… Please help me."

"Shrimp?"

"Yeah, that's them. Coon, he knew that I could not, if the Devil himself was on my tail, say that word. So, ever time we found ourselves in Nawlins, as they call it; when we was in Orleans, as I called it, he always takin' us to this place where all they serve up is swimps. Even the 'ssert was swimps; swimps custard, swimp soufflé, somethin' horrible like that." He laughed. "Don't get me wrong I love t'eat 'em, just can't call 'em by name." Amos was grinning, thinking about it.

"'What you gonna have, Billy?' 'Why I believe I'll have me a big platter of them fried swimps.' 'Bout you, Horn Player?' 'Ummmm, those barbecued swimps sure look good to me.' 'An' you Amos..?' So then there was that silence, you know. They all waitin'. They can't wait to see my acrobatics."

Amos slapped his thigh and bowed his head in laughter. He started coughing, and coughed for a long time before continuing.

"Ever body in the place seemed to be waitin' for me to attempt the impossible. Talk about perfect time for a drum roll." Amos was laughing so hard he started coughing again. "They knew I could not say that word. They all knew it. My boys knew it. Waitress, she knows it too. She seen me in there enough times; she's standin' there waitin'. 'Oh, I guess I'll just have whatever Billy's havin.' And they would crack up."

Amos began laughing so hard that he started wheezing.

"You can't say shrimp?"

"Still can't, no."

There were tears in Amos' eyes when he looked at me and he was beaming with a schoolboy delight.

"Had me a friend, Bad Boy Big Billy Murdock—horn player from out of Memphis—tryin' to secretly educate me, give me instruction, whenever we met up. We tried breaking that word down into three parts and that didn't work. We tried enunciating exercises that involved every word in the book that looked, moved or smelled like swimpses, but that did not work."

He looked at me, "Go ahead an' laugh. Old black man can't say swimps; the very essence of humor."

It was kind of funny and I did laugh.

"But, that's the point, Charlie…if there is a point. What we went through tonight… down the road, that'll make a good story; time you went into the Jubi and come out with your skin still on. One piece. Uncut!"

"I'm still frightened," I admitted.

"You'd be a fool if you wasn't. Hell, man, I'm frightened too. Dogs was frightened. But, I know you, you're clever, and in time, it'll make a good tale. You'll prolly end up beatin' the black off Jerome or Rashid X or whatever it is he calls himself these days… been nothin' but trouble since he was a kid… in time you'll be puttin' your foot right through his skinny black ass. In time it'll evolve that way in the tellin', you'll see."

We sat there on the bench laughing about it, but my eyes were on Harrison Street the whole time, looking for that car.

"Don't worry. They won't come up in here," he said and patted me on the thigh. "They won't come up this side a Broad. How'd you get into that fix anyway?"

"A friend took me there."

"Oh that's right, you done already told me that."

He sat, pondered. "Some friend."

58

A really peculiar little note (nonetheless true):
>In 1988 (so that's like 20 years after this event) I was in
a little blues dive called Larry Blake's, in Berkeley
California, one night when Lonnie Brooks was playing
there. In between sets the bass player takes the mic. and
he tell us this very same tale, almost note for note, but
it's about himself. Only difference was, he called 'em
shimps, not swimps. He can't pronounce shimps, the
band knows he can't pronounce shimps, whenever
they're in 'Nawlins', they make a point of taking him to
a place where everything on the menu is shimps.
>I almost fell off my chair.

As Amos once told me, it's funny how Life works itself out.

REGGIE (1968 or there about)

That year, for some reason which I could not comprehend, girls seemed to find me irresistible; I'd been finding them irresistible for years. What was new was, my skin had cleared up. I also had a little money; I had a few friends; I had a car. My work (writing) was moving along steadily, nicely, and I had gained some note as a painter. I was doing alright; for someone who didn't know what the heck he was doing, let alone why; I was doing alright. So, I thought I'd give a little back, as they say.

I called an organization which puts fatherless boys together with young men, so the kid might know what it's like to have a male figure in his life—someone who cared about him and set an example of what it was to be a man. I had a phone put into my studio specifically so that organization could call me and, when a kid was assigned, I could call him. They sent me a packet with a brochure and some forms to fill out. And I must admit I looked pretty good on paper.

Before long I was assigned a kid; his name was Reggie. I was given his home phone number and another pamphlet to read, and told to talk to his grandmother, his guardian. Then I took a deep breath, picked up my new phone, and set up a date.

The pamphlet stressed that I must prove myself reliable in the eyes of this kid. If I made a date with him to meet up and go somewhere, the most important thing on earth was that I kept that date; these kids had already had enough disappointment in their lives. If I wasn't willing or able to do that, the pamphlet urged me strongly to quit before even meeting the kid, and save everybody the sadness. But I was ready, willing, able, and on top of it, I was eager. So, after making arrangements, I drove over to the frightening little neighborhood where the kid lived, and I parked my car out front, and I bounded jauntily up to the door, and I knock-knock-knocked.

An old black woman looked out through the narrow crack that the chain bolt allowed, and eyed me.
"Is Reggie here?"
"You the man from the organization?"
"Yes."
"Well," she hesitated, then opened the door enough for a skinny little black kid—he must have been 10 or 12—to slip through. He tugged on a baseball cap and stood there looking up at me, ready to go.
"When will you be bringing him home?" she asked from her safe position behind the door.
"I guess in about two hours."
"TWO HOURS? No, no, no, no, you had better get him home 'fore that, now."
"I thought we'd go to the park and then maybe have some ice cream somewhere."
"One or the other," she said in a commanding voice. "You choose what y'all are gonna do together, but you have him back here in an hour... and a half. OK? No more than that."
She looked at her watch and tapped it with her finger.

I think both of us could still feel her presence behind the door, as we climbed into my car and drove off.

During the ride Reggie did not look directly at me even one time that I was aware of. From the glances I took of him, he was delighted to be going out. We talked a little and I asked him what he would like to do. He shrugged; he didn't know, he didn't care. I offered him the park and I offered him ice cream, and ice cream was the resounding winner in a race that wasn't even close.

I'm not a political person, but I'm not completely unaware of the political pulse of our society either, and I made a kind of weird decision to go to a place where they had previously denied me service: The Plantation Room. By the time this event took place the working theory was that a freshly scrubbed, properly attired black person could now sit at a soda fountain just like your average big fat sweaty redneck in dung spattered overalls. We were about to test that theory.
I had no idea what they would think of me.

So, we drove right up to the Plantation Room, just like we belonged there, and we marched right in, just like everybody else, and the hostess looked at us as if something foul had been dragged in on the sole of someone's shoe. Did I say there were brand new federal laws in place? She led us, without a spoken word, to a booth. Reggie scooted into a seat and I scooched into the seat across from him.

As he looked around, he saw only wonder; as I looked around, I saw only cold reality. People throughout the entire section were gawking. There was such a hum about the place that people in the adjoining rooms were standing up and craning their necks to discover what that vibration was about. I didn't know if it was because the kid was black or because my hair was long or the peculiar combo, but the good customers of that very fine establishment had no qualms whatsoever about staring and mumbling things under their breath. Little beady eyes squinted at us disapprovingly from round pink faces wherever I looked.

Reggie was oblivious to it all. He was delighted to be there. This, after all, was THE place to go if you wanted the very best banana split anyone could get in all of Richmond. So, I managed somehow to talk him into having a banana split, and I somehow managed to talk myself into a chocolate malt.

When the waitress came, she had nothing to say; just stood there with her pencil poised and waited. Somehow the very process of taking our order seemed to irritate her. I was jovial, but she was having none of it. After taking our order, she disappeared, martyr to a greater cause.

When the good stuff arrived, it was dumped coldly upon the table and a bill was torn from a pad and slapped down on the tabletop, face up. The message, as I read it, was, "Eat up, pay up, and get out." I didn't know whether the unspoken pronoun was nigger lover, or hippie, but we ate, and we enjoyed ourselves.

As we ate, we talked a bit—though neither of us was much for talk—we talked. We talked about how good that ice cream was, and after checking to confirm, we had to admit that it was very good indeed. For the entire time, I was aware of waves of hatred wafting in our direction, but I'm absolutely sure that the kid wasn't. (If I had thought for a moment that he'd noticed, I would have taken him by the hand and left that place.)

As said, we had a good time. But, when we were finished, instead of pushing it, I took the bill directly to the hostess, gave her the sum in round figures, and smiled as we walked out the door. "Boy, the air is sure fresh out here," I said to the kid as we stepped outside. After driving Reggie home, I went back to my place and collapsed.

The next day I called Reggie's grandmother wanting to set up a meeting for the coming week and she said, "Oh, you know, the fella down at the organization asked me to tell you to call him."
"The fellah at the organization wants me to call him?"
"That's what he said."
"Ok," I said, "I'll do that, but, what about next week?"
"I think you better call that man first."

So I called the fellah down at the organization, and he told me that, well, you know, things being what they are and all, they really didn't need any more volunteers at the moment, and someone else, you know, another really well-qualified young man, had been waiting patiently to have a kid assigned to him and, you know, he'd been over-looked somehow, and he was sorry but he didn't think they would be needing me any further.

I never knew if it was because I was white, or because I had long hair, or because I took Reggie to that place and that was seen as putting the kid in danger, but they could hardly admit to any of that. You couldn't say I hadn't been warned though; what dream had I been living in? My entire Richmond experience should have prepared me for this, but I was gutted.

After putting my foot right through one of my paintings, I broke down into tears. In those days I did that sort of thing.

Someday I hope to walk away from that phone conversation; meanwhile writing about this has been like opening an old wound.

CARL BROWN (1964)

Until Andre West showed up, relegating my brother to second fastest sprinter in our district, Carl Brown and his sister were 2/3 of the black kids at East Brunswick High. The third was a girl whose name I never knew—one of those solid A+ students who, in her own quiet way, made the rest of us look and feel stupid.

Carl was one of most mysterious kids I'd ever met. He didn't say much, if anything, ever, to anyone; though he laughed a lot. The look in his eye seemed to say that he found most of what was going on around us to be ridiculous. Though purposefully self-alienated, Carl was also one of the strongest kids around and therefor gladly accepted on the wrestling team.

So, I don't recall exactly how this happened but, (I was a freshman at the time), one day the 141 pound weight class was open on the varsity team and, at 140 pounds soaking wet, I felt like I naturally belonged in that slot. Carl Brown, at a natural and muscular 132 pounds, was more perfectly suited for the 136 pound weight class, but, Coach, Jay Doyle thought Carl would be best at 141. Carl had a year or two more experience wrestling; he was strong and quick and hard to get a hold of, not to mention impossible to pin. But, I wanted it, and asked the coach if I could try out, wrestling Carl Brown.

During the summer I'd attended a wrestling camp at Lehigh University, and came away with a lot of clever ideas about take-downs and escapes, and I was absolutely convinced that, with that knowledge, my longer arms and legs, and my 8 pound advantage, I still didn't stand a chance against Carl Brown. Carl Brown knew it. Coach Doyle knew it. My own brother— who wrestled heavy weight—knew it. Everybody on the team knew it. I couldn't beat Carl Brown and—who was I kidding?— I knew it, going into that match.

When a wrestler finds himself on his back, about to be pinned, if he has the neck and back strength for it, he can bowing his neck back until a 'bridge' is created, lifting his back off the mat—thus avoiding the loss—until he can get out of that predicament. Carl Brown had the strongest bridge anyone had ever seen. When Carl rose up in a bridge, you could have stood upon his chest and jumped up and down and he would not have collapsed. We'd all seen it. In more than one meet, we'd witnessed the frustration his opponents felt at trying to break Carl's bridge. If you were going to beat Carl Brown, it would have to be on points; nobody had ever pinned him.

So, there we are, me and Carl Brown. The whistle blows, and we come at each other. Carl Brown is basically jeering at me as I try some of the moves I learned at Lehigh. And, first period, whatever I do, I cannot get a grip on any part of Carl Brown.

In the second period—with Carl Brown on top and me down—I manage to escape and, picking up a leg, slam Carl Brown to the mat. He's on his back, and BAM—in an instant Carl goes into a bridge. I throw myself on top and I'm tearing away at his arms and his legs and I'm basically bouncing my full weight on Carl Brown's chest... Carl Brown seems to be perfectly relaxed in his bridge; he might as well be reading a book. I'm doing everything I can think of to bring him down, but all of my efforts are futile. I'm frustrated and practically in tears, I want that 141 spot so badly. It means so much to me that I find myself whimpering, through my mouth guard, "Goddamnit, Carl!"

And Carl Brown, from his unbreakable bridge, says quietly into my headgear, "You really want it, huh?"
And though nobody else could possibly have heard Carl Brown say that to me, I'm sure none of them really believed what happened next, when I pinned Carl Brown.

After the coach raised my hand, and declared I'd be wrestling 141 in the up-coming meet, I quickly followed Carl Brown into the locker room, and I started to say 'thanks'. He just looked at me like he had no idea what I was talking about.

But he had that clever Carl Brown glint in his eyes.

THOATS (1968 or 1969, I don't know)

Leaving the University of Kansas one fine December day, we found ourselves discussing the fact that we had, to that point, never picked up a black hitchhiker.

I cannot tell you WHY we were discussing that—I can't tell you why we hadn't picked up any black hitchhikers either, we probably hadn't seen any—but, at that very moment, like a miracle, there he stood, with his thumb out, on the side of the road. Since we could all read the signs when they're in large enough print, we picked him up.
"Where you headed?" Rick asked.
"Where are y'all headed?"
"Los Angeles."
"Well, I ain't going that far, but I'm going that way."

So, I got in the backseat with Ginger, our honored guest got in the front next to Rick, who was driving. "We were just talking about…" Ginger whispered to me. I was equally amazed.

Nothing was said for several minutes as we got underway again. Then, as if inspired, our friend the hitchhiker said, "You know, I could slit y'all's thoats!"

Rick, a scholar yet still a man of action, yanked the wheel smartly and brought the car to a skidding stop on the graveled edge of the road. I leaned forward to let the guy know I was still there. Rick sighed and then spoke directly to him, "Get out of this car!"

The guy seemed honestly surprised by our reaction and responded, stuttering "I said I COULDA slit y'all's thoats, not I WOULDA slit y'all thoats."

I growled, "Get the fuck (pardon me, ladies) out of this car."

He popped out, totally confused, and we drove off leaving him on the side of the road, a mile and a half from where we'd picked him up.

After a few moments Rick turned to me and said, "I didn't like the way he said 'thoats'."
I agreed.
Ginger too: "There *was* something creepy about that."

We could let the coulda/woulda thing go, but saying thoats like that was just expecting too much from us educated white folks.

NO VACANY (1997)

I was working in the only beachfront motel in Del Mar, California. I worked from 6 PM until 2 AM during the summer months. Since it was the only beachfront motel in Del Mar, and since we only had 50 rooms, we were often sold out; during the summer, we were always solidly booked well in advance. There's a world class horse racing track in Del Mar, so nobody was forced at gunpoint to go there. In brief, we never had any problem filling those 50 rooms.

So, one night, during the horse racing season, I arrived at work to see the No Vacancy sign up, in the parking lot and another one—as was usual—hanging on the office door.

A little after midnight a black guy comes in and asks for a room. I say, "Sorry, we're solidly booked."
He says. "What? You don't have any rooms? You don't have even one room?"
I say, "Nope. Sorry. It'll probably be difficult to find anything in Del Mar tonight; maybe you should try heading down toward Solana Beach."
He says, "You don't have even one room?"
I say, "That's why that No Vacancy sign is on the door."
"Yeah," he says, "when you saw me coming, you hung it up."
I said, "That's nonsense; that sign was up when I came in this evening at 6 PM. We've been booked for weeks."

And then the guy says this—while looking me in the eye, he says this: "Racist!"
I say, "What did you say?"
He says, "You're a fucking racist. You see me pull into your parking lot and UP goes the No Vacancy sign."
I say, "As I told you, that sign was up when I arrived here at 6 PM; it's been up for weeks. It has NOTHING to do, whatsoever,

with you. If my own mother walked in that door right now, I'd have to turn her away."
He says, "You're a fucking racist!" and turns and walks out.

I follow him outside and, as he keeps walking, I shout at his back, "You owe me an apology."
He shouts, over his shoulder, "Fuck you, Racist."
I watch him as he gets into his car and drives off.

Then I walk to the entrance to our parking lot and I look at the sign that's posted there, declaring, in solid block letters: "NO VACANCY".

A stopped clock is wrong almost all of the time.

BO DIDDLEY Provides the Free Entertainment

One of the most delightful things I have *ever* witnessed took place just outside the Sacramento Blues Festival in 1986.

I was there to interview Bo Diddley—the old, self-taught, bluesman; who became a legend by playing one unique rhythm, which he claimed to have invented, and mostly in one key. Diddley was a genuine natural born entertainer, and well worth seeing.

When Bo Diddley shows up at the Blues Festival, he's driving this HUGE white Cadillac, with gold wire wheels, gold hood ornament, gold grill, gold pin-striping and, if I recall correctly, there might have been some gold on that car somewhere. He parks this imperial carriage up near the entrance to things, where it cannot easily be ignored. A lot of people break stride to eyeball the vehicle and say, "I bet that's Bo Diddley's car". But, whoever's car it is, the thing is rigged with an alarm system so, if someone steps too close, a warning message comes on; a threatening voice commands, "Step away from the vehicle! You have 10 seconds … nine… eight… seven… six… five…"

So, there are these skinny little black kids—this is where it becomes beautiful and unforgettable—there are three or four of them; my guess, they are like 7 to 10 years old. It's summer, and it's unbearably hot in Sacramento on that day and, basically, the only thing the kids have on is shorts and flip flops.

They've tested this alarm system enough to know where the boundary lies and, seeing it as a challenge, they're taking turns, one after another, stepping into the forbidden zone. They want to see who can stay in there the longest, while the thing counts down, before turning and running away.

When I arrived, a crowd had already gathered to watch these kids. I stood and watched for quite a while myself; and though tempted, I did not partake… I mean who wouldn't want to test their skills against such a device?… but, it was their game. Besides, they were having so much fun that the rest of us were thoroughly engaged just by watching them. We understood every delightful aspect of that game, viscerally.

We were right there with each kid as, giggling and looking back at his friends for encouragement, he hopped into the forbidden zone. We were there with him as the alarm issued its warning: 'Step away from the vehicle!' We held our breath as that thing counted down. 'You have 10 seconds… nine… eight… seven… six…' While each brave challenger, shuddering with fear and delight, held his ground, our hearts beat quicker. And when, squealing and flailing his arms as if electrified, our hero turned and dove frantically outside the forbidden zone—just in time to prevent triggering the dread unknown penalty—we cheered wildly. It was wonderful!

What I liked most about those kids was their playful defiance; standing there proudly, arms folded, staring directly at the highly polished grill of that monstrous vehicle… until the moment when the squealing from his friends, and the shouting of the crowd, drove the young challenger to bail.

I wish I could explain it better. I wish I could say it in such a way that you might feel how neat watching those kids was.

They never stayed in there beyond the count of four; so, we never found out what might happen if that countdown hit zero. But, seeing those little kids screw with that device was a beautiful thing.

It was TRULY a beautiful thing.

GUNS in AMERICA,
as I know it

BILLY, KEN-TUCK an' ME

One day in 1968, at 6:30 AM I met with a guy named Billy, and his partner, Ken-tuck at an industrial warehouse. We all climbed into a big truck and drove over to a cement plant, and through that plant to a mill, where we—this team of three—were painting the structural steel that held the roof on, 45 feet above our heads. Billy, 'as in Hill-Billy', came from Tennessee, and Ken-tuck, from 'guess where'.

They showed me what I needed to do, to work below them, to keep them working above. They worked on the 16 inch wide catwalk overhead, 35 feet in the air, spraying structural steel with grey paint. Below, I mixed paint, I poured paint, I ran equipment up and down on ropes, I cleaned spray guns and kept the pumps working. What was nice about working for these two rednecks was that they didn't expect me to do anything that didn't need doing; as long as the pump was running, the paint didn't run out, the needles in their guns were clean and the lines ran without kinks, they seemed delighted to have me working with them. They called me 'Guitar', "'Cause you look lack you oughter be in some kinda gull-darn rock'n'roll band with all that hair."

My third day working with these guys, they asked me if I would like to go above. And although I have been scared of heights my entire life, I liked these guys so much and wanted so badly to please them, that I said "Sure." The eagerness in my voice sounded foreign to my own ear. But, that's why I was standing on a 16 inch catwalk, 35 feet in the air, working on my spray pattern, when a pickup truck came speeding into the building below, horn blaring. Billy stopped his technique lesson and looked down. I looked down and almost fell.

Below, a couple of guys jumped from the truck, as soon as it came to a stop, and ran over to Ken-tuck, who looked up at us and hollered, "Shut it down! SHUT it DOWN!"
"Why? What's happening?"
"Kerik is folding," they shouted.
We let down our equipment with ropes, tied off the cat walks, made our way down to the mill floor, piled into our trucks, and sped off, back to the warehouse.

One of the informants rode with us, on the way there, and he explained that he'd seen some tax people go into the offices, along with Kerik accountants and lawyers, and when they emerged a few minutes later, he'd overheard them discussing how they'd pay off *all the big guys* they owed money to, first.

When we arrived out front, there were pickup trucks all over the place and good honest, trusting, salt of the earth, hardworking fellows gathering in clumps and talking animatedly. Billy told the guy who rode with us to go over and sit on the boss' Buick and to not let ANYONE drive off with it. Then he went to his own truck in the parking lot and leaned in and took something from the glove compartment and shoved it inside his overalls under his belt. Then Billy and Ken-tuck and Guitar went right into the office.
The secretary seemed surprised to see us.
"What's this we hear about Kerik folding?"
"Oh, that's just..." she looked around behind herself, nodded '*Yes*' emphatically and continued loudly, "That's just a rumor."
"Well," said Billy, "We'd like to get paid."

Right then a guy in an ill-fitting suit with a huge pot belly emerged from the inner offices and demanded, "What's going on out here! I thought I told you to lock that door."
"We'd like to get paid," said Billy.

"Don't you worry," said the pregnant fellow, "everybody's going to get paid."

"We want paid right now."

"You'll be paid on the 15th just like always," he said calmingly.

"We want paid now," said Ken-tuck moving forward in a threatening manner.

The guy in the suit eyed him for a bit then said, "OK. I'll go in and write you guys a check right now." He asked the secretary in a courteous whisper to go over and lock the front door, and she did that while he backed smilingly into the offices. Ken-tuck sat on the secretary's desk and I sat down in one of the chairs reserved for clients, and Billy paced around in front of the door the guy had disappeared into.

After what felt like a very long time the guy emerged with two checks and gave them to Billy and Ken-tuck. "Here you go, fellahs; everything we owe you."

"Guitar too," said Billy.

"What? I'm afraid I'm not sure I und…"

"Guitar," said Billy, pointing to me. "He's gonna want to be paid today too."

"Oh. OK," said the guy. "I see no reason why we can't do that," he said, and slipped back into the offices.

While we were waiting, Garret appeared out of those offices, eyed us critically, spit on the carpet, and walked out through another door. Garret was my former supervisor; a man who'd hated me when I worked under him, and hated me more now that he no longer had authority over me.

When the pregnant guy came out again he handed me a check. But when he started to go back into the office, Ken-tuck had blocked the door.

"Now," said Billy, standing up and walking over to the man, "You're gonna cash 'em."

"Now, boys," said the man, "there's no reason for that. Just take your checks to the bank in the morning and they'll be glad to cash them for you."
Billy looked at the guy; the guy looked at him. Ken-tuck stood there with his arm across the door, blocking his retreat.
"These checks are perfectly good. I assure you."
Billy reached inside his overalls and revealed something to the guy—which later I learned was the handle of a gun. The guy in the suit, borrowed a pen from the secretary, asked us each to sign the back of our check, and went back into the offices.

Shortly after, the boss' son emerged and leaned up against a wall, with his hands behind his back, and stared at us. After several minutes of loud voices from within, the guy came out again, said, "There's really no need for this," and counted out what was due to each of us, in cash, on the secretary's desk. "Lock that door again after they leave," he instructed someone and stormed back into the inner offices.

We went outside and everybody in the parking lot looked to us. They wanted answers. They wanted to know what went on in there. We said nothing. Ken-tuck made a gesture, declaring, "It's every man for himself, boys." Billy said to me, "Get your car, Guitar, and folly us, we gonna go spend some of this money while IT'S still good."

And we did.

The PRICE of BEER in PARIS, after the LIBERATION (1944)

My father told me that after the liberation of Paris the soldiers of his division were each given, in turn, a day off, to go into town and try to forget about things for a brief moment. When it was his turn my father went into the city, found a little bistro, walked straight up to the bar, and ordered a beer. When the beer was placed before him he placed a single note on the counter. It was the smallest thing he had, the only thing he had, the equivalent of about one month's pay.

The French gentleman behind the bar made much of the fact that it was a big note, gesticulating broadly and rolling his eyes heavenward for help, and opening the till to reveal its lamentable emptiness. My father demonstrated that it was the only thing he had. So, the barkeep shrugged and, making a gesture suggesting that he might find change in the back room, took the note and disappeared behind some curtains.

After finishing his beer my father spoke to the guy behind the counter in his best French, asking for his change. Oh, he was sorry, this French gentleman, but he did not understand what the good American soldier was trying to say. Did he want another beer? Non? Well what could it be then? What could he possibly want? My father, first in French and then in English, asked once again politely for the change. Oh, but, he did not understand, this poor French fellow; after all, unfortunately, he did not speak English. He was sorry. Regret was written deeply upon his sincerely furled face. He was very sorry, but he could not even guess what this American soldier was trying to communicate. Perhaps it was one of those small mysteries that must, alas, remain a mystery.

My father, having just been through four months of unrelenting Hell, was wearing a side arm at the time, a 45 automatic.

So, "just to clarify things" he thought he would take his side arm and lay it gently upon the bar... a mere suggestion. Of course, whatever your intentions, two pounds of cold steel hitting a marble countertop can make what my father called "a substantial clunk"—Clack!, as the French might say—and it raised a few eyebrows. Suddenly the place went dead silent.

As suddenly, the barkeep remembered that Monsieur had not yet received his change. Oh la-la la-la! How could he have forgotten? He ran through the curtains and, returning as quickly as he departed, laid the change nicely upon the counter. The poor French man could not understand my father's French and, unfortunately, he did not understand any English, but that handgun spoke a language he understood perfectly.

My father was 19 years old at the time, about the same age I was when Billy's handgun spoke on my behalf.

The IMPLICATION of a GUN

During the 1990s I worked with an ex-Marine named Mike in a Del Mar beachfront motel. Mike was a tough guy, who many people, for some reason which he could never understand, seemed to think was rude.

On summer weekends, when the place was open until 2 AM, Mike would, on occasion, stick a handgun in his belt, in the center of his back. And, whenever someone came in who clearly meant trouble, he'd emerge from his office with his right hand tucked behind his back, resting upon the butt of that gun.

One time, a loud belligerent drunk came in and, thinking I was there alone, started threatening me. From inside his office, Mike monitored what was going on and, when he thought it had gone far enough, he came out with his hand tucked behind his back.

The drunk looked at Mike, noted the hand behind his back and, guessing what that might mean, bowed, apologized to me, smiled at Mike, and quickly backed out the door.

"Mike," I said, "I don't think a gun was really necessary."
Mike said, "Me neither." And, as he turned to go back into his office, I saw that his hand was tucked into his empty belt.

So, I can tell you this first hand: at times, just the implication that there might be a gun present can quell a problem.

DRUGS in AMERICA,
as I know it

ONE HIT WONDER

If anyone on earth was born to be an artist in the grandest sense of the word it was Ducky Ryan. Everyone who knew anything at all about painting recognized his enormous talent instinctively. Better yet, people in the position to help Ducky attain greatness seemed eager to do whatever they could for him. Beyond that—whether they knew him as a great artist or not—every man, woman, child, dog, cat, bird, cop, thief, swindler and politician (if such a fine line can be drawn), not to mention drooling idiot, loved Ducky on sight. There was just something about him; women were overcome with the surging desire to bed him, and men wanted to claim him as their friend. Ducky was a celebrity from the moment he set foot on campus.

My honor is that Ducky and I both had a piece stolen from the Emerging Artists' Show, at the Virginia Museum of Art. Ducky, however, **sold** three pieces and **won** Best of Show. Still, to have my humble entry stolen, along with Ducky's, was something.

In those days painting at RPI was predominantly hard-edge. That means large cohesive, un-modulated fields of color bordering each other with crisp, clean, typically straight, lines. These paintings were usually executed on very large canvasses. And, although scale is a matter worthy of investigation unto itself, I'm not sure any of us understood that at the time; our justification for painting large—as any other atrocity committed in the world of art—could be found in Art Forum. However, we were mainly influenced by the Washington color school—professional painters from nearby D.C.—and they painted BIG.

Meanwhile, Ducky was shaking things up locally by producing work that one awestruck painting instructor described as, 'incorporating the hard edge approach with traditional classic painting techniques'.

Feel free to snort derisively at that idiotic remark, I just did.

Basically, Ducky painted the bottom two thirds of his long vertical canvases with wavering un-modulated locales stacked like geological strata, and dashed off some painterly, relatively unconvincing, clouds in the upper third. This won him awards and notoriety, and a growing pool of fawning followers, both instructors and students. My work at that point was strictly, and somewhat defiantly, neither large nor hard edge. Unfortunately, my stupid little paintings were also dull, predictable, easily understood; serious work which was readily dismissed.

Ducky was one of the first people to recognize my work for what it was, and at some point he invited me over to his place. Anyone might tremble with delight at such an invitation. Not really a social creature by nature, I trembled with fear.

When I got there, it was Ducky and a kid named Wayne—who looked like a partially civilized Mick Jagger—a kid named Aaron—who everybody adored because his cranium, from every indication, contained no brain—and a nameless unobtrusive chick who had taken it upon herself to wait hand and foot upon Ducky. After she left, Wayne pulled out a reefer and these guys began to pass it around. When offered, I said, "I don't smoke, thanks," and that was OK. But, after a while of breathing in their exhaust, I reconsidered my position and announced meekly that I'd, you know, maybe, if it's still on offer, give it a try.

After instruction, I took a small hit and watched them as they watched me for a while, before they moved on to other things. When my ears began to get really hot, I interrupted to ask, "Is it normal for your ears to get really hot?"
"Your ears are hot?"
"Yeah, my ears are cookin'" I said.

And, as it turned out, that was very possibly the most hilarious thing anyone had ever said in the entire history of mankind.

When I finally stopped coughing, I looked up and noticed that Ducky had the head of a rabbit, Wayne had the head of a donkey and Aaron looked a great deal like a sea-going turtle. I thought that was a little peculiar but, at the same time, those transformations seemed alright with me; I'd found myself in an accepting mood.
"How do you like it?" asked the donkey.
"It's OK," I said.
"Are you feeling alright?"
"Yeah, except for these hot ears."
"You realize that you're now a felon," said the rabbit.
"Worse," said the turtle, "is the paranoia."
"Well, I don't know why this should be illegal," I said.

As for paranoia, this was one of the very few times in my life that I felt perfectly comfortable; better still, I felt like I belonged.

"Oh, no!" said the donkey suddenly, and pointed toward the ceiling. We all looked up where he was pointing. There was a poster taped up there depicting a large hole in the ceiling; a cop was looking down at us through the lath and plaster; and another was already stepping through the hole on his way down to nab us. I cracked up, but soon found myself thinking about my stroll around campus the first day I arrived at RPI.

I was walking toward the site of the future library, when a young man, barefoot and bare-chested, came running down the street, chased by a man in a dark suit. Seconds later, a blue Ford sedan came speeding down the street, jumped the curb, and screeched to a halt inches from the kid. The doors flew open and three men in suits popped out. They dragged the young man to the ground, and started swinging away wildly with their fists.

After exhausting themselves, they yanked the kid to his feet, threw him in the back seat of the Ford, backed out, and drove off. "Wow," I said to a campus cop who had just arrived huffing heavily beside me, "what was that about?"
"Dope," he said smugly. "Those men are federal agents. It's really great to see the good guys in action isn't it?"

"Look at this," said the goat, jarring me back to my senses. He handed me the album cover of Beggar's Banquet. "Look inside." And so, I did. And it was the most remarkable thing I had ever seen in my entire life; I had never seen anything like that. I'd never even imagined anything like that. I began to study it.

And, I studied it so deeply and for so long that when I surfaced again Ducky, Wayne, and Aaron had all departed. I didn't remember them leaving, though I did vaguely recall acknowledging something one of them had said. I looked to the cops above and snorted. At that rate, those guys were never gonna catch me.

I got up and made my way down an exceptionally long hallway and out the door.

The day was brilliant. Looking around I realized for the first time that street signs lead a quiet little life of their own… which I could not help but admire.

One Day Package Delivery Service (1968 or so)

I was playing chess with Howard on the steps of the Grove
Avenue apartment building where he lived along with the
Richmond branch of Motorcycle Morons of the Confederacy,
MC. I was probably doing my usual job of it—feeling
unreasonably confident into mid-game—when Howard asked
casually, "How would you like to make three hundred dollars?"

That was the equivalent of asking me if I would like to win the
lottery. "Well, sure," I said. "What do I gotta do?"
"You go down to a place I tell you to go, and a guy will give you
a package. You take the package to the address he tells you and
the guy who takes the package from you will hand you $300
cash. It's yours." Howard shrugged.
"How far between the place I pick this thing up and the place I
drop it off?"
"Three blocks," he said. "It's right over here on N. Harvie. Three
hundred dollars..." he urged. "You want to do it?"
"But, Howard, I don't get it," I said. "I go somewhere and pick
up a package, and I deliver it to a guy three blocks away, and *he*
hands me three hundred dollars?"
Howard said nothing, but, he took my queen.

"Howard!" I protested, "Why didn't you tell me to guard my
queen?"
"Do you want the job or not?"
"It's a courtesy, Howard," I said, taking one of his knights. "I
don't understand why the guy doesn't just go and pick it up
himself."
"Check," said Howard. "You want the job or not?"
"Why don't you do it?" I interposed a pawn.
Howard just blew out steam and shrugged as if to say, Me?... for
a mere three hundred bucks? And then he said, "Checkmate."
"When do I have to do this?"

"You can do it right now."

"I pick up a package and deliver it three blocks away and the guy hands me three hundred dollars and that's all mine to keep?" I really couldn't believe it.

"Yes," Howard was becoming bored with my density. "Yes, yes, yes, yes, yes," he said, answering any further questions I might have, in advance.

"That's a hundred dollars per block."

"DO YOU WANT the job?"

"Can I go home first and get some stuff?"

"Be quick about it."

I had no idea what might have been in that package, but I'm not an idiot. I thought the best thing to do would be to attire myself like a painter—which I was—so as not to attract any undue attention while delivering this package. So that's how I ended up walking down Grove Avenue with a large stretcher over my shoulder—my usual thing—and a bag full of various jars of paint—also typical behavior for me—and carrying a paper bag with who knows what in it, to a guy who opened the door, *said nothing*, took the bag, looked in it, and handed me THREE HUNDRED dollars CASH. (Three HUN-dred Dollars CASH!)

I still don't know how that worked. As I write this I'm more than 70 years old and I guess I must be as naïve as I was back then; I still don't know why the delivery guy should walk with $300. Back then, I didn't care. I lived off that $300 like a king for months; it was, after all, the equivalent of about 10 months' rent.

Despite the monumental nature of that windfall I never did such a thing again. For one thing, Howard never offered again, but for another, it just didn't seem worth it to me. That was the longest 10 minutes I'd ever spent in my life, and three of the longest blocks I ever wobbled along weak-kneed.

JUST DOING THEIR JOBS (1970)

One fine day, with nothing better to do, I dedicated myself to finding someone who might want to drop acid with me. I spent the entire morning and part of the afternoon looking for Susan Ensley—whose mind it would have the least effect on. The next thing I knew—being what I was at that time—I'd taken the thing by myself, alone.

As soon as I realized I was tripping, being a man of some experience, I purposely avoided all mirrors; but, acid, being what it is, I soon found myself hallucinating pretty heavily. I felt like I was adrift alone in a tiny boat, in dangerous waters, and I didn't really take to the relentless pounding drums that followed me wherever I went. The drums seemed to be speaking to me, telling me horrible things about imminent catastrophic earthly events. (That's as close as I can come to it.)

Of course, for a kid who had spent most of his college career convinced that he was not going to live to see the age of 25, such fears were somewhat undignified. If I had been true to my own convictions I should have taken the opportunity to climb up to the top of a very tall building, and while clinging to its spire, shouted, "Pound on, ye drums of doom!" Then I would have laughed in a hysterical/maniacal (you choose) manner and sadly/ proudly (your choice again) whispered, "I knew this was going to happen," before casting myself off, to flutter away.
But I didn't.

Instead, despite my fright, I knew that I needed to get quickly to someone I could trust. By what miracle I do not know, I found myself at Joanie's place and I told her that I was sick and worried and frightened and I needed to go to a hospital. Incapable of explaining precisely what I was experiencing, I somehow managed to form the phrase, "I did some bad acid."

I'm pretty sure—fairly certain actually—that Joanie was not the very proudest that she had ever been of me, at that moment. But she did her duty, as a true friend, and took me to the campus police.

While driving me to the hospital, this big beefy redneck with the shaved head, this campus cop, told me, "I do NOT like what you did. In fact," he said, looking at me in the rearview mirror, "I HATE what you did." He waited until he could conclude the thought calmly, "But, it's my job to get you to a doctor and to see that you get treatment." I was not so stoned that I did not recognize a hero when one spoke to me in earnest, in good old plain American. His statement cut through the all drums and the rest of what was going on in my greatly distended mind, and it stuck with me. I still admire that man for his principles.

We arrived at the hospital and a specialist in bad trips—such were the times that a small southern university had a crew of doctors on duty to handle bad trips—took me aside, into a little room, and asked, "What's your name?"
I said, "Name?"
He said slowly distinctly, "Your name; do you know your name?"
I said, "I don't even know what *name* is. What is *name*?"
He told me, "It's a word, or a couple of words that each person has that identifies him as an individual. It's a word that stands only for you."
"Oh, OK," I said. I thought about the concept.
"Like, my name is…" He looked down at the pin attached to his smock as if reading it… "Doctor Hartley. Louis Hartley. That's my name. We all have one. This is Nurse Simms. Her name is Nancy. You have a name too."
"Wow," I said, "I like that idea!" It did sound like a very good idea at the time. "I REALLY like that idea!" I said with delight.

But, I had no idea whatsoever what my name might be. I truly did like the idea that I had one, though.

He helped me take out my wallet and found my driver's license—a couple more ideas which I also found absolutely fascinating. "Your name is Richard," he said.
"Wow," I said, "I like the sound of it."
"That's you," he said pointing a finger at my chest.
"Man," I said, "This is such a GREAT idea!" I couldn't get over the inventiveness behind it. "I really like it."

I looked at him dumbly for a while waiting for the next step in our adventure together. While he asked me questions about what I had taken and how long ago and what it had looked like and what was going on in my head, I continued to marvel at the name thing. The drums, by then, had somewhat diminished.
"Look," he said, "I'm going to give you something that should neutralize the hallucinations a little bit for you, but it won't do anything about whatever the acid was cut with. With luck it was cut with something simple, like speed."
He gave me a shot, and said, "I'd like to show you something."

He led me down a hallway, to a room where a young woman my age was wrapped in a straightjacket and ramming herself against the walls of her little cell, screaming in horrible fear.
"You want to avoid that if you can," he said to me.
I was astounded at his insight; the guy seemed to be reading my mind; I DID want to avoid that.

So, then he took me into a room where Joanie was waiting for me, and he said a few things to her before he handed me off to her. He turned to me, put a hand on my shoulder and said, "Is there anything else you feel you might like to know before you go?"
"Yeah," I said. "First though, thank you."

"That's OK, that's what we do here."
"No, but really, thanks," I said.
"That's OK. Was there something else?"
"Yes, can you explain how these names are selected?"
He laughed genuinely. "I think your friend here will be able to explain that to you on your way home."
Then, we just walked out the door.

The drums were gone completely and things were looking pretty nice outside. As we walked away I asked Joanie, "Do they just let insane people walk away like this all the time?"
As we walked along I looked up at the palm trees that lined the boulevard, and I asked Joanie, "When did we arrive in L.A.?"
She answered sweetly, but she was obviously concerned.

Later that day the hallucinations ended and I discovered that the acid had indeed been cut with speed.

I didn't sleep for three days.

STORIES FOR PEOPLE WHO DON'T BELIEVE BEER IS A DANGEROUS DRUG (1969)

In those days, if we weren't going a very long distance in a car, we didn't go at all. I mean if it wasn't New York City (600 miles), or Cape Cod (further), or California (three days and nights of sleepless non-stop, tag-team driving), what was the sense of packing up and climbing into a car?

We were walking around in New York City one very cold January morning—on our way, first to Cape Cod and then on to California—when Rick stopped me mid-stride and said, "Bob Dylan owns a couple of these apartment buildings on this block."
"How do you know that?" I asked.
"We have our way of knowing these things," he assured me.
"And," he added knowingly, "I understand he's a pretty lousy landlord."
"What does that mean?" I asked.
"Let's just say that he's not very giving."
"Is a landlord supposed to be giving?" I asked. "But, forget that—how do you know Bob Dylan owns one of these buildings?"
"A couple of these buildings," Rick corrected me.

At that point we were directly across from the White Horse Tavern as two huge (HUGE) black men emerged, wearing big fur coats. They stood on either side of the door like sentry. As Rick and I watched, a little guy in a huge white fur coat and a broad brimmed hat came out and walked down the street with the two huge black guys pacing him at about three feet.
It was Bob Dylan.
"Wow," I said to Rick, "You started talking about Bob Dylan and he materialized before our very eyes."
"THAT," said Rick, "is exactly why I make a point never to mention Perry Como." (He may have said Vic Damone.)

There were not many people of that sort (famous) who I either knew much about or felt like I cared to know much about, but Bob Dylan was one of them; so, I was happy. Went to New York, saw Bob Dylan coming out of the White Horse Tavern. So far, it was a pretty cool trip.

When we got to Provincetown, we drove out to a bar at the very end of the point (is it Stingray Point?), a place where Provincetown locals hung out. There we discovered an old schoolmate, Ed Gearing, sitting at the bar. We took a table and invited Ed over to talk with us about life in P'town.

Apparently he was caretaker and child-care giver for Norman Mailer. He looked after the house, when the Mailers weren't in town and after the kids when they were. Maybe 2, maybe 3 beers later, Norman Mailer, who everybody knows was a Golden Gloves Champion, and who then was known locally as Provincetown's reigning resident celebrity hard-ass, came through the door. Mailer shoved his way through the parting crowd, swaggered over to our table, and started shouting at our friend, Ed. Ed stood up and, defensively, apologetically, started to offer a reasonable explanation for whatever the problem might have been, but Norman Mailer wasn't satisfied. Apparently, he felt it was his right to humiliate Ed loudly and openly in public.

He was well underway when, inspired by the quest for justice which dwells deep within me after three beers, I rose to my feet, bottle number four in hand, and placed myself directly between Norman Mailer and Ed.
"Excuse me," said Norman Mailer, in a tone that any celebrity might use in speaking down to anyone who is not. He tried to step around me to get to Ed, but, as he moved I moved too, blocking his way again.
"I'm trying to talk to my au pair," Mailer complained, and I remained solidly, exactly, where I stood.

I didn't know what an au pair was, but I was pretty sure, whatever it was, the job didn't require verbal abuse in the public arena... and especially if that au pair was an old friend of mine. At that point in my life I'd never done anything like this before —although I've done it since, each time 'in the name of justice' —but, when Mailer moved again, I moved again. Each time I repositioned myself so that I was standing directly between Norman Mailer and my friend, Ed.

This dance didn't last long. Mailer gave me a look which made no impression on me whatsoever at the moment, but later—after I'd heard that he'd stabbed his wife, for example—gave me much to think about. I think Ed may have saved me when he said, "I gotta go," and simply departed. That left me and Norman Mailer evaluating each other at very close range.

He was looking at me coldly, while I, inadvisably perhaps, looked down at him, bemused. I stood my ground with a silly drunken look on my face until Norman Mailer snorted, observed me for a brief moment, sneered, and walked away shaking his huge block-like head. I'm told that the local crowd sighed a massive sigh of relief... or disappointment; I wasn't told which. At any rate they all returned to their drinks while I remained standing, bottle raised in glorious victory. I was drunk!

Rick tugged on my sleeve and said, "Mailer used to be a Golden Gloves champion, Richard." I snorted loudly in disregard. "Yeah," I said, "and I used to be sober!"
(Much of this story is pieced together from the eye witness reports of others who were seated at that table that night.)

So, at that point in the trip it was: went to New York, saw Bob Dylan emerging from the White Horse Tavern; wandered up to P'town where Norman Mailer considered cleaning my clock, but didn't; and we were on our way to California, by way of Aspen, where we stopped in for another beer, or three or four or more.

We were coming out of a place called Pinocchio's and, for some reason which I cannot either understand or explain, I had a small cigar hanging out of my mouth as we picked our way carefully, drunkenly, across the icy street toward our car.

Rick, who smoked Parliaments, had no matches on him. I'm fairly certain those little plastic throw-away lighters had not yet been invented, or, if they had they were too expensive for us dolts. So my cigar remained unlit. When Rick whispered, "Hey, look, it's Paul Simon," I got an idea.

As Paul Simon approached I pointed at my cigar and said, "Hey, buddy, you got a match?"
Paul Simon said, "I think so…" and started searching through his pockets. "Wait a minute," he said, then went over to his car—a discreet little black Mercedes—opened the door, crawled around in there and emerged with a matchbook. He raised it to show us, then tip-toed his way carefully across the icy pavement to us and lit my cigar. He was very very nice.
(I think I should tell you that.)

I took a few puffs, to see that it stayed lit, and said, "Thanks, pal." In my foggy mind, I wanted to make it clear to him that I didn't know him from Adam. (Even though I admired his work.) "You're welcome," he said simply, walked carefully back to his car, got in, started the engine and took off.

For some reason my own obnoxious behavior pleased me greatly. (Who can explain such stuff?) I was delighted by the fact that Paul Simon had lit my cigar. I was even more delighted that I had called him "Pal". Rick was amused too.

So was Ginger who said, "I thought you were going to pat him on the back there for a minute."
"HA!" I laughed. "I was thinking about patting him on the head," I said, "but I'm not that drunk."

So, at that point in the trip it was: went to New York, saw Bob Dylan emerging from the White Horse Tavern; wandered up to Provincetown where Norman Mailer considered cleaning my clock, but didn't; stopped in at Aspen, where Paul Simon lit my cigar, and we were on our way to San Francisco.
My God, Liberty is a wonderful thing!

Sometime, later that afternoon perhaps, I detected Ginger deep in thought. I asked her, "What are you thinking about, Ginger?"
She said, "I'm trying to figure out at what point you started becoming such a smart aleck."

It was like a blow to the head. It was like the punch Norman Mailer never threw. It was a very good question; an excellent question. How had the excruciating shyness upon which my entire character was so shakily built become buried so deeply in rank belligerence?

With a few beers under my belt, I had certainly become creatively destructive, as well as predictably unpredictable. I, like Lucius, had been turned into an ass and there were no roses anywhere in sight.

The question that began to haunt me, at that point, was: Had I become a permanent jackass?

THE GLIMMER OF INSIGHT

Sometime around 1978 I was thrown out of an Irish bar in San Francisco because of my tendency to be overly honest, even in the midst of a hostile crowd.

Things had been peaceful enough until I thought I'd offer my unsolicited apolitical views to the drummer of an ideologically driven Irish band. They'd spent the last three hours revving up the crowd with loud, raucous revolutionary songs and, while they were busy up there challenging the gods with their shouting, I was reflecting. If you can agree with me that once you've heard three Irish revolutionary songs you've heard them all, at least twice, then you might guess my state of mind.
I'd had a few beers as well.

So, during a break between sets, after the other band members had put down their instruments and made their way through the adoring crowd to the bar, I shoved my chair back, rose, steadied myself, turned and stumbled to the apron of the stage to address the drummer. He was conscientiously tuning one of his drums when I came up, and I waited for him to acknowledge me.
"I guess it must be pretty easy playing the part of the big bad revolutionary 6000 miles away from all the action," I slurred.

Of course, he was shocked; when he saw me approaching he had expected to hear me gush about how great their show was. And, because poseurs seem to take offense at any uncalled-for intrusion of reality into their act, he decided almost instantly that he didn't like me. He thought his band-mates might not like me too, and signaled them to put down their drinks and come back quickly, to hear what I had to say. Meanwhile, he wanted to be sure he'd heard me correctly. "What did you say?' he asked.

98

I know that simple undeniable truth often treads upon the bloated self-assurance of mindless ideologues, but I wasn't trying to insult the guy; I was merely making an observation. "I SAID," I began arrogantly, "it must be pretty goddamned easy for you big tough revolutionaries singing about the glories of violent revolution 6000 miles away from all the action." I gave him my most charming smile.

As fate would have it, rather than clarify things, repeating my statement only lead to further misunderstanding and I soon found myself surrounded by a swelling crowd. I remember it somewhat in a haze. That throng and I were like magnets of the same polarity; as the mob advanced upon me some unseen force propelled me on ahead of them, and right out the front door.

The next thing I remember clearly is standing on the sidewalk with a very large—massive—bouncer warning the others to go back inside. He shut the door behind them smartly before turning to me. "Are you soom kind oov a fookin' idjut?" he asked.

I looked at him for a long time, studying his face. It seemed like a reasonable question, so I was giving it the thought it deserved. It was certainly one explanation for my behavior. "Are you?" he demanded. "No," I said meekly. (Actually, at the moment, I wasn't sure.) He looked down on me with the tortured kindness of an older brother, shook his head, sighed and said, "Jist go hoom then."

He turned and walked back into the bar, leaving me alone on the sidewalk to think about things for a bit. Then I wobbled off in a generally homeward direction.

And, I think, on that very night I managed to cross a street all by myself, unassisted, with only 40 or 45 years' experience.

COCAINE (1986)

I'll tell you what I know about cocaine.

By all accounts it is addictive. NOBODY would deny that; nobody would even consider denying it; cocaine is highly addictive and that's that. The addictive nature of the damned stuff is one of the things addicts like about it.

Despite what anyone may say about cocaine being a "recreational drug", it is anything but. Cocaine is a desperation drug. It's used by people who want to get as far away from reality as they possibly can, as quickly as they possibly can.

From my own experience I can tell you that under the influence of cocaine you feel that you can do anything; moral or immoral, legal or illegal, rational or irrational, sane or insane—and get away with it. Given the opportunity—and by that I mean unless something steps in to prevent it—you'll try.

I did cocaine one time, and I didn't like it.

When I found myself attempting to break into a locked display case in an antique store full of customers, in order to steal a Persian rug, I knew something was wrong. Only later, when I remembered that I'd actually walked twelve blocks back to my truck to get a crowbar—after my fingernails had failed to gain access—did I realize precisely how wrong. With cocaine in my system I found myself doing something that never would have even occurred to me otherwise.

The only thing I could see of myself in those stupid actions was a genuine appreciation for the beauty of that rug, and the fact that I wanted to steal it so that I could give it as a gift to a friend—I was sure she'd enjoy it as much as I did.

100

I was surprised and ashamed at what I'd done. So, I dropped cocaine cold; never did it again; never considered doing it again. Cocaine is no friend of mine.

After my experience with cocaine, I realized something.

I realized that politicians all act as though they're on cocaine — each and every damned last one of them. And, if they were, they'd act no differently than they do today.
Nor would they feel any shame.

LIFE BEGINS TO WORK ITSELF OUT (NOV. 1971)

So, pretty quickly now. Just to wrap things up: I found myself hanging out near the restaurant where a junkie I knew was manager, and he made a point of seeing that I was fed. And when I needed a place to stay but had no money, he took me in.

It was a big house, and the people who lived there fitted out the garage so that I could paint and sleep out there; and, when the opportunity came up, they hired me at the restaurant as a dishwasher. I got involved with the junkie's girlfriend, who took off a week from their ages-old, on again off again arrangement to move into the garage with me, for a few awkward days.

She promised me she would kick and, one day soon after that promise, I walked into the main house and saw her curled up on the living room floor, alternately sweating and shaking with body wracking chills. She was as white as a ghost and, when she looked at me with hollow eyes, she didn't recognize me. I didn't recognize her either. I felt terrible and didn't know what to do. I couldn't just stand there and watch her. When I went to him agitated and concerned, Henry said, "Leave her alone. She'll be alright. She always goes through this when she tries to kick."

A day or two later she asked me to take her downtown to a methadone clinic, and I was glad, even proud, to do so. It meant she was taking this idea of kicking seriously. While she was inside the clinic, I waited outside on the sidewalk among junkies and whores, the only sober guy for miles. After a long time, she came out and went directly up to a tall black man in a full-length black and white leather coat and kissed him full on the lips. They then shook hands like lovers parting and—while he sipped from a paper cup—she came to me and said, "Let's go."

I was furious. We walked in silence back to the car. After we got in, before I started the engine, I asked her bitterly, "So, who was that guy?"

"Which one?"

"That tall black guy you kissed?"

"Can you do me one more favor?"

We sat in the car for a bit at loggerheads.

Eventually I said, "Tell me who that guy was and I'll do you the favor."

"OK," she said, "The truth is, I don't know who that guy is. I've seen him at the clinic before but I don't know his name."

"You walked up to a guy, who you don't even know his name, and kissed him on the lips?"

She unfolded her hand to reveal a crumpled wad of moist bills.

"What is that?"

"That's what he gave me for the methadone."

"What methadone?"

She looked at me for a long time thinking, I suppose, that I could work this puzzle out for myself. But, when I couldn't, she explained, even though it pained her to have to. "I go in; I get my dose; I come out; I spit it in the mouth of someone who distributes; he pays cash. It's a good deal all around. Now I want you to fulfill your promise," she said cheerily.

"I thought they ask you to open your mouth after you get your dose."

She smiled as if she possessed some secret elfish wisdom.

"Now," she said, "it's time for you to fulfill your promise."

So, things are happening pretty quickly now, and as we drive out to the farm near the James River, I'm telling her that I will NEVER EVER EVER again either give her money or drive her anywhere, even to the methadone clinic... especially to the methadone clinic… or ANYWHERE that has anything at all to do with heroin. She accepts that with alacrity.

At the farm, as I pull in, the seemingly empty old house becomes animated; there are faces looking out of the upstairs windows and two guys with handguns in their belts come out and casually lean on the wooden rail that leads up to the front door. She tells me to park about 50 yards away from the house, under a big tree, and to wait in the car.

The guys on the steps are looking directly at me and each of them has his hand resting solidly on the butt of his weapon, as she hops out of the car and skips like a child toward the house. As she bounds joyfully up the steps she nods to them and they respond NOT AT ALL—they are staying focused on me. One of these guys moves along the porch to a position where he can, I'm thinking, get a view of my license plate number. I am, of course, trying to look anywhere but at these two guys. (You should try THAT some time.)

She goes into the house and comes out several minutes later with treasure clutched in her tiny hands. She gets into the car beside me and joyfully shows me what she has. It just looks like two pills to me. "Where to?" I ask coldly.
"Right here," she says, and out of her purse come the necessary items. I have my head turned decidedly away from her as she does whatever it is she does. Not that it was anything I hadn't seen before; it was just something I didn't care to see again. I had had enough; I just hadn't realized it until that moment.

I couldn't shake the image of her kissing the black guy and now, while she's hitting up beside me, I suddenly realize that he was not sipping FROM the cup, but spitting INTO it. Of course, she had pretty much told me that but, at the time I was so angry that I didn't fully understand what she'd said.

Here's a question for you: How much would you pay for a cup of *slightly used* methadone?

While I sat there, I was thinking about the times I gave her $20 and watched her walk away. I was thinking about the time I drove her to a certain corner in a part of town I had never been in before, and didn't feel comfortable being in then, and upon her frantic insistence that I leave her there. I was thinking about the time I drove her to the hospital to be tested for I forget what and her asking the nurse if she could draw her own blood.

I remember the look on the nurse's face; first the shock, then the repulsion, before she turned white and wobbled at the thought. Meanwhile her patient took the tourniquet from the tray and almost joyfully strapped it on.

This was a struggle for me because, I remembered one evening, around Thanksgiving, when Robin arrived in the house looking extraordinarily pregnant and proudly produced a turkey and all the fixings from under her coat, including two cans of cranberry sauce. I could not believe that. Meanwhile, as Margaret prepared to cook the bird, Henry sent Robin back to the store to steal a couple bottles of wine and, she came back with two bottles of Blue Nun. I couldn't believe that either. While all of this was going on, I just sat around amazed at the way these outlaws lived their lives; for them that was all just good fun.

And, of course, I remembered her lying in my arms out there in the garage as we looked up at the Richmond starlit night, through the skylight in the garage roof.

When the university from which I'd graduated discovered I was working for them as a part-time janitor, and thought it might be better to let me go than to keep me employed (that's how much they thought of their own degree), these people, these junkies, these low-lifes, took me in. They made sure that I was fed and gave me a place to stay. Most importantly, these good people— outlaws who lived their lives beyond the protection of the law— told me directly that they wanted to be sure I had a place where I could continue to paint. Once in a while, such was their support, I'd return to discover tubes of paint where, when I left, there had only been crumpled empty tubes.

The other side of that, the other undeniable aspect of it, is that any one of these good people would look Christ himself straight in the eye and, without blinking, lie to him in order to score a hit of heroin.

When next I looked, Robin had kindly replaced things into her purse and her head was back, resting on the seat of the car; her eyes were barely open, and she was smiling.
"This is the very last time," I said coldly as I started the engine.
"It's the very last goddamned time."
She said nothing.
Her head lolled as I drove away from that dreadful farmhouse.

So, then, as I recall, word came down within the community that there was about to be a big bust and that it was going to be a heroin bust, and distribution had been halted for a bit. Good luck to those who needed dope of any sort and did not already have it… which was everybody who used. You don't put heroin aside for a rainy day, you get it and you use it. Expiration date: NOW, this very goddamned minute; the stuff just doesn't seem to keep.

There I am, Mister Innocent, having never shot drugs in my life, mister painter-part-time-dishwasher guy, out in the garage slapping paint on canvas while the outside world tears itself apart. To my mind, as I recall I was doing some pretty nice work at that time; for the first time in my life I was working large, because, for the first time in my life, I had the space for it.

I had stretched a couple of beautiful 6 X 6 canvasses, and had some drawings pinned up on the garage wall. It was going nicely. I had plans. I had nothing but time. My mind was reeling day and night with the wonderful possibilities ahead.

That garage was situated on an alley. The main house, in which my acquaintances lived, and to which Robin had returned after I put an end to helping her score her drugs, was situated on a pleasant little tree-lined street. The garage had two windows facing that alley and, as I worked, I would look up when I heard anything going on out there. Those windows were my TV.

So it was that I looked up one day and saw a cop's car drive slowly by the first window, then slowly through the next. I saw the profile of the cop in the passenger seat as they rolled by. Ten minutes later I saw the same profile of the same guy as they drifted by again. By the time they drifted by my window the third time I was out the door and up the back steps, into to the main house, and frantically telling them inside what I had seen. They knew.

Henry said matter-of-factly, "We may be next."
"Well what are you going to do?" I asked.
"What do you want us to do?" someone said.
"I don't know… get out, go away. Flee." I was nearly hysterical. They laughed at that.
One of them said, "Pah, it's easier to get heroin in prison than it is to get it out here."
"What?" I said, but they'd moved on without me.
"It's also better stuff," someone else said.
"What?" I said trying to remain calm, trying to make sense of how relaxed they were.

I recalled once when they discussed ways to make needles out of things like cigarette wrappers, even though there is— according to these same people—no lack of good needles in the joint. It was just a casual little evening discussion among friends. Their extreme calm had me almost insane. I dashed out onto the front step and took a seat and watched with Jim and Margaret as a cop car rolled slowly down the avenue, through the dappled light, under the lovely overhanging Richmond summer trees. Then Henry came out and sat down quietly beside me. As the cops roll by, he asks, "Are those the ones?"

I lift my head up and find myself looking directly into the eyes of the cop on the passenger side. It's him. I wonder if he can discern the difference between Henry and me. "Yes," I say, "They're just going around the block and around the block and around the block."
Henry snorts knowingly. He gets up and goes to the front door, leans in and says something. Before long the entire family is out there on the steps. Someone is saying, "I think it's going down soon." They sit and watch as that same car goes by yet again and the cop on the passenger side looks casually in our direction. He's got all the time in the world.

On the steps, I'm the only one trembling in fear; for my friends this is a grotesque kind of entertainment. Someone cocks a finger and aims it at the cop car as they round the corner.
"Jesus…" I whisper, "Don't do that." And this proves to be the most hilarious thing anyone has ever said.

I run through the house and go down the back steps and into the garage. I draw the old threadbare curtains that are hanging there. When I hear the tires on the cobblestone outside, I peek through and see the cop car go slowly by. I look at the working drawings I have hanging up on the wall. Goddamn it.
I look at the beautifully stretched, primed, nice-sized canvasses that are begging for paint. I'm practically weeping.

I look at my set up—the garage, the part-time job with money coming in, the friends, junkies though some may be. I look at my brushes, my paint, the stupid saggy mattress on the floor.
Now I am in tears.
I hear the crunching of the tires as the cop car rolls slowly by outside again. God damn it!

I don't even remember how I got to the airport.

COPS in AMERICA,
as I know it

ONE HALF INSULT ONE HALF INJURY (2012)

One morning, my very dear wife and I stepped out of the hotel on our way to take the dogs to the beach, and there was a car lying completely upside down on the sidewalk, against the façade of the Sushi Man restaurant. The Sushi Man himself was standing there in a kind of jovial shock, amongst a crowd of curious onlookers, cops, and tow truck drivers.

The trajectory of the incident could be traced backward through the side-swiped cars it had left in its wake as it came careening down Bush Street. They'd all been re-arranged and had come to rest at strange new angles to the curb, with dents and scrapes and broken windows along the street side.

The last one hit, apparently, had been struck so hard that it had been driven up over the curb, and only the street-side wheels remained on pavement. As my wife and I were taking all of this in, and remarking at how astounding it all was—it looked like a scene out of a movie about the end of civilization—I noticed something even more astounding. There was a meter maid bent over the windshield of the car which had been driven up onto the sidewalk, checking the VIN. She was in the process of writing that car a ticket.

I told my dear wife, "I guess she thinks that guy doesn't have enough troubles."
My wife—who may have picked up a bad habit or two by hanging around with me—said, "She's probably just giving him a warning."

HOW TO CROSS A STREET UNASSISTED,
with only 45 years' experience (1978)

It's maybe 2 AM and I've just been thrown out of an Irish pub; I'm on my way home on foot. I arrive at the intersection of Clement Street and Park Presidio (three lanes in each direction, divided by a concrete median barrier). From where I stand, you can see almost a mile in one direction, and maybe two miles in the other. The light is red in my direction and there is a sign flashing "DON'T WALK". I look in both directions; there is not a car in sight. I decide it's ridiculous to stand there, and I cross the street.

When I reach the other side, there is a patrol car parked at the curb, right there on the corner. There are two cops in the thing. They bump the siren and, rolling down his window, one of the cops put a flashlight in my face.
I say, "Get that light out of my face... please."
He says, "Did you see the don't-walk sign?"
I say, "Get that LIGHT out of my face. Please."
He turns off the flashlight and says, "Did you SEE the sign telling you not to cross?"
I say, "There is not a car for a mile in either direction. It's 2 AM. I just want to get home and get to sleep."
He insists, "<u>Did you see</u> the don't-walk sign, sir?"
I say, "I'm 50 years old; I've been crossing the street on my own for more years than you have been on this planet, and you can either give me a ticket or let me go; that's entirely up to you."

The other cop leans over to get a look at me and, after studying me for a bit, says, "Have a good night, Sir."
The window goes up, and I'm on my way again.

UNCLE BILLY (an event from mid 1930)

I told my father about how I'd managed to cross Park Presidio on my own, unassisted, at 2 AM, with only my instincts and common sense to guide me, and he told me about Uncle Billy.

His telling went something like this:
One time, when I was a kid, we were out visiting Uncle Billy—he lived way out in the country, outside of DeLand (pronounced DEE-land). He decided he had to make a trip into town and he asked me if I'd like to ride along with him—I was just a kid at the time.

Uncle Billy had this old open-air car which he had converted into a truck by removing the back seat and building a flatbed on the frame. There weren't many cars on the road in those days, and we came up to this crossroad in the middle of nowhere, with a stoplight... a *stoplight* in the middle of nowhere. You could look down the road in all four directions as far as the eye could see, but some local authority decided that it needed a stoplight.

Of course, it was red when we approached, and Uncle Billy just flew right on through. I said, "Don't you think you should stop for a stoplight, Uncle Billy?" And Uncle Billy said, "I'm a grown man. I'm not going to let some damned fool light tell me what I can do and what I cannot do."

NIGHTSTICKS and STONES (2007 or there about)

My wife and I were walking somewhere; I'd tell you where but
I'd be making it up. (We were probably going to visit an elderly
lady upon her death bed, to feed her homemade soup.)

We were passing a hospital when something went whistling by
my ear and slammed into the metal garage door behind us.
"What the heck was that?!"

While I was looking around to see if I could identify the thing,
my dear wife spied some kids—young men—on a roof across
the street from us, crouched behind the parapet. One of them had
something in his hand pointed in our direction but, when we
made eye contact, they all ducked behind the wall. A few
seconds later they emerged, each rising up to his full height, in
defiance. At that moment, for an instant, I truly yearned for the
ability to reach that roof in a single bound and just beat the hell
out of those stupid little bastards, but alas…(despite what
younger generations may believe, life is not a comic book.)

Instead of messing with those young idiots, I marked the house
in my mind and escorted my wife across the street to their side,
where they'd have less of an angle on us. We hugged the
buildings until we made it to the nearest corner.

"Where the hell are the cops when you want one?" I said bitterly.
"Those stupid little bastards could have really injured one of us."
"I think that was their intent," my dear wife said.
"There are never any cops around when you need them," I
concluded. And, just to make me look bad, as we rounded that
corner, Fate had arranged for two cops to be dragging
themselves slowly out of a squad car down at the far end of that
block.

I ran up to them, saying, "There are some kids on a roof around the corner, and they are shooting something at people… Red house, tile roof."

"Wait. Wait. Wait a minute, sir. Wait, sir," commanded one of the cops.

"No," I said, "this demands attention right now; those kids could really hurt someone. Red house, tile roof…"

"Sir, you are going to have to wait. We need for you to answer some questions, first."

"Look," I said, "There's no time for questions. There are kids, they're up on a roof across from the hospital and they are firing something at people, and somebody is going to be seriously injured."

"Sir, you are going to have to stop talking and let us ask you some questions."

"We're walking down the street, across from the hospital and kids on the roof fired something at us and it nearly hit my wife. You need to do something before someone gets hurt," I said.

That did not go over well with the cops. They didn't like me telling them what their job was—even though they didn't seem to know what it was without my instruction.

"Do you live around here?" one of them asked.

"What does that have to do with… ? Look, pal…" I began, and at that point the cop put his hand on the butt of his gun.

He said, "You look, *PAL*, we're not going to be able to do ANYthing until you slow down and allow us to ask you some questions."

"Nope," I said, "No questions. I'm telling you for the last time. Then, you do what you feel you have to do. There are kids on the roof, across from the hospital, and they are firing projectiles of some sort at people walking on the sidewalk near the hospital. One of those things almost hit my wife. They are on the roof of the fourth or fifth house in from the corner; it's red, it has a tiled

roof. That's it. That's all I have to tell you. I know no more than that. There you go; do whatever you feel you gotta do."
The cop looked at me as if he were tempted to arrest me. Then his fellow cop—a pear-shaped woman—spoke to me, saying snidely, "Thank you SO much for your cooperation." Then they both waddled off slowly (very slowly; not a care in the world) around the corner from which we'd just come.

I started to walk away, but my excellent wife suggested I put childishness aside, go back around the corner, and point out the place for the cops. She was right of course. So, I went back around the corner and discovered these officers of the law standing at the doorway of the first house on the corner, ringing the doorbell. Only an idiot could imagine what they were expecting to accomplish by that.
"Yes, who is it? Oh, yes, actually we were up on the roof just now shooting at people… Is there something wrong, officer? Here, let me buzz you in, so we can talk about it over tea."

"What are you doing?" I wailed, "I told you it was like the fourth or fifth house down the block, I told you it's red and there's a tile roof." Then the female cop took her nightstick in hand and—this I will attest to in a court of law—she tapped me lightly on the chest and snarled, "Thank you for your assistance, *Citizen*."

THE GENERATOR and How Experience Works (1999)

I was coming home, just around 8 AM, from my stint as night guy at a small, privately-owned French hotel. Right outside the alley, where I lived, there was a cop car, a crew of people standing around doing nothing, and one or two men talking animatedly to two cops. Just curious, I went over to one of the idlers and asked what was going on.

He told me that someone had walked by and had locked their generator down with a padlock. He showed me the switch where the padlock hung, with the big machine in OFF.
I said, "What are you gonna do?"
He replied, "First, we're gonna catch that son-of-a-bitch!"
I laughed, walked up the alley, went up the steps to my place, put some water in the Bialetti, and waited for the coffee to brew.

I was pouring that good coffee into a little cup when a knock-knock-knock came upon my door. I opened the door to find two cops and the guy I'd just spoken to standing there. The guy pointed at me and said, "That's him; that's the one!"
One of the cops said to me, "What is your name?" and I told him my name. He asked, "Were you just down on Upper Grant at the construction site at the end of this alley?"
I said I was.
"That's him... I recognize him!" interrupted the construction worker. "He was wearing those same clothes; that's the guy!"
At this point the other cop took the construction worker aside.

The cop that remained asked me what I had been doing there, and I told him I was passing by, on my way home, after a night of work. He asked me where I worked and when I had gotten off. I gave him the details. At that point the construction guy interrupted again and declared, "THAT IS THE GUY! That's the guy who locked down our generator. I recognize him. I saw him.

That's the guy." It was a kind of whining complaint.
I stepped around the cop and said, "I have nothing to do with
your problem. You saw *me* when I stopped to ask *you* what was
going on, about seven minutes ago. The cops were already there
when I came by."

After an exchange of knowing looks between the cops, my cop
turned me around as the other cop led the construction guy away.
He asked me a short series of questions: When did I leave work?
How long does it usually take me to walk home?
And then he apologized.

He explained: "It's not unusual for an eye witness to identify
someone as the perpetrator, who just happened to be at the scene
but had nothing to do with the event. That's what's going on
here," he said, assuring me. "I've seen it before; it happens all
the time. Whoever locked down their machine did it before you
even left work. Thank you for your cooperation, sir." And
turning to smile at me, he said, "Enjoy your coffee."
And that was that.

Experience and training led to swiftly delivered justice.

A COP of COMPASSION (1998)

There is this stop sign in Encinitas where nobody stops because if you go straight ahead the road becomes a dead end in about 100 yards. However, if you take a right turn there, as everybody does, it heads downhill to two very large, very popular shopping malls—which is where everyone who finds themselves at that corner is headed anyway. So, as said, nobody really *stops* at that stop sign; we all just kinda slow down a bit before drifting through the turn.

Once in a while the Encinitas police put a motorcycle cop up there—just beyond the bend, just out of sight—because it's easy income for the city. That lucky fellow could probably ticket every single car that takes that turn, from dawn 'til dusk, for failing to stop, and most of 'em for not signaling as well.

So, there I am one day coming up to this stop sign, and the guy in front of me does something peculiar—he stops.
"What the heck is wrong with that idiot?" I ask myself. "Come on, come on…" I touch the brakes to slow down enough to make the turn and, as I do that, I look, and there's the cop on his motorcycle. He's looking directly at me.

At this point I'm already halfway through the turn, but I slam on my brakes anyway—kind of a token to the man—and come to a complete, sudden, somewhat jerky stop.
I look at him.
He looks at me.
I shrug theatrically and raise my eyebrows in an overly exaggerated plea of innocence… and he does this:
He drags the back of his gloved hand across the brow of his helmet as if wiping sweat from his brow—the classic gesture for 'Man, *that* was a close one'—and he smiles.

ROUSTED (1969)

Late one afternoon, just before the Fall Semester was to begin—
there were new students with their parents everywhere you
looked—an entire herd of winos was gathered in the park. They
weren't drinking; they weren't bothering anybody. Slim and
Amos were sitting on one bench, a redneck wino named Harlen,
was standing in front of them lecturing. I was sitting on the other
bench with an out-patient from the local infirmary.

I was thinking about something pretty deeply and hadn't seen the
cops drive up. My thoughts were disrupted when a cop spoke
with the voice of authority.
"Alright, party's over. All you winos, out of the park! Dog-man,
Slim, let's go."
The out-patient said, "Oh-oh," and got up and walked right
across Harrison Street, without either looking or looking back.
"You too," the cop said to Harlen.
Harlen stood his ground, folded his arms across his chest and
demanded, "Why are you rousting us?"
"Gotta put on a pretty face for the parents," said the cop.
"We don't have the constitutional right to congregate any more
in this country?"

The cop looked at the redneck wino while Amos and Slim
worked on the process of getting their weary old bones up and on
their feet.
"What's your name, troublemaker?" the cop asked Harlen.
"My name's None Of Your Business, that's MY fuckin' name,"
said Harlen. "What's your badge number?"
"You can see my badge number right there," the cop said,
touching a finger to his badge. "OK? ...You NOW HAVE 10
seconds to leave this park unassisted."
As Amos and Slim were squeezing their way humbly past the
confrontation, the cop stopped long enough to say, "Do yourself

120

a favor, Slim, check in at the V.A. hospital, sober up. Dog-man, let's go! You too, None-Of-Your-Business."

"I'm not going," said Harlen. "I want to know why you're rousting us."

The cop sighed, "What's your last name, None-Of-Your-Business?"

"I told you MY fuckin' name. What about him?" Harlen said and pointed toward me.

"I'm talkin' to YOU," said the cop. "What's your last name?"

"Moseby," said Harlen, defiantly.

"You related to Beverly Moseby?"

"He's a cousin of mine."

"Well, you're a crazy as he was."

"You're wrong about that, officer," said Harlen, "I'm crazier. And smarter; AND, I know my fuckin' rights."

"OK, good for you. But, listen, I'm just trying to do my job here. You don't want to get in the way of someone just doing his job, do you? So, why don't you..."

"Pure crap," said Harlen.

"What do you do for a living?" asked the cop patiently.

"I'll tell you what I DON'T do," said Harlen, "I don't go around threatening people. AND I don't need a gun and a fuckin' nightstick to be a man."

The cop walked a couple steps away from the redneck wino and said something into his walkie-talkie. "Van's on its way," he said to those of us who remained. Harlen just stood there staring at the guy until a police van pulled up to the curb. The cop gestured for him to turn around, and he did so.

"So, now you're gonna arrest me?" Hey! So, now you're gonna arrest me?!" He placed his hands, interlocked, behind his head. "This is pure crap."

"Last chance. You go away now, without assistance, or you go home with us in cuffs. It's your decision."

"What for?"

"What for? For being yourself; for being a public nuisance, and a disgrace to humanity."

"What about him?" Harlen said pointing at me, in an effort to involve me in his nightmare.

"What about him?" asked the cop.

"All you see is us winos? You don't see him?"

"All I see," said the cop, "is a kid sitting quietly on a park bench."

Harlen glared at me. "I see an over-privileged white, middle-class punk."

When the cop came over to me I felt a chill run up my spine. I shuddered as he leaned toward me. "You want to leave this area for a little while for your own protection," the cop advised me quietly. I bowed and, as I got up to leave, Harlen was yelling at my back. "Yeah, you better leave, Charlie!"

(Harlen was another one of those who called me Charlie. My landlord's wife, Mrs. See called me Bill; the nice old woman who owned the house next door to the Laundro-Mat called me Mitchell, for reasons I've never understood; the winos in that park called me Charlie. My skin had begun to clear up, girls were everywhere, I was flexible.)

I looked back and saw Harlen standing there with his hands clasped behind his head and the cop putting handcuffs on him. "This is justice?" he was yelling. "This is justice?! THIS is bullshit! This is BULLshit. CHARLIE, you're a witness! THIS IS…"

A day or two after the rousting Slim was really angry with me. When I ran by there on my way to work at 5:30 AM he turned his back on me, in a comic, greatly dramatic gesture. I went over and sat and looked at him until he coughed up.

"You're not down and out like some of the rest of us, so I don't know why you're doing it."

"Doing what?'

"Livin' like a low-life; actin' like a low-life. Hangin' around with us low-lifes."

"I was just sitting here in the park. I like this park. I live right there." I pointed.

"Do you want to be a low-life? Is that it?" Slim asked.

"Nope," I said...and I think I may have patted him on the knee. I had to get to work.

FISHIN' ALONG 101 (1983)

The average speed between San Francisco and Santa Rosa is probably something pretty close to 80 miles per hour. Some parts of that stretch are posted 65, but no one without car trouble ever slows down that much. For your own safety, you keep up with the crowd. These folks are all desperate to get away from work and anxious to get home, and only a fool would get in their way. Believe me, they want to get there.

My friend, Peter was flying along with the flow of traffic on this route one evening on his way home from work, when a Highway Patrol officer pulled him over. As Peter tells it, that cop came out of nowhere (an ability of which the CHP is justifiably proud). Documentation is demanded with hollow courtesy, and handed over with a somewhat sheepish smile.

While the officer fills in the blanks, Peter feels compelled to offer an explanation, saying, "I wasn't going any faster than anyone else. And," he adds, "other cars were passing me." "Sign here," said the cop. So, Peter signs.

Despite the officer's overly obvious lack of interest, Peter is driven by curiosity to ask, "Why did you choose me?" The cop smiles and says, "If you were shooting fish in a barrel, which one would you shoot?

FEDERAL RAVEN PROTECTION (2016)

My wonderful wife and her pretty damned wonderful dog and I
were parked near Crissy Field (in San Francisco) one Sunday.
We were about to go for a little walk together along the beach.
It was a nice clear day—a beautiful day.

We'd just been to the French bakery and had an abundance of
bread in the trunk. While my wife was putting on her walking
shoes, I opened the trunk, tore off a bit of bread from a baguette,
and tossed it to some ravens, who were hanging around.

Instantly, there was the bump of a siren and a Federal cop of
some sort appeared in front of me. He got out of his car and
came over to me, demanding my name. I was bewildered and,
for some reason, I laughed.
"What's the problem?" I asked.
"Do you realize what you just did?" he asked me with severity.
"No," I said, quite honestly. "What did I just do?"
"You were feeding something to those birds."
"Yes," I said. "I tossed them a little bread…"
"Do you realize that there is a Federal Statute against feeding
wild birds on Federal Property?" he asked.
I said, "What? You're kidding me. You're telling me that there is
a law against me tossing bread to birds?"
"Yes. And I should ticket you right now."
"Wait," I said, "You're telling me that *it is illegal* for me to feed
bread to birds?"

He glared at me for a while, and then he said something like…
(I cannot honestly remember it all because it just sounded so
idiotic that it was beyond belief)… he said something like this:
"If every visitor to our parks were to start feeding these wild
birds, the birds would soon become used to it, and they would
start making demands on the visitors. And then, if you stopped

feeding them, they might attack a child and pass bird-borne diseases on to that child; and that child might become sick and die. So, yes—though you may think it's a joke, or maybe you think it's just innocent fun to feed these birds, but it's a serious matter. The action you took just now could have very serious consequences. So, put the bread away, and don't let me see you feeding birds around here again."

This occurred in 2016; and though I didn't see it at that moment, it was harbinger to the madness that was about to engulf the rational world.

ANNOYANCE and the LAW (1984)

When we were driving anywhere at night and Gail saw a car
with only one headlight working, she would declare, "Padiddle!"
and lean over and give me a kiss. If I saw a car with only one
headlight before she did, I would say, "Padiddle", and she would
lean over and give me a kiss. If we both saw the same car, with
only one headlight and happened to say padiddle simultaneously,
Gail would lean over and give me a kiss.

Those were better times; and I think Gail had a better grasp on
things, padiddle-wise, than the female cop who pulled me over at
about 3 AM one night, in San Francisco.

I saw the flashing lights in my rearview mirror as I was crossing
Geary, but didn't stop. The cop car behind me, bumped its siren,
but I didn't pull over. The bullhorn came on and a female voice
said, "Pickup truck! Pull over", and I didn't.

At that point I was about 60 feet from a parking spot which I
could see, on the corner of 15th and Clement, where I lived. So, I
continued on and pulled into that parking space.

The cop came up to me and knocked on the window. I rolled
down the window, and she said, "When an officer of the law
commands you to pull over, you pull over!"
I said, "I did."
She said, "You did not pull over immediately."
I said, "Because, I could see this parking spot open—I live right
there (I pointed)—and I didn't see any reason to stop in the
middle of the street when I could park in a legitimate spot."
She said nothing for a while. Then she said, "Do you know why
I wanted you to pull over?"
I said I did not.

She said, "Doesn't it annoy you when you see a vehicle with only one functioning headlight?"
Reflecting briefly on Gail and her response to such 'vehicles', I could not help but smile.

"Well?" she demanded, "Doesn't it annoy you to see a vehicle, travelling a night, with only one headlight?"
I said, "I'm guessing that one of my headlights is out."
She said, "Yes, that's why I pulled you over. Did you already *know* that only one of our headlights is working?"
I said, "If I knew that, I would have fixed it."
She said, "Well doesn't having only one headlight annoy you?"
I said this: "What does annoyance have to do with it? It's either legal or illegal; annoyance has nothing to do with it."
She said, "You have 10 days to fix it," tore a piece of paper from a big pad and handed it to me.

Three days later, after I changed out the old headlight for a new one that worked, I walked into the Richmond District Police Station. Behind the thick glass sat a beefy sort of thoroughly bored guy in uniform, who knew I was there but found things to do which were more important than acknowledging my presence. This went on for quite a while, until I slapped the ticket I'd received up against the glass. Then he looked up and, saying not a word, pointed to the slot where I was to slide it through to him.
He glanced at it and, without looking up again, asked me, "Did you get it fixed?"
I said, "Yes."
He took the ticket, set it aside and made a gesture that told me to go away.

I have to be honest with you; I found every aspect of that experience annoying.

128

THE NEWS in AMERICA,
as I know it

One evening, in 2016 (I think) I heard on the local news that a woman in San Jose (CA) had been attacked by FOUR pit bulls.

According to the report:
"A neighbor, witnessing the event, ran to get the owner of the dogs, and he managed to get control over all but three of them."

I told my wife, "Well, that certainly describes Life as I know it."

The NEWS from NICARAGUA (1983)

My father once told me that he had never witnessed any event—
or had taken part in one—and found that what had been written
about it later, in the news, was either accurate or even honest; not
once. He was 92 years old when he told me that. He said, "It was
like they were reporting on something entirely different than
what I had seen." I knew that to be true, personally.

For example, one time when 250,000 people made an attempt to
shut down Washington DC—in protest of the war in Vietnam—
the official account dismissed them as merely a tiny little,
insignificant crowd of 35,000. (I'd gone there to observe that
event, because someone had told me that protests are less about
politics than they are about 'getting laid'... a statement that in
time has since proven, more than once, to be true.) And although
I make no claim at being a crowd estimator of any sort, I know
what Wrigley Field looks like fully packed, and believe me,
you'd need several ballparks of that size to contain all the people
I saw in DC on that day. The feds must have thought so too,
because when they started arresting people they first began by
tossing them all into Robert F. Kennedy Stadium, which holds
about 43,000 malcontents seated properly, and who knows how
many standing shoulder to shoulder on the playing field.

When I was in Managua (1983), all of the US newspaper and
weekly news magazine reporters were staying at the Inter-
Continental Hotel. In fact, the lobby of that particular hotel was
the standard meeting place for many travelers, whether they
stayed there or not. So, in the morning, that is where I would
meet up with someone to go out amongst the people, and check
things out for ourselves.

Meanwhile, almost immediately after breakfast, all those hotshot
reporters took to the bar and settled in for the day.

Or, at least, it certainly looked that way because, they were there when I left and, when I came back from my excursion, in the afternoon, those same big-time foreign correspondents were still in that bar. From appearances, they hadn't even moved from their seats.

At three o'clock, a silent alarm went off and they would all get up and dash out of the bar, across the lobby toward the phone banks, and grab the first available phone. There, they would call home and file their report for the day. At that point (comma) one afternoon (comma) I took a seat on a couch nearby and listened to them (comma.) as they dictated their columns (period.) It gave me great insight into the manner in which this was done (period. Next paragraph.) It was a process that hadn't changed in 60 years (end).

After listening to several of them, I had the distinct feeling that while I was out in the countryside poking around under an ever-oppressive sun, these guys had all stayed inside, in that nicely air conditioned bar, only getting up, when necessary, to empty their bladders. Who knows the source of the information they used in those daily reports? What I heard being relayed by phone, from that hotel lobby in Nicaragua, sounded a great deal like the US State Department reports which floated around there daily—with some hearsay, mutually-contrived non-existent events, and what they overheard from people, like me, returning to the hotel after being out in the real world.

One day I was much sicker than usual and hung around the hotel lobby all day and, as I'd suspected, discovered that those clowns did not leave that bar for the entire day. YET, when three o'clock struck they all dashed toward the phone bank (comma) and filed their reports as usual (period, end end end.)

Of course, if correspondents for large respectable newspapers and weekly news magazines were winging it, that was none of my business. What did that have to do with me?

Still, when I got home sweet home again—back in the US of A—I fired off a brief note to the Editor in Chief of U. S. News and World Report. I told him where I'd been and what I had seen in pretty much the same way I've just told you, and ended my note by saying: 'I'm surprised and somewhat saddened to discover that U. S. News and World Report should swallow whole whatever the State Department puts out.'

Lick it, seal it, stamp it, and drop it in the old mailbox... Congratulations; good work, citizen!

In response—almost immediately—I got a scathing letter from the Editor in Chief of U. S. News and World Report, saying (amongst other things), "We DO NOT swallow whole anything from any source!" That letter was signed with enough fury to impress his signature into the surface of that paper; I could actually feel it.

And, although I admire that gentleman's passion for the integrity of his publication, I must say this: Just because you don't want to hear the truth, it doesn't make it any less true (period. new paragraph). Things happened down there (bold cap) EXACTLY as I told you they had (period, end end end)

You can believe the guy sitting in his office in Washington DC, or you can believe someone who occupied the same table as one of his reporters, at a bar in the InterContinental, in Managua.

And that's everything I have to say about that.

THE GROVE AVENUE REPUBLIC RIOT (1969, maybe)

The day following the Grove Avenue riot, the college newspaper
came out with several pictures of that event on the front page.
The largest was a shot of a squad car with the word OINK spray-
painted on the side of it. There was a shot of the banner hanging
over the street, declaring 'Grove Avenue Republic'; and a couple
shots of what might have appeared, at first glance, to show riot
police beating kids, who were cowering in an attempt to defend
themselves from the blow of their nightsticks. The story, what I
read of it, began by stating that the police had been attacked by
this large angry mob.
I thought about that.

Then, I asked myself this question—going into battle, how
would I prefer to be equipped? Would I choose: a t-shirt, torn
jeans and worn-out sneakers, and arm myself with jeering and
shouted insults? OR, would I choose body armor, helmet with
face shield, a night stick, a semi-automatic handgun—with a
shotgun available to me in my nearby, fully-equipped squad
car—and a walkie-talkie to coordinate my movement with the
rest of my similarly attired team, by way of the helicopter
hovering overhead? Would I arm myself further with vicious
dogs, tear gas and water cannons, or just go with pebbles, empty
bottles and spray paint?
It was a tough question.

Reading the story, as it was written though, you'd have to feel
sorry for the poor cops, who'd been so savagely attacked.

I tried to go back to staring at my painting but—having witness
that riot myself—my work was disrupted by political thoughts.
I had to believe that, on the motivational level alone, the cops
had the advantage. Let's say you're a young person living fairly
casually, pretty much hand to mouth, eating, sleeping, drinking,

maybe smokin' some dope, going to school once in a while, sleeping with every pretty little girl that passes by and, for some unexplainable reason you get it in your head that a bunch of self-serving millionaire lawyers and career politicians in DC, dressed in expensive suits, with badly chosen ties, do not represent you. Your motivation to riot is ephemeral at best; easily reduced to something as lame as the slogan, *Down with the Establishment!*

Now, let's say you're a cop and your world view is pretty much that everybody is a criminal or, at very least, a potential criminal, and those goddamned long-haired college kids are the worst of the lot. Up until this very moment you've been operating under restraint; laws and that kind of crap have prevented you from just cruising up and down the streets and knocking all their heads in. Sure, you've managed to harass a few of these little bastards occasionally and, from time to time, you've throw a handful of them into jail for no apparent reason; perhaps you've even gotten away with beating up one or two on the side, but where's the satisfaction? It has to be frustrating; you've got the equipment, there's no doubt in your mind that you've got societal approval, but the authorities above you have you on a short leash.

Now, today, here you are facing hordes of the arrogant little bastards and the word comes down from above that it not only OK to swing for the fences, it's an order. The Chief of Police himself commands you to lay into them. Who in their right mind would overlook this opportunity? What a glorious day this is! To add kindling to that fire, some smart ass has spray painted OINK on the side of your squad car, and there's a skinny little fucker up there on the roof who just chucked a brick down and hit Dwayne on the shoulder. Now, *that's* what you call motivation.

After this calm analysis it was pretty clear to me who had the advantage, motivationally speaking, in that little tussle on that golden day. But, you'd never read that in the newspaper.

Personally speaking, I don't know how it came to that; the last time I visited the Grove Avenue Republic I'd been drawn by the tribal rhythms of the Grove Avenue Republic Spontaneous Assembly Rhythm Band. They were all sitting on the curb, thirty-some strong, and celebrating Liberty with wooden spoons and garbage can lids. Seeing me coming, Howard scooched over, making room for me on the curb, and handed me a stick and an empty tin can.

That gathering probably fit the definition of a riot, but, you'd never read about that riot in the newspaper.

Now that I've had 50 years or so to think about it, I suppose it was proper use of the word Republic that had the authorities so upset.

WAR in AMERICA,
as I know it

SOMEONE WAS LYING, and it wasn't me

When I was the age of the kids who now run the world, the old folks were in control and they made that clear in every possible way. For example, I recall one time when 250,000 citizens tried to send an unequivocal message to the President of the United States that, in our opinion, the United States of America was conducting a vicious, stupid, unproductive and, possibly, even immoral war over there in Viet Nam. In our innocence we thought that our opinion counted for something, and that The President would take our presence on his door step as a sign that the American People were, possibly, beginning to get a little disenchanted with that war.

But, after being told about the little gathering outside, The President, a politician not a psychic, sent the lowest underling he could find outside with a microphone to tell us to shut up and go back to wherever we had come from or be arrested. In essence his message to us was that our opinion on the matter did not count. Then, almost immediately, without further warning, they came at us in hordes, like wasps, on Vespas, with helmets and night sticks and tear gas, and, after driving us to ground, rounded us up like cattle, arrested every goddamned last one of us, and threw us all into Robert F. Kennedy Stadium, which made an excellent make-shift prison for anyone whose opinion bore no weight whatsoever but rankled nonetheless.

For additional proof of who was in control, we need look no further than Lawrence Welk or Lucille Ball. Their continued presence in our lives sent the clear, unequivocal, pie-in-the-face, message that our opinions, our ideas, our desires meant *nothing* to those in control. Though we were the largest segment of the population (and I believe we might still be, for a while) what our generation might have liked to see on TV did not matter; the old folks were in control, and, like it or not, where there should have been Iron Butterfly (or at very least Peter, Paul and Mary), there was Lawrence Welk; where there should have been Firesign Theatre, there was I Love Lucy. Game, set, match, Old Folks!

Sometime around 1969 (I'm guessing here) I had come home during a break from college, and one evening, the President of the United States was on TV loudly, vehemently, denying that U. S. troops had ever crossed over the border and entered Cambodia (or maybe it was Laos—I forget which). Apparently crossing that particular border was forbidden for reasons which I didn't understand at the time... and have never cared enough to think about since. I was, then, as I am today, basically apolitical, relatively uninformed, and both pleased and somewhat proud to be so. And, I honestly believe that I am much saner than I might otherwise be because of that stance.

Nonetheless, I felt compelled, during this particular speech, to stand up in my parent's living room, point an accusatory finger at the television, and state unequivocally, "That bastard's a liar." (The bastard I referred to was the President of the United States.) Then I strode out of the room in a kind of overly-staged, morally superior huff. (That's the way I did it in those days.) It was all very dramatic.

My father, who had landed in Normandy, who had a hand in the taking of Metz and driving the Nazis back into Germany followed me out of the room, clapped a fairly meaningful hand upon my skinny shoulder, spun me around, looked me squarely in the eye, and demanded to know what could have motivated any son raised by him to make such a statement about the President of the United States.

Basically what he wanted to know was how an Art student—a kid who divided his time, in relatively equal parts, between painting, sleeping, and fornicating—could claim to know anything at all about what was then going on in Vietnam. I have to admit that it did seem a little weird for me to imagine I might know as much as the President of the United States about a war I only wished to avoid. However, despite my purposeful un-involvement in the matter, I did. And, more damning still, I knew the truth. My accusation was that the President did too; he just wasn't revealing it.

In those days I really wanted nothing more than to be left alone to paint and to smoke a little dope and drink an occasional beer, and sleep with whoever wanted to sleep with me. Nevertheless, somehow, through that process, a few days before heading home, a small group of us artists-hopeful spent a couple of weird evenings with a young soldier temporarily back from that war. He was telling anybody who would listen—and that seemed to be limited pretty much to us—that not only had we gone into Cambodia (or it may have been Laos... I forget which) but, that such incursions were regular and on-going.
He knew this because he'd taken part in them.

Apparently, from what this soldier told us, whenever our guys crossed that forbidden border, they carried no picnic baskets.

So, between accepting what the President of the United States said on TV, and the word of a soldier who had just come back from over there, I chose to believe the soldier.

After the fact, I am pleased to report, that was the correct choice because, years late, what that soldier'd told us proved to be perfectly true—and everybody, whatever their previous stance on that matter, admitted as much. But, back on that inglorious evening in 1968 (if that was indeed the year), when I told my father the source of my information his ire was quelled. He too preferred the word of a man in uniform over the unblinking insistence of any career politician.

140

When I got back to college, while in the print shop pulling stone lithographs, I overheard two graduate students discussing that war. One of them said: "Vietnam is like… you're making your way down a stairway in the dark and you bump into somebody and knock them down a flight of steps. Then the lights come on and you discover it's your grandmother. So, you knock her down another flight of steps. And that continues. You continue kicking your grandmother down the steps until you find yourselves both trapped in the basement, up to your waist in mud and soaked in your own blood."

I had no idea what he meant by any of that, and I didn't know if it was a good analogy or not, but I liked the way it went together so I remembered it clearly.

The other grad student laughed and said, "Vietnam is like…you hear that some people you've never seen or even heard of before are having a little family argument in their kitchen on the other side of town. So you get on a bus and after a very long and uncomfortable ride, you decide to walk the final 14 blocks in the blistering sun. When you get to their place, you kick in the back door, rush into their kitchen and, after putting yourself in between these people… you get on the phone and start calling people asking them to come over and take your side."

I thought about what they were saying, and since I knew as little about that war as anybody else, came up with an analogy of my own. So, you're sitting on the bank of a river when a pick-up truck pulls up and a couple of big guys in cheap suits grab you and force you, at gun point, into the bed of the truck. You are told to shrug on some ugly overalls while you go bouncing down the highway. You shout, Where are we going? And, *apparently* they don't hear you. You shout, Where are we going? And they say, 'Never mind, you'll find out when we get there.' They drive you out into the country somewhere, hand you a gun, and kick

you out into an open field. Before driving off, almost as an afterthought, one of them leans out the window and shouts, "By the way, they're twins…"
The other guy winks and says, "Don't shoot the wrong one."

In those days I felt that if members of Congress felt strongly enough about events in some distant land to declare war, they should also feel strongly enough to shrug on the uniform, fly over to wherever those events were taking place, and risk their own lives in the horrible bloody madness.

Now of course—50 year later—after observing politicians from a safe distance and giving the matter a great deal of thought, I still feel that way.

MY FATHER TOLD ME THIS

During their push through France, driving the Nazis out and liberating villages along the way, a new Lieutenant came on board to command the platoon in which my father was a mortar gunner. Where the previous lieutenant had gone was a mystery; one day he was gone and the new guy arrived to replace him.

Apparently, my father had failed to take the time, during the shooting, the killing, the dodging of bullets and heavy munitions fire, to properly salute this new Lieutenant every time he strolled by. So, from the very beginning, that Lieutenant didn't like my father very much.

After several grueling days of slowly, building by building, meticulously driving the Germans out of small villages, the new Lieutenant decided they would spend the night inside a particular building which he had, for no apparent reason, taken a liking to. As the others were rolling out their sleeping bags, my father approached the Lieutenant and said, "Don't you think it would be advisable to check out the basement?"
The Lieutenant said, "Oh, sure, I guess that would be a good idea." My father took out his side arm and started down the stairs, with the Lieutenant right behind him.

When it was all clear, my father suggested, "Don't you think it would be wise to set a sentry, since we're all going to be sleeping in here?"
And the Lieutenant snarled, "That would be a good idea," and appointed my father to the task.

A few days later, immediately after clearing out another village, with a break in the fire, the Lieutenant came stomping up to my father and said, "What's wrong with you, Mansfield, is that you have no respect for your superiors!"

My father replied, "I have no superior; I am an American soldier. In America all men are created equal." (Knowing my father, he looked the man directly in the eye when he said it.)

The Lieutenant insisted, "I am your superior, soldier!"

And my father said, "In what way are you my superior? I can run faster than you, I can march farther than you, I can carry more weight. I can assemble a rifle quicker than you, and fire it with greater accuracy. I can set up and fire a mortar with greater accuracy than you. I am stronger than you and better educated, and I'll compare my intelligence to yours anytime. In what way are you my superior?"

The Lieutenant shook his head and said, "You don't BELONG in the Army, Mansfield."

My father replied, "Well, we can agree on that."

The Lieutenant said, "And, I expect you to salute me, soldier."

My father snorted and said, "When we get to Japan, and we find ourselves on the battlefield, face to face with the Japanese, I'll be more than glad to salute you."

My father says that, before this contention came to a real head, the war—thanks to Harry—had come to a sudden end.

An Interlude:

My father landed with the 95th Division, 377th Infantry Regiment on Omaha Beach in Normandy in August 1944. Shortly thereafter, the 377th Infantry faced <u>103 consecutive days of combat without relief,</u> and suffered the highest number of casualties in the 95th Division; they also received the largest number of combat decorations. During that time, against heavy resistance, the 95th Division re-captured first, the forts surrounding Metz, and, on November 22, the city itself.

Lieut. General G. S. Patton, Jr. recognized the good work that the 95th Division had done in a commendation stating, among other things: *In the course of this attack you successfully (1) made four assault crossings of the Moselle River at its high flood stage, (2) penetrated the line of defending forts, reducing those necessary to accomplish the mission, and (3) greatly contributed to the destruction of an entire reinforced German division. Against these fortifications which had never before in modern times fallen by assault, in terrain favorable to the enemy, and under almost intolerable weather conditions of rain, flood, and bitter cold, your officers and men met a most searching combat test which required not only individual courage, skill, endurance, and determination, but also sound tactical judgement (sic) coupled with an insatiable desire to close with the enemy. This achievement has added luster to the glorious history of American arms, for which you and all the officers and enlisted personnel of your division and attached units, are highly commended.*

Later these good men came upon a small village and found themselves immediately involved in a skirmish with the Germans holding that place. They were exhausted because they'd traveled hundreds of miles and had liberated 160 cities, town and villages along the way. They were cold, because it was the dead of winter.

This particular village was somewhere in the war-torn region that could have been either Belgium or France—in war, I'm told, such things are often confused. Wherever they were, just minutes after the Germans had been run off, the battle won, and the last shot fired, two women emerged from a farm house nearby and came slogging through the frozen mud to them. One of them carried a tray full of porcelain cups and the other carried two large steaming kettles, one in each hand. After the first woman had given each soldier a cup, the second came along right behind her and poured hot liquid simultaneously from the two kettles. (You'll see why my eyes are welling up with tears in a second.)

My father says that was the most wonderful thing he'd ever tasted. He said he will remember it for the rest of his life. The fact that it was just a few days before Christmas made this gift all the more remarkable to him. "What is this?" he asked in French, and the woman replied, "It is café au lait, Monsieur."

As my father tells it, you could see the smoke from the fire fight still hanging in the chilled air; the resound of the final shots had not yet died completely in the hills beyond, when these two good women emerged with rattling porcelain cups and their hot liquid gratitude.

It would be impossible to paint a nicer picture than that.

When my father received the Legion of Honor for having "played a significant role in the taking of the heavily defended fortifications in the area of Metz", M. Francois-Xavier Tilliette, Deputy Consul General of France, Los Angeles, referred to this same story in his speech. He followed it by saying, "Our message, Monsieur, is a simple one, but it could not be more heart-felt: Merci...thank you." At that moment, if my eyes had not been already full of tears, that certainly would have done it.

July 18, 2017:
My 92 year old father, from his hospital bed, just asked me if there was anything *he* could do for *me.*

I didn't know that that was the last time I would see my father, or that those were the last words he would speak to me.

Earlier that same day, he had offered me this bit of wisdom, drawn from years of personal experience, concerning accountants: "Stick two of them in a room together, with nothing to do, and in three days they'll both be working overtime."

I laughed and said, "I think that's the way government works." From the glint in his eye I could tell he was proud of me.

I've always considered it an honor to be my father's son.

NOR RAIN NOR DARK OF NIGHT (1968)

A peculiar thing happened one fine rainy day as I was walking
down Harrison Street, coming back from a class called
Introduction to the Static Arts. A bus stopped near the theatre on
the corner, and as it pulled away a guy in the back leaned out the
window and hollered, "Hey, you forgot your umbrella!" Then, he
tossed an umbrella at me. My instincts allowed me to catch it,
but I hadn't been on that bus.

I looked around for the people who might have gotten off that
bus, but they had dispersed pretty efficiently into the drizzle,
with the exception of a very slow-moving old black woman. She
seemed to be struggling as she tottered her way down Harrison
Street. I didn't know how the guy could have confused me with
her, a hunched over old woman in a long dark shiny plastic
raincoat, but I ran after her anyway, on the chance. When I
caught her I touched her sleeve. She stopped and looked up at
me wearily. "Is this yours?" I asked her. She just looked at me.
"Did you forget your umbrella on the bus?" I asked. She shook
her head and started off again on her slow and torturous journey.

Despite the fact that I believe the umbrella is one of the greatest
inventions mankind has ever come up with, I had never, until
that very moment, possessed one. I popped it open and
discovered that I liked owning an umbrella. It leant a kind of
phony-baloney dignity to things. I don't know why I had
deprived myself of such joy in the past.

Maybe it was because, in a world where pigs go for 50 cents a
dozen, I couldn't afford to buy an imitation of an oink. I'm not
an umbrella-cost historian but I believe a good umbrella, in those
days, probably cost $10; my monthly rent was 27.
I didn't know quite what to make of this wonderful gift, until
that evening.

148

It was raining heavily that night and I decided to take a break from staring at the painting propped up before me. I looked out the window, through the driving rain to the street below, the trees, the park, and I saw a figure sitting on one of the benches, alone, glistening wet. Even at that distance, in the dark, through the sheeting rain, I knew it was Slim. Even hunched over like that, with his collar up and his hat drawn down, I knew it was Slim. Slim, I was convinced, had had enough misery in his life; so, I grabbed the umbrella and went galloping down the stairs.

I popped open my new umbrella and dashed across the street. I stood before him.
"What are you doing out here in the rain?" I shouted.
"Sittin'. 'Bout you?"
"It's raining pretty hard; don't you have any place you can go?"
"Is that what they teach you in that art school?"
"Let me sit down."
Slim made room for me but knocked the umbrella away with one gloved hand. "Git that... away…"
I tried to put it up over us again, but he struck violently at the umbrella, knocking it away again.
"Git that thing… OUT. Git out of here with that thing. Don't want it. Is that clear enough for you?"
"But it'll keep us dry," I explained.
"That's what they teach you in that school?"
I tried one final time to place it over his head—stretching my arm up high so that maybe he wouldn't notice—but he got up and walked over to the other bench and sat down.

I shouted, "I just thought you'd like to get in out of the rain."
Slim said nothing. "It's only an umbrella!" I shouted.
Slim shouted, "How old are you?"
"What?" It wasn't that I couldn't hear him, I just didn't understand him. He pointed at the umbrella.
"It's that thing, Tin roof. I don't want that sound."

I felt like a fool sitting there with an umbrella while he sat just feet away drowning in the shower. "I can't hear you…" I said. "You want to hear me bad enough, you know what to do," he said.

I folded the umbrella, walked over and huddled beside the man. I adjusted my collar to keep the rain out and leaned over closer. "What are you doing out here in the rain anyway?"

"You think this is a proper place to conjugate?"

I laughed. "What? Conjugate?"

"Simple terms," he said, "I—that's me—want to be alone. I didn't know anyone was dumb enough—that's you—to come out here in the rain just to bother me."

"Yeah, but, I saw you from my window. I live up there, over the Laundro-Mat."

"Yes, I know," he said. "And I suggest, you go back up there, *over the Laundro-Mat*. I don't want none right now."

I thought about this.

The entire scene seemed idiotic. I was getting very wet and my hands were beginning to freeze. The guy seemed immovable. "OK, if that's the way you want it, I just thought that…"

I popped open the umbrella and raised it.

"Bah! You didn't think at all. That's the problem with you college kids." He turned his head violently away from me.

I just left him sitting there in the rain.

Sometime later that year Amos told me that, during the war, Slim had been abandoned on an island in the Pacific; that he'd been captured, and held in a big pit with two other guys, under sheets of corrugated tin. One of those guys died in that pit.

I think Slim died a little too, but not until he got home and realized that nobody really gave a goddamn about what he'd been through.

POLITICAL INVOLVEMENT,
as I know it

The GROVE AVENUE REPUBLIC (1969, I'm a-guessin')

I was crawling in through the back window of my apartment
building, having just come down from the roof, and Mrs. See
was there to meet me. She was angry.

"Bill," she said, "No up on roof. NO up on roof." She wagged a
finger at me.

I said, "OK. I'm sorry, Mrs. See."

She said, "Bill? OK? No up on roof." She wanted a firm
commitment.

So, I said, "I'm sorry, Mrs. See," and started to walk by her. At
this point Mr. See was coming up the steps to see what was
going on. She told him, "Bill up on roof." Mr. See shook a finger
at me, "No roof."

"I'm sorry, Mr. See," I said, "I won't do it again."

Mr. See disappeared down the steps again shaking his head, but
his wife remained. She called my name, "Bill?"

I was standing at the door to my room now, I looked back.

"No up on roof, Bill. No roof."

"OK, Mrs. See. I'm sorry."

I went into my room, and if it had had a lock I would have
locked it. Instead, for the next hour or so I would sit there on the
floor in silence, with my back against the door, hoping that I
wouldn't hear the sound of cops arriving at the top of the stairs.

Three days earlier I'd gone out in the morning and found a loose
crowd had gathered on the corner to watch a small band of
young belligerents, all dressed like washing machine repairmen
—muted work shirts, matching work pants and work boots—as
they came marching with marked defiance right down the middle
of Grove Avenue. My guess is that there were no more than
twelve of them. They were marching in the direction of the
school's campus. They were chanting something catchy but not
so catchy I could remember it. The crowd seemed to like them
though.

152

In fact, they seemed to be in awe of them; some of them ran forward to join them.

"Who are these guys?" I asked someone.

"The Weathermen," he told me, and in one clever step moved closer to the action and further away from the complete idiot who didn't know the Weathermen when he saw them.

In fact, I was more of an idiot than he supposed. Not only did I not recognize the Weathermen when I saw them, to make things worse, I didn't care. And by that I mean, I really, honestly did not care. When I tell you that, in those days, I just wanted to be left alone to work on my painting, I'm telling you the truth.

Of course I knew that the Weathermen were serious radicals, but I want to say this as clearly as I did one drunken night when I said it to a lovely young lady, "I am not THEN, and was not NOW a political am-nimol." That remains true today. I am not then, a political am-nimol (hopefully never will be). Still, I knew the Weathermen had something to do with riots, burning cars, the FBI's most wanted list, and blowing up government buildings; which lead to riot squads, police dogs, people beaten at random, arrested en masse, and senseless mayhem wherever and whenever they showed up.

I didn't think that was going to happen in the Fan District of Richmond though; Richmond was, for me at least, a land of painters and poets and long wavy-haired, willing young lovelies.

If I *had* to choose between the two fragments: The hippies, with their peace and love, their beloved pot, their music, and their vans scrawled over with the dayglow warning, "We've Come For Your Daughters"… and the anti-war crowd, with their petitions, leaflets, placards, marching, chanting, bricks and bottles and pipe bombs… I'd have sided with the self-proclaimed goofballs.

Actually though, I didn't really relate in any way to either of them. I never once used the word groovy, and only went to a protest in DC to observe the generation I'd been born into. I preferred solitude; I wanted to paint: I haunted the library. I liked warm girls, and I liked sleep. That's the world I was immersed in, willingly. But I could not ignore what was going on around me, so, I watched at a distance, as the Weathermen marched by.

On campus, when I came around the corner that day, there were loudly chanting mobs of students carrying placards and picketing in front of the RPI cafeteria. They didn't wear work clothes, but they still looked pretty serious. Crowds were also gathered, in chanting clumps, in front of the library and administration building. Somebody standing on a stone wall had a bullhorn, and from time to time he'd blare out something inspiring, which I could not understand, and the throng would all raise their fists in the air and shout something incomprehensible in response. I asked someone in the crowd for an explanation and I was told that they wanted things. They wanted Afro-American Studies; they wanted more Women's Studies; they wanted RPI to take a public stand against the war in Vietnam.

Here comes Steve Podlewski. He's got his apron rolled up in one fist and he's already wearing that stupid little paper hat they make you wear while you're working away, in utter disgrace, in the university cafeteria.
"Where are you headed all dressed up?" I ask.
"Goin' to work," he says, matter-of-factly.
"Well, you're gonna have to fight your way in." I observed. Steve just shrugged.
"You're not going to cross that picket line are you?" I asked, not that I cared about such stuff.
Then Steve Podlewski said something which I will never forget. He said this: "When these people are finished playing revolution, they're gonna be hungry. It's my job to feed them."

154

I watched Steve Podlewski, a quiet man of action, as he walked right through the screaming protestors and on inside. Later on I'd go through that picket line myself, not because I was taking a side but, just as Steve had predicted, because I was hungry. There was food in there; I wanted some.

It was about three days later that I found myself up on that roof.

I'd looked out onto Harrison Street to observe the day and noticed that the park below was full of people. There were cops' cars parked in every direction near Grove Avenue, which I couldn't see entirely from my vantage point, and I could hear mayhem; screaming and shouting and someone giving orders over a bullhorn. I must have been pretty solidly involved in my painting because I hadn't heard any of this from inside my little studio until I opened up that window to get some air.

Finding this scene curious, and wanting a better view, I went out the back window and climbed up the fire escape ladder to the roof , and over the brick barrier that separated See's Laundro-Mat from the apartment building next door. I went to the edge of that building and looked down upon the action.

This is what I saw. There was a large banner hanging over the street declaring "GROVE AVENUE REPUBLIC". Grove Avenue was closed off, with two squad cars parked nose to nose, and there were cops in riot gear down there swinging night sticks around wildly at kids (for that is what we were) who were taunting them.

The cops had a few vicious looking dogs on leashes; those leashes were stretched out to their limits; those dogs wanted to bite themselves a few hippies. Kids were throwing things and screaming and there was debris all over the street; obviously this had been going on for some time.

And, in the midst of all that, some clever fellow had managed to crawl forward and spray paint the word "OINK" in large awkward letters on the side of one of the squad cars. That was pretty good, I thought.

As I was watching this from my safe perspective above, a guy who I had never seen before appeared silently beside me. He looked down; he pried a brick loose from the parapet; he took aim, he fired that brick down upon a cop in riot gear. The brick hit the cop squarely, knocking him to the pavement. The guy then ran off, leaving ME up there alone.

Another cop, while assisting his felled teammate to his feet, looked up to see who had thrown the brick. He used his nightstick to raise his face shield to get a clearer view and, as I stood there dazzled by my predicament, he looked directly at me.

There was no way that I could possibly explain to that man, at that distance, what had actually happened. No gesture would have helped. Sticking around so he could get a more lasting impression of me didn't seem like the prudent thing to do either. So, I ran from that spot. I leapt over the brick barrier between the two buildings, ran across the roof of the Laundro-Mat, and climbed as quickly as I could down the metal ladder. As I was crawling back in through the window I looked up and saw Mrs. See. She was angry. "Bill," she said, "No up on roof. NO up on roof." She glared at me and stamped her foot.

I said, "OK. I'm sorry, Mrs. See."

A TRIP TO SAN MARCOS (1983)

During this trip, from time to time, for no apparent reason, the bus would arrive at a roadblock and Honduran soldiers would come on board. They'd make as much as they could of their slow walk through the bus, staring sternly at people, selecting someone at random and demanding their papers; frightening everybody. The soldiers would then spend an inordinate amount of time looking over the papers with magnificent disdain, before tossing them back, with grand indifference, into the lap of the poor trembling suspect. I saw this acted out so many times that it had become theatre.

During these stops they always took one or two frightened people off the bus, for no reason that any of us could determine. These people went like sheep—frightened sheep, but sheep nonetheless—and when we pulled away without them, nobody on that bus, including family, friends, neighbors, myself, turned their heads to look back. It may have been theatre, but it was chilling theatre.

What's peculiar is that these soldiers *never* asked either of the two women I was traveling with, or myself, for our papers. It was as if we didn't exist; it was as if they didn't even see us. I felt fairly secure because I was traveling with United Nations credentials, but it was frightening nonetheless whenever the bus was flagged down and the soldiers came aboard. After several hours of travel, we came to a different kind of check point. It wasn't just an armed man in uniform stepping out in front of the bus and signaling for it to stop; this time there was a striped wooden barrier stretched across the road with a little hut beside it. It was like something out of a movie. This time the soldiers came aboard as usual and looked down the aisle as usual, but, instead of making the slow walk down, demanding papers, they saw us, turned, and quickly left the bus.

I watched them as they went into the hut. And I watched as someone of superior bearing, presumably of superior position, stepped back outside with them. There was some pointing, a nod, and the soldiers were given instructions. This time, when they entered the bus, they marched quickly right down the aisle, directly to us and demanded to see our papers.

We each handed them our credentials, but they didn't even look at them. "Where are you going?" the soldier demanded coldly of one of the women I was traveling with, handing back her papers. "San Marcos," she said hesitantly.
"And where are you going?" he asked the other.
"San Marcos," she stuttered.
"And you," he said, handing my UN credentials back to me, "where are you going, señor?"
"San Marcos," I said.

And then that man uttered the most chilling words I had ever heard spoken. "This IS San Marcos," he said.

THAT GOOD OL' SAN MARCOS WELCOME

The soldiers escorted us off the bus and into the hut where, behind a desk, sat the better-looking, better-groomed, superior officer. Like in a movie, he had a nicely-trimmed little mustache; like in a movie, he ignored us completely. He was busy reading a document of some sort; and it must have been an extremely complicated document because it took several very long minutes before he put his signature to it with a great flourish, and placed it aside. Then he looked up and was surprised to see us there.

We stood before him and waited for him to speak. He first spoke to the soldiers behind us, in Spanish, and they responded with a kind of snap-to-it precision. I didn't understand a word of it, but assumed it had something to do with us and our destination—the Salvadoran refugee camp at Mesa Grande. Then he looked at the women and demanded their passports. They complied, stepping forward quietly and placing their passports gently upon his desk.

Without looking at me he asked for my passport. The women were both quick to interpret—"Give him your passport," they whispered urgently. So, I did.

He looked at the passports one at a time and studied them carefully before tossing them back upon his desk.
"What are you doing in San Marcos?" he asked in Spanish.
"We are here to visit the camp at Mesa Grande," one of the women said.
"But to go to Mesa Grande, you must first enter San Marcos," he said coolly. We waited. "And, to enter San Marcos you must have my permission," he concluded. He smiled at the women.

We'd been standing there all this time while there were two wooden chairs sitting along the side of the wall. I went over and took the chairs and placed one behind each of the women.

This was an act which stunned the women, startled the guy behind the desk, and infuriated the soldiers who both stepped back as if to prepare for the inevitable attack the placement of chairs no doubt heralded.

"Have a seat," I told the women, but they would not sit.

The guy behind the desk was glaring at me.

"Have a seat," I urged the women.

They looked to the guy behind the desk for approval, and when he finally deigned to nod, they sat.

Then he started speaking to the women at length. "What's he saying?" I asked repeatedly and, each time, they shushed me. When I insisted, by asking louder, one of the soldiers behind me stepped in so close that I could feel his breath on my neck.

When the guy behind the desk finished his speech, he waited while my traveling companion interpreted. "He tells us that in order to go to the camps we must have United Nations approval." Nothing could be simpler. I reached inside my vest and pulled out a plastic bag that contained my UN credentials, stepped forward and placed them on the desk.

When I stepped back, I took the opportunity to look at the guy who had been pressing the length of his rifle into my spine and he took the opportunity to make it clear that he disliked me. I tried to pretended indifference, even though Americans had been known to disappear in that neck of the woods.

The man behind the desk looked at my credentials casually then tossed them toward me. He spoke; my associates interpreted. "He says we must get the approval of the LOCAL United Nations Representative... *she* must stamp our papers... and *then*, we must return here."

"OK," I said, how do we do that? Where is this local U.N. Representative?"

160

"She is in San Marcos."

"Please ask him," I said, "where we should go precisely to get this approval."

Then he opened the top drawer of his desk, swept our passports into it, and closed the drawer.

When he spoke it was with great condescension, and basically a repeat of what he'd already said. I understood it to be something like this: "I will allow you to go into San Marcos, to the U.N. Representative, but then you must come back to me to get my signature in order to enter San Marcos."

This was perfectly idiotic of course and I pointed that out to my traveling companions, who told me to shut up.

"Will you do me a favor?" I asked one of the girls—the prettiest one with the best command of Spanish.

"What?" she asked peevishly.

"Will you tell this gentleman this: We want our passports back."

"What?"

"Tell this gentleman behind the desk that we want our passports back."

He held up his hand and said (in Spanish) you will get your passports back when you return with the stamp from the local U.N. Representative."

"No," I said, a word which I was sure needed no interpretation. "Tell this gentleman behind the desk that he will give us our passports back now."

He glared at me, and the soldier behind me gave me a tiny little nudge with his rifle. The guy behind the desk then rattled off a long string of things, which I didn't get, and which my friend did not interpret for me.

When he was done with his fit, I said to the woman, "Tell him what I am saying."

She looked at me as if I might be insane.

I said, "Tell him *exactly*, word for word, what I am saying." And she did. She told him word for word what I was saying as I said this: "We are citizens of the United States of America. The passports that you have taken from us are not ours; they belong to the United States government. You have no right to take them; you have no right to hold them. You will return them to us."

Everyone in that tiny shack was looking directly at me with the very same look—can this guy be serious? And every one of them could tell that I was. I was very tired; I'd been violently sick for many days, and had no fear whatsoever. Also, I've never really enjoyed anybody assuming they have authority over me.
You tell him this, I continued: "We are not leaving this room until we get our passports back. Tell him that!"

Honestly, I thought I might be facing death (soon to be delivered by the little coward who stood directly behind me). But if that were so, then I guess I thought it would be better to just get it over with, rather than continue dicking around with these tin soldiers. If that's what we're gonna do, then let's do it. Either way, let's stop playing footsie. That was my thinking at the moment. As said, we'd come along way, and I was very tired.

The man behind the desk looked at me for a long, long while. I could practically hear the girls' hearts beating in their chests as they waited; they were horrified at what I had just said. I'm pretty sure the little bastard behind me was hoping to receive the order, "Drag this stupid American son-of-a bitch out of here and do whatever you want with him!" I think he was dying to do it. And I think the guy behind the desk was clearly drawn between giving that order and laughing it off. He did neither though.

Instead, after giving the matter enough time to demonstrate his authority, he just opened his drawer, took out the passports, and slid them across the desk to us. All the while he continued staring at me. "Enjoy your stay in San Marcos," he said in English, while still looking at me.

I picked up my UN credentials and my passport, and we left that hut in a very quiet, very nervous little herd.

After we'd walked about two hundred yards down the dusty road, under a blistering sun, in complete silence, I said, "Wow, just like in a movie, huh?"

But my travelling companions were having none of it. After a few more steps one of the girls stopped, turned to face me, and shrieked, "Are you out of your mind? Are you? Are you out of your mind?"

That was, I think, the very last thing that woman ever said to me.

It was certainly a reasonable question.

The Unfair Fight Between OPINION and FACT (2003)

One time I said something to my old friend, Bruce—I forget the specific matter, but it was a commonly understood, long accepted, scientifically-proven fact—and he responded, "I don't believe that."

Because this was not the first time he'd responded in that peculiar way, I was not surprised. But, because it was not the first time he'd responded in that peculiar way, it was also not the first time I considered strangulation as one option for bringing him around to a clearer way of thinking.

"Bruce," I said, "this is not my personal opinion, it's a fact; it's universally recognized, commonly accepted, fact."
"Well, I don't choose to believe it," he repeated.
"You have no choice in the matter, Bruce," I said. "This is a fact. You can't NOT believe it. It's a fact. It exists. That's the way it is. It's out there. It's undeniable. It's real. There is no other option. It remains the same from any point of view. Personal opinion does not enter into it."
He looked me in the eye, shrugged and said, "Well, I don't choose to believe it."

So, here's a little guessing game for you. Which one of us— Bruce or the surly, explosive guy—is what they still insist upon calling a 'liberal', and which a conservative?

"It's plain, goddamned undeniable, FACT, Bruce!" I shouted at his back as he walked away.
"Well, I don't choose to believe it," he muttered from a safe but cowardly distance.

So, what was I supposed to do about that?

Here was a dear old friend of mine, a person who has known me for years—and yet continues to hang around with me—who seemed to be purposefully infuriating me.

He was sure that I was wrong; I was dead-certain that he was; and there was nothing neither of us could do about it.

That I had fact on my side meant nothing when thrown up against his unshakable opinion.

WHY NOT JUST DON'T (1983)

I first started thinking seriously about keeping my mouth shut when the US government was involved in something that, I felt, was none of its business, in Central America. At that time, I hadn't yet come to realize that it was also none of mine.

So, occasionally I could be found spouting my views on the situation in El Salvador and, when I spoke it was clearly, unquestionably, the voice of authority. It would take a year, and a little trip down to Central America for me to realize that spewing a few secondhand 'facts' is not the same thing as knowing what you are talking about. However, I *should have* realized that, because whenever I started huffing and puffing about Nicaragua someone always asked, "When was the last time you were *in* Central America, Mr. Mansfield?"
Well, so, OK, game, set, and match, wise guy.

In a childish act of defiance, I signed up with the Church of the Brethren to go down there and look around for myself.

After a month in Honduras, one brief frightening moment when we found ourselves actually *inside* El Salvador, and a very, very sick week in Nicaragua, gathering real information—and by that I mean, what I'd seen with my own two eyes—I was convinced that the US government was, in undeniable fact, involved in something that was absolutely none of its business. Better yet— though I didn't know it—I was getting pretty close to making the tiny leap necessary to admit to myself that it was none of mine.

Naturally, when I returned, full of righteous fury, I jumped right in again; quickly joining a protest down at the Federal Building. There was a huge crowd. We were all out there shouting in front of a big marble-clad building and, to add to our rage, we were being completely ignored.

166

Outside, people were coming and going just as if we didn't exist, while inside, business was tripping along nicely, as usual; even the armed security guards had their backs to us—they'd seen it all before.

So, there I was, screaming my fool head off about something I still did not really know much about—despite my noble trip. At the point when I found myself shouting at some poor woman who was coming out of that building, something clicked. Why was I screaming at her? What did I think she had to do with it?— for all I know she'd just gone in there to use the bathroom.

At that very moment I began to really question myself. What was I thinking? Why was I standing out there, shouting at a building? What did I believe all that screaming would accomplish? And, most importantly, if we couldn't reach people who were walking by within inches of us, how on earth would we ever reach some career politician in his office on the 34th floor? Our screaming wasn't going to change anybody's mind, and it wouldn't do anything at all for the good people in El Salvador. The futility of my actions sickened me.

At some point in our lives we must each take a look around and determine what affects us and what doesn't; what things we can do something about and what things we wish we could, but cannot. On that day, I had just about reached that point, when a young woman stepped in front of me holding a cardboard tray with two cups of coffee and some hot dogs. She was looking around for someone but, after a while not finding them, she shrugged, turned to me and said, "You want any of this?" I said, "What d' you got?" She said, "Cappuccino; the girl over there at the hotdog cart makes a pretty good cappuccino." So, you know, I took a cup.

Then she said, "I bought it for a friend, but I can't find him; I guess he left. You want a hotlink? I got two."
"Thanks," I said, and I took one.

At that very moment, despite the odds against it, I think I may have learned something—apparently, the hotlink was precisely the impetus I needed. And, I cannot tell you why, but we just start walking away together. We left all the shouting and shrieking behind us, and just drifted away, like in a dream. Without knowing why, or even how, I had freed myself.

I came away convinced that nobody has ever changed another person's mind about politics through reason, let alone by screaming at them.

We were walking along, munching on hotlinks, sipping cappuccino, when she said, "After they get finished protesting, they're gonna want some of this, and the girl with the hotdog cart 'll be long gone."

There it was; laid out so simply and so clearly before me that I could not ignore it. This was the second time I'd heard that wisdom spoken... and each time, it had to do with food.
I asked her, "Who are you?" And, she said, "I may be the only one around here who has any common sense left."

Then, I asked myself why had I been standing out there for hours, screaming at the top of my lungs at an indifferent marble-clad edifice, over something I could do nothing about, when, all that time, I could have been strolling around eating hotlinks, drinking cappuccino, and flirting with the only one around there with any common sense left?

THE LAST TIME I SAW OTIS RUSH (1989)

The final day of the 17th Annual San Francisco Blues Festival word had gotten around pretty quickly... but not quick enough... that there was to be an impromptu gathering of noted blues guitarists (Otis Rush, Ronnie Earl, Duke Robillard, I think Walter Trout may have been there as well) at Sweetwater, in Mill Valley. By the time we arrived the place was packed and the big galoot guarding the door was NOT letting ANYONE in.

At the time I was the publisher of a small Bay Area blues magazine, and I somehow managed to convince the guy that I was *somebody* and, that Otis Rush was not really there so much to play guitar as to be interviewed by me. He held my friends ransom, at the door, but he let me in to talk to Otis Rush. (It's amazing what a press pass can do.)

After fighting my way through the crowd, I discovered Otis Rush leaning back in a stick chair, in the passage between the stage and the stairway that leads down to the room where the infamous *Tribute to Percy Mayfield*/pool table incident took place. I went over to him and introduced myself. He smiled and shook my hand. He told me he remembered me, though I was sure he didn't. Then I pleaded with him—as well as a man might plead with Ronnie Earl's guitar scorching the hairs on the back of his neck—"Can you get us into this place?"

Otis Rush studied my face for a while; he moved a toothpick from one side of his mouth to the other, nudged the brim of his cowboy hat up a bit with one knuckle. He smiled and motioned for me to lean in. I placed an ear within inches of his mouth. "You're already in," he said.

There you go; that's the message. That's wisdom itself. You're already in. Enjoy the show.

WHY NOT JUST DON'T 2 (May 12, 2021)

Just today, I received a 3 page letter from a government agency, which confirms everything I thought I knew about government.

Let me tell you only two things about that letter and see if you can spot *at least* two things wrong with it.

.

1- On page one of that letter, at the top, in bold type, it said: **THIS IS NOT A BILL**
2- Three pages later it said: YOU OWE $0.00, and advised me that it was due immediately.

The fact that my taxes were spent in the composition, execution, and mailing of that letter would probably infuriate me, if I thought it would do any good.

Instead, my excellent wife and I took the puppy to the beach.

WOMEN in AMERICA,
as I've had the great good pleasure to know them

SHE SHALL NOT BE MOVED (1991 or so)

I was living in a small room in a wealthy woman's house in Del Mar, California. The house was one of only three residences that shared a private road; a densely treed ¼ mile-long cul-de-sac which ran steeply downhill from the public street above.

One day, I was sitting quietly by myself, contemplating the vast emptiness that was my undeniable future, when what sounded like a fog horn went off right outside my window. I peeked out and saw nothing. Then the horn blasted again and I got up and went outside.

I walked down our little private road toward the entrance and there on the steeply descending slope, in the very middle of the road, was a small woman, nicely dressed, in high heels, standing directly in the path of a huge (HUGE) Peterbilt, semi-trailer truck. The idling engine of that truck sounded like a house-sized cat purring, until the driver blasted his air horn again. And when he did that, that excellent woman did not budge; she did not move a muscle. I was witnessing a confrontation between a monstrous mechanical beast and a tiny, very nicely attired, Del Mar aristocrat.

When the truck horn blasted again, she crossed her arms and actually stepped closer to the grill of the monster. The driver of that truck had to open the door to his cab and lean out in order to see her; and when he shouted something at her—which I did not hear—she shouted something back. Then he blasted the air horn again, holding it for a long and threatening time.

And, here's where it becomes beautiful. In response to that loud demanding blast, she jumped up and slapped the shiny chromed radiator with one tiny hand. Then she shouted something and took up her position again in front of the truck.

When the truck driver got out of his cab, climbed down and came around to confront her, she folded her arms across her chest and stamped her nicely-shod little foot upon the pavement. After an exchange of words, it became clear that she wasn't moving; that truck was NOT driving down *our* road.

The driver stared at her for a while before he turned, went back and climbed into his cab. Then, he just sat there in silence for a very long time with the big engine purring, before releasing the brake and putting that huge truck in reverse. With smoke pouring out of both stacks, he opened the cab door, leaned out so he could see beyond his trailer, and began backing slowly up the road and back onto the publicly owned pavement.

After the truck had departed—and it took some doing to maneuver that thing uphill backwards—she walked down the slope and disappeared into her luxurious little house. That woman—my neighbor—had just become a hero, in my mind.

At the time, for some reason—though I was without a doubt the poorest man in Del Mar—I had a bottle of truly excellent tequila, unopened, in my little room. And, I had the strongest urge to take that bottle of truly excellent tequila, cross our little private road, tap upon that wonderful woman's door, and say, "Look, this is all I've got; please take it as a sign of the sincerest respect for what I just saw you accomplish. YOU WERE GREAT!"

It's a shame I didn't have the nerve to do that.

MY AMERICAN ROOTS: **My Mother**
Elizabeth Ann Mansfield 1928- 2017

The most remarkable thing about my mother was her innocence. In a world that ignores innocence, often makes a mockery of the innocent; a world almost perfectly designed to crush innocence, my mother remained herself. She was never affected by the indifference of this world, because she was, by her very nature, an innocent; it was, simply, who and what she was. To say that she was an innocent is not the same as saying she was naive. She was not.

What she was, was trusting, caring, continually joyful and kind. She was also an extraordinarily shy person; there was not a single moment in my mother' life when she wanted to draw attention to herself. Additionally, she wanted nothing for herself; she was a giver. She would look at something; a book, an object, a picture, and say to herself, "I bet so-and-so would like that. And, if you were that lucky person, that thing would show up in the mail, with a little note saying, "I thought you would enjoy this." She looked at everything that way; not as something that would please her, but as something that might please someone else.

One time, more than 50 years ago, when I was in college, she saw a 1960 Dodge Coronet, and she thought, "I bet Richard would like that.", and she bought that car for me.

It was a big weird-looking thing, difficult to ignore because it had, quite possibly, the largest tail-fins ever sported on an American-built car. It was a very cool car. She bought it, had it put in good mechanical order, and she had new tires put on it. And, the next time I arrived home, she handed me the keys. She told me, "I saw this car, and I thought you would enjoy it."

I did enjoy that car. It had push-button transmission: something I have never seen since. In fact, I loved that car, because it was a gift from my Mother.

She was an artist, and looked at the world through an artist's eyes; as if it was all new to her. Her beautiful deep brown eyes always sparkled with the light of discovery. There was brightness and joy and playfulness in her glance.

Recently, while Mom was in a care facility, my wonderful sister created a wall of photographs; a dozen or so photographs of various stages of Mom's life; and pasted them up where Mom could look at them and enjoy them. One evening, as my Father and I were walking to the car, he said, "Did you notice that in every single one of those photographs she was smiling?" I told him that I did. But I noticed something else as well. I noticed that in every single one of those photographs my Mother was looking at someone else, and smiling.

In some of those photographs she was looking at Dad; in some, it was a baby she holds in her arms. It might be one of her children or one of her grandchildren, or one of her great-grandchildren. If you were to look at 900 photographs of my mother, in every one of those photographs, she'd be smiling at someone else. It was as if, in each case, the photographer had said, "Alright, everybody, look at the camera and smile; except you Elizabeth; I want you to look at someone you love, and smile.

My Mother was an innocent, and an absolutely unique individual. Her innocence allowed her to enjoy her life. And, more importantly (I think she would say) it allowed her to offer her joy to us, those she loved.

I miss you so much my very dear Mother.

AN INNOCENT IN ACTION (1955)

My sister, Darla, was extremely shy and quiet as a child. But, when she arrived for the first day of school, in the 2nd grade, her strength of character was immediately called into play. The teacher, calling the roll at the beginning of class, called out, "Darlene?" My sister looked around to see who it was with a name so close to her own. But no one was raising their hand. So, she guessed that the teacher must have read her name wrong. She raised her hand meekly and said "Here... but, my name is Darla."
The teacher responded, "No it isn't; it's Darlene."

My poor little sister 'was terrified', imagining an entire year of that teacher calling her Darlene and getting into trouble for not answering, or—more likely, since she was a Mansfield— repeatedly correcting the teacher. She knew she would be 'going up against the biggest authority figure she had ever met, outside of our parents' and it scared her to death. Nevertheless, her family-imbued resistance to idiocy forced her to speak up.
"My name is Darla," she repeated, quietly.
In a suddenly snarly voice, the teacher responded, "No it's not. That's a nickname. Your name is Darlene, and that is what we'll call you. And when I say, Darlene, you will respond!"

Darla knew it was hopeless, and she also knew, without a doubt, that that teacher harbored an immediate dislike for her, because of this disagreement. She felt doomed; she foresaw a year of snarling, unwarranted criticism, bad grades, and continually facing the dilemma of how to respond whenever the teacher called, 'Darlene?' She could hardly keep the tears back. But, when she got home, and our mother asked how the first day of school had gone, she burst into tears. Between sobs, she told Mom the entire Darlene incident.

Many years later, my sister recounted: "Mom got up immediately, and went off down the hall, into her and Dad's bedroom. After a few minutes, she emerged with her hair combed, lipstick on, and purse in hand. She said, "Come on, we're going to THAT SCHOOL".

Darla said, "No, no, please, the teacher will hate me and be mean to me ALL YEAR!"

Mom said, "Oh no she won't!" And off they went to the school.

Holding my sister's hand tightly, Mom went straight to the principal's office. She told him the story and pulled out, from her purse, my sister's birth certificate. She put it on the man's desk, pointed at my sister's name on the certificate, and said, "Her legal name is Darla. DARLA. It's not Darlene and it's not a nickname; and THAT TEACHER had better start calling her Darla. And she had better not be mean to her or give her bad grades over this, because my daughter is a good student, and I will know if something is going on." And, if I know anything at all about my mother, I'd guess that, during all of that, she looked that principal right in the eye.

The principal—not a stupid man—said, "I am so sorry about this Mrs. Mansfield. I will talk with her teacher immediately; I will take care of this matter myself, today, I assure you."

The next day, the teacher called out, 'Darla?' at roll call and, from what we've been told, she even forced a little smile.

She called my sister Darla ever after. And, my sister told me, "From that day on, I knew, with certainty, that Mom would always have my back... always."

MY AMERICAN ROOTS: My Father's Mother (2013)

The only advice I can ever recall getting from Grandma—my father's mother—was when I was a very little boy. I don't know what I was doing or what I had said, but she took me aside, placed a hand on my shoulder, looked me in the eye, and told me sternly, "Say what you mean, and mean what you say."

While watching my mother sleep—while recovering from a stroke—I told my father of that memory. He said to me, "And she lived by that too... and everybody knew it." Then he told me this story:

"There was an 'Animal Control Officer'—a dog catcher—one time in our back yard. That was one of those appointed positions —he'd done somebody a political favor—and that gave him license to go around catching dogs and hauling them off to the pound. Then, the owner was forced to come in and bribe the man to get their dog back.

So, one time, my mother looked out the kitchen window and there was a man in a suit dragging our dog by the collar toward the alley. In the alley was a panel truck with the back doors wide open. My mother went out onto the back step and said, 'What are you doing with my dog?'
The man showed a badge and said, 'I'm taking him in. So-and-so, down the street said your dog was on his property and tried to bite him.'
My mother said, 'That dog has never left this property, and you're not taking him anywhere.'
See, our dog had a long chain to his collar, and it didn't reach beyond the edge of our property line.
'Well, he's going with me,' said the man.
'Wait, just a minute, please,' said my mother, and she went back in the house.

The man waited willingly of course, thinking he was about to be paid off.

When my mother emerged again she had a double aught six—a shotgun—cradled in her arms."
I asked Dad, at this point in the story, "Was that a single barrel or a double barrel shotgun?"
"No," he said, "it was a double barrel."
"Oh, one of those things with two barrels side by side?"
"No," he said, "over and under."

"So," he continued, "My mother said, 'You're gonna chain that dog up just like you found him, and then you're gonna get off my property.' And the man did just that. He had no doubt whatsoever that my mother meant every word she spoke. She'd always been that way."
"You're certainly that way," I observed.
"We're all that way," said my father.

At that moment I felt a familiar glow within. I have always been kinda proud to be part of a family that, when we speak, nobody who has any sense has any doubt as to whether we mean what we've said.

UNDER THE OLD BAGWORM TREE

It was apparent that I liked women pretty much right from the beginning. What was to become a lifelong fascination was undeniable, even while I was still of crawling age.

One day my mother stuck me outside in a playpen under the ponderous limbs of the old bagworm tree and, as the story goes, she came out a little later to find me no longer in confinement. Several of the solid oak bars of that pen had been shattered, and I was nowhere in sight. However, my absence did not launch a mother's frantic search for her missing child; apparently I'd done it before, and she knew just where to find me.

Sure enough, I was three doors down the street, sitting in a neighbor woman's lap, calmly eating cigarette butts.

My mother says, when she came upon us I was nestled up against the woman just as happy as can be, shoving the foul things into my mouth with both fists. I always like to imagine that I was using the more advanced, alternating hands technique (something in the manner of the way Bubba eats ribs). And, knowing me, I probably stepped up the pace when, at a distance, I spied my mother coming.

The kindly neighbor's name was Gladys Schoelein. Her husband was a long-haul truck driver; I think his name was Phil. That's about all I know. The rest is only what I've been told. But, I can tell you this much firsthand: it wasn't the tobacco that called me, gave me the strength to shatter those oak prison bars, and filled me with the necessary resolve to crawl a hundred yards of gritty, glass-strewn, concrete sidewalk on my tender, puffy little hands and knees. It was Gladys. I'm told that I loved her dearly…and what's nice is that, by all accounts, she liked me too.

She was always glad to see me, always offered me a lap and as many cigarette butts as I could chew on.

Although I was expendable—as the second son in a family then wanting only a daughter to achieve the ideal balance— and though I'd made my own desires clear enough—by repeatedly escaping and making the treacherous journey alone—I was nevertheless unceremoniously scooped up and returned home.

As said, I don't remember any of this. I cannot picture Gladys Schoelein, but at times I can almost feel her arms around me. At times I can almost taste those cigarette butts too. Maybe that's why I never took to smoking in any serious way. Thank you, Gladys, for all of that.

A bit later on in life—toddling age—because of that unswerving compass within me, I had a migratory compulsion toward the kitchen whenever we were at my grandmother's house. I recall her running me out of there countless times, because boys didn't belong in the kitchen (at least not while the women were cooking). "What in Sam Hill are you doing in here again?" I can hear her say. "Now, you go on out there with the rest of the men; we'll let you know when it's ready." She thought I was there for the food. But, I slipped back in again as soon as I could, and stood quietly, unmoving, in the nearest corner with my back pressed flat against the wall, hoping (that means with rapidly beating heart) not to be noticed; because I wanted to be close to my Aunt Carolyn.

To me she was everything that a woman should or ever could be. She was a trim, dark, intelligent creature invested with that mysterious calm that the very best women always seem to possess. She was strong and opinionated, like her mother yet, also like her mother, she was good-natured, kind and warm and even-keeled. And like all truly fine, strong intelligent women, she had absolutely no idea how beautiful she was. That is a marvelous trait in a woman.

I adored her. She married a line of idiots.

And that's probably enough said about that. (I probably should have stopped with 'I adored her.')

That outlines, almost perfectly, the beginning of a life driven by an unquenchable desire to be in the presence of, to impress, and to please women.

Respect for females is embedded in my very earliest memory: I'm walking down the sidewalk under the assistance of a kindly old gentleman. He is holding my hand to keep me upright— apparently at that stage in the game, I had some navigational problems. The kindly old gentleman says, "When you see someone coming down the sidewalk toward you, look them right in the eye, smile and say, 'Good morning.' If it's a lady, you tip your hat… I guess we're gonna have to get you a hat."

That is my earliest memory.

ODILE (around 2001 or so)

One afternoon, one of this hotel's best desk clerks (young, beautiful, charming, chirpy, and exceedingly French) was observed in the appalling, completely unacceptable act of insisting that a guest admit the truth.

I forget the details, or maybe I never knew the details, it hardly matters, but the scene was interesting because in this business the guest may not always be right but we, the staff, are always wrong. Always. Whenever one of these matters goes to trial before the owner, things like facts, truth, and reality are never allowed to stand in the way of a swiftly delivered guilty verdict. We are all, each and every one of us, guilty from the moment we are hired.

When I arrived in the office that day, there was a noticeable chill in the air. The opening shot had already been fired, and the smoke still hung in the air. The desk clerk, Odile, was seated behind the desk and the guest was very properly seated, ramrod straight, across from her; they were glaring at each other in silence. The guest held her purse clenched in her lap as if Odile's next move might be to quickly lean over the desktop and snatch it.

Somewhere in there, during the ice cold silence of the check-out process, the guest felt compelled to tell Odile—apparently yet again—that she had been misled by something Odile had said. In response, Odile denied having ever said it. The guest then, assuming that Odile was restrained by her position as mindless and spineless servant to the hotel, demanded that she confess to having said this thing, whatever it might have been. Odile not only refused to admit it, she went so far as to correct the guest. "I never told you that, Madame," she said flatly.
The tone of that statement certainly got my attention.

At this point the guest's beady little eyes began to narrow as she sensed something less than the anticipated boot licking subservience which one might normally expect from a lowly desk clerk, and things soon escalated.

The guest stood up abruptly, saying, "You told me…"

Odile stood up on her side of the desk just as quickly and cut her off by saying, "That is not true, Madame, and you know it is not true."

The guest then fled the office while shouting over her shoulder, "You said it. Admit it."

Odile followed her out into the hallway shouting, "That is not true, Madame."

"Admit it," screeched the guest without looking back.

"No, you are wrong, Madame. I never told you that."

The guest stopped with her hand on the front door, wheeled and shouted, "You said…", but seeing Odile in close pursuit, escaped outside without finishing the thought.

Odile, while dashing down the hallway, was shouting, "That is not true, Madame. You are wrong Madame." She actually followed the guest outside onto the sidewalk, and was heard shouting out there, "That is not true, Madame!" as the guest, successfully routed, scurried away.

The owner had long since emerged from his office to find out what all the shouting was about. And as we stood there in the hallway together, awaiting Odile's return from her crusade, I had a barely restrained grin on my big stupid face. The owner, I noted, did not. What I saw as an act of heroism, he saw only as the willful breaking of convention.

When Odile returned she went stomping into our office with the owner following her. He was furious and had a lot of things to say to her in French, in cold, subdued tones. She had my complete approval however; I was delighted, practically giggling

184

with delight. In my mind, she was the one true champion of a very good and too-long neglected cause.

Like Odile, I don't always thoroughly enjoy guests treating us as though they might have been royalty in some previous life and now recognize us, in this one, as the foul ingrate peasant who once sullenly tended their generously overflowing fields. Even less do I enjoy it when they think nothing has changed from that life to this.

So, I was delighted to see someone other than myself reject the universally accepted concept that humiliation of the staff is simply part of any good hotel experience. Fresh sheets, clean towels, full breakfast, talk down to the maid; insult the desk clerk on your way out the door... an excellent stay... I'd recommend this place to anyone.

I think we may have won that little skirmish. The enemy had certainly been driven from the field of battle.

The owner called Odile into his office, and shortly (by French standards) she returned to the front office to pick up her purse, slam a few drawers around, grab her coat, and make her way, head tilted nicely upward, out the door, never to be seen or heard from again.

As she was gathering her things, I told her, "I don't know what that was about, I don't even know if you were right, but I certainly applaud your spirit." I smiled.

Odile looked at me in that way the French look at anyone who doesn't speak French and expelled a puff of air, dismissing me entirely. She didn't want and certainly didn't need any American's approval (and, you know, I'm good with that).

Just as a note: I'm sure Odile would want me to make it clear right here that she was not fired from the hotel, she quit. She quit with the kind of drama that we all dream of bringing to our quitting. Her departure was glorious. She looked great.

Of course, though the guest may not have been right, Odile was clearly very wrong and, as said, guilty from the day she was hired. So, she had to go. But, she'd stood up against the ridiculous tyranny that some guests feel they have the right to impose upon the hotel staff, and won.
In my view Odile was driven out by her own heroism.

Odile, wherever you are today, I salute you.

AMY (1967 or 1968)

One night in the Village Tavern, a kid came up to the booth I
was poetically sulking in and sat down across from me. I'd seen
him around; I didn't know who he was or where he fit in; we'd
never met. I only knew his name: Spencer Something or other
III. He was very serious when he spoke, serious and secretive.
"You know Amy?" he whispered.
"Amy?"
"You know, she always hangs around with us… the theatre
crowd."
"Theatre crowd?"
"Tiny little thing with stringy blonde hair, wears yellow chucks."
"Oh. Yeah, I know her… with the big eyes?"
"That's her. She's so cute, don't you think?"
I shrugged, nodded.
He continued, "Well anyway…she told me that if I ever had the
chance to tell you something I should tell you. And, well, since I
saw you sitting here alone, I thought this would be as good a
time as any… to tell you."
"She wanted *you* to tell *me* something? I don't even know that
chick," I said.
"Still, she asked me to tell you; she begged me to tell you."

At that time, (who can explain such things) I'd been working on
raising one eyebrow independently, and had developed it to the
point where I thought I'd give it a try in public, without the
mirror. I'm not sure I even knew what the implication of that
gesture was, (still don't) but I hated to waste the opportunity; this
seemed as good a time as any. So, in response to what he'd said,
I raised one eyebrow. In response, Spencer Something or other
III just sat there looking at me. Hadn't he noticed?

"What is it she wanted you to tell me?" I asked, bored to tears.

He looked around cautiously, then leaned across the table toward me, and breathed out, "Amy said that she really wants to — ———————-."
That certainly got my attention.
"She said she'd love to," he concluded.

No longer a virgin, but a boy of limited specific experience, I couldn't believe what I'd just heard. I shook my head in disbelief. Was I dreaming? No female that I'd ever known had ever uttered such a phrase… in my sexual fantasies they were more temperate. I leaned across the table toward him.
"She told you that she wants to ——————-?" I whispered.
"Yes. Those are her exact words."
"She wants to———————————-?" I whispered, with equal parts shame and hope. (Admittedly, perhaps I was leaning just a little more toward hope.)
"She wanted me to let you know that."

I drank my beer very slowly. I was stunned. Delighted, of course, but, stunned. Curious, of course, and eager, but stunned. I tried not to show it. I wanted to be clear about this, though; I wanted to know that I'd heard him correctly. Or, maybe I just wanted to hear it again.
"*She* told *you* to tell *me* that she wants to ————————-?"
"She REALLY wants to ———————-," he said, and raised both eyebrows as if to say, 'how y' gonna top that?' She told me, 'Tell him I'd ——————— any time, anywhere; he doesn't even have to ask, all he has to do is show up.' Oh, and she told me to give you this."
He handed me a scrap of paper which, once unfolded with trembling hands, revealed her address.
"Any time," he repeated.

I remained stunned; flattered; nonplused; floored and speechless (not necessarily in that order) for quite a while… and, though

188

seated—I have to be honest with you—I felt a little weak in the knees. I didn't know what to say or do.

For a while I couldn't say or do anything. I looked down at my hands, at the beer, at the table, around the bar. I was thinking. I mean I was trying to think. 'She's a cute kid,' I reasoned. AND, I was, after all, above all and, maybe especially below all, a living breathing male type creature. To go along with it made a kind of unassailable, natural, good sense.

This had to be some kind of a set-up, though. Girls didn't go around saying things like that, did they? No, something was wrong here. Someone wanted to get me to a certain location where they could beat the life out of me without witnesses, or worse, with a crowd of jeering witnesses. I studied Spencer to see if he was setting me up, or simply messing with my mind, and decided that he was as honest as he was flamboyant; he was pretty damned obvious. So, I thought about it some more. I mean there isn't a free man on earth that wouldn't want some pretty college girl to————————.

I was a free man. And I was on earth—though not firmly attached at that moment. Amy was a very sweet looking, little charmer. Basic arithmetic should have helped me to figure it out. Still, I remained cautious. "Why are you telling me this?"
"Cause we're friends, Amy and I. Cause she asked me to. Cause I want to see her happy." He shrugged. It was all pretty simple.
"You want to see her happy?"
"Yeah, we were sitting around the other day and we were talking about Happiness and I said, 'Dear, dear Amy, what would make you happy? I mean, what would make you really and truly happy?' She bubbled up immediately and said, 'You know what would make me crazy-happy? …that painter guy, Richard? I'd like to————————. That would make me ecstatic.' Well, of course I was shocked!" He mimed shock for me.

"She said that?"

"Yes, that is what I'm telling you, you numskull!" he said with obvious frustration (heterosexuals can be so trying at times). He reached across the table to slap the back of my hand. "She said it would make her deliriously happy." He took a dramatic pause before turning peevish. "Why on earth would I make up such a thing?" That, indeed, was the question. I must have had a glazed look in my eye because he repeated the tale one more time with appropriate gestures for emphasis. "Are you hearing me? Do you get the message?"

It was true that I didn't know what to say or how to respond, but, believe me, I got the message.

"She told me that if I ever ran into you I should tell you that if you want her to————— ——, just drop by her house, any time day or night."

"Please don't say it again," I said, and sat in silence for a while. I folded my hands properly in my lap, then placed them under my thighs, then placed them back on the table and twiddled my thumbs. I think I said, "Yikes."

"She'll do it too," he added.

"Alright." I said. "Don't say it again. Please…"

He slumped back into the booth and stared at me impatiently. Was he expecting me to send him back to Amy with a response? *The gentleman is pleased to accept your kind invitation… and will arrive there as soon as his cloven hooves can carry him to you.*

"Well, I've done my job," he said with a sigh, and tapped the paper with her name on it with one finger. Then he got up and drifted out of the Village, leaving me to ponder a world in which lovely creatures with saucer-like eyes plead for the chance to push our lust-driven dreams down the steep slope of salacious expectation, over the cliff, into the pit of carnal carelessness.

As someone who had only recently 'lost his virginity' I had to decide if I was ready for that. I just felt maybe I needed a little more time to prepare for my descent into delightful Depravity.

Ultimately, (just joking) I decided to take full advantage of the offer that Amy had made me (of course, and naturally). And, (of course and naturally) I realize that 'shameful' is not really an adequate word to describe my behavior. I offer no excuse… though I really think it would be fair for biology to take some of the blame.

Back then… at the beginning, she lived less than two blocks from me. So, I thought it would be rude for me to walk by her place and not drop in once in a while, if only to say hello; it was merely a matter of courtesy. And when she moved out of the neighborhood, to an apartment 20 blocks away, it was sort of a pain to get there, but courtesy has its demands.

Here's the true weirdness: Amy didn't want a relationship, she didn't want a lover, she didn't want my friendship or the advice an emerging painter might offer her, concerning the theatre arts. It was pretty much as Spencer III had laid it out for me that day in the Village; she just wanted to… And, just as he'd predicted, it seemed to make her deliriously happy. I was very nervous about all of that, you know, at first, and thought about it a lot.

And this is what I came up with.
The Bible has it all wrong, concerning Job. The Devil should have challenged God to GIVE Job whatever he wanted, instead of challenging Him to strip Job of all his fine possessions. If you really want to drive a wedge in between any vital human male being and any overwhelming benevolent being, give him wealth, give him success; see what happens. Or, better yet, take the direct route and just give him a girl like Amy. Take away all his earthly possessions and God may be the only thing the poor man

has left, but give him a girl like Amy and, Excuse me, God, would you mind just taking a little walk?

Confusion aside, every time I knocked on Amy's door I sang a thousand silent songs of thanksgiving. I was truly, truly, a very, very thankful young man at the moment she opened that door. My heart, my mind, my body, my soul all resonated with the purest ringing gratitude every time I crossed that blessed threshold. Soon, I became a devoted convert.
Man, was I devoted.

There were times when I walked those 20 blocks, and times I ran. I covered that distance sober, drunk, stoned, delighted and regretful, shameful and shamelessly, but always eagerly. Above all, *of course*, I wanted to make sure that Amy was happy. Sun, rain, snow, dark of night, nuclear war, nothing prevented me from honoring my commitment to this young woman's happiness. I would have crawled if necessary. Through broken glass, if it came to that. And, in those torturous times I took the bus, I had plenty of time to think.

While the bus piddled along, I wondered about Amy; what she thought she was doing, why she was doing it, and I wondered, of course, about my own culpability, my soul, my damnation, my pleasure, my happiness, my greed, my apparent insatiability…and, of course, whether or not any of it mattered.

With all hope utterly lost, of ever becoming a decent human being again, reason told me that I might as well enjoy my sub-human existence. Whatever the depth of my thoughts, the anguish of my concerns, I always arrived at her door without so much as a single thought in my head. Well, one, but, I didn't even need that one… Amy would take care of that for me.

The last time I saw Amy, I arrived at her place in the middle of a bright sunlit Sunday afternoon, and a clean, casually dressed gentleman, about my father's age, answered the door. I asked if Amy was there, and he invited me in. On the couch sat a perfectly proper woman and her prim young daughter, both flowery in Spring-like dresses. In a chair sat an unnecessarily clean-cut teenaged boy (he could have been me three years earlier). That sure was one very nice-lookin' American middle class family.

The gentleman took a seat on the couch next to his younger daughter and patted her on the knobby knee. Amy appeared in the hallway, introduced me to her parents and then, taking me by the hand, lead me quickly down the short hallway, into the next room... and... pushing me up against the door with real urgency, proceeded to do what Amy did.

My crime, and who could see it as anything less, was that I only struggled briefly. I'm sorry to say that with time this tale has not evolved into one of my most charming or endearing moments.

After 20 minutes or so we emerged; her father stood up, we shook hands, smiled and looked each other directly in the eye; him questioningly, me unblinkingly innocent. Then, we both agreed it had been a pleasure to meet one another. Her mother smiled wanly and looked down at her prayerful hands as if knowing more than any mother might want to know about her daughter (women have such instincts), and I began to wobble drunkenly toward the front door.

At the door, Amy caught up to me, took my hand and explained quickly that she was moving back home and, since this was the last time she'd ever see me, she wanted to tell me something. I was surprised; I had no idea what she was about to say. But also, this was the first time I could recall her ever holding my hand.

She held it in both of hers and swung it about like a young girl with a crush. As she stood there in front of me, a tiny little saucer-eyed beauty, she smiled sweetly, and took in a big breath before speaking. "Thank you," she said.

"Thank *you*," I responded and purposefully stopped short of saying, "the pleasure was all mine." I hoped with all my heart that wasn't perfectly true.

Then, Amy stood up on her tip-toes and kissed me very softly on the cheek. It was the first time I can ever remember her kissing me. "Gosh," I said.

And, believe me, I meant every word of it.

SOMETHING BETTER TO DO (1969 or so)

In those days we were always returning home with the sunrise. I don't know what we did; talked mostly, smoked some dope and talked. Drank some wine; laughed. Laughed a lot. Sometimes a single word would set us off. We'd be sitting around listening to music (there was always music), or gazing blankly at each other, and someone would utter a word and we'd all be snorting and rolling around on the floor holding our sides. That's the way I remember it anyway.
(Hopefully, others harbor more dignified memories.)

We were a good-natured lot. No animals were harmed in the making of this lifestyle.

So, one morning, after such a night, Ginger was on her way home alone. She was passing a lovely little house with pristine white picket fencing all around and willow trees which overhung the sidewalk (I'm sure there were flowers involved too), when a young black kid—post pubescent—came out of the lovely little cobblestone alley, climbed upon Ginger's back and, while clinging to her like a monkey, rubbed himself against her.

Ginger managed somehow to shrug him off, and then she turned to face the kid. Apparently, though she was perturbed by the kid's strange animal-like behavior, she was not angry.
"Haven't you got anything better to do?" she asked him, somewhat peevishly.
Naturally, the kid was surprised by Ginger's reserve. (We'd all been surprised by Ginger's reserve at one time or another.) But, he was so thoroughly disarmed that he didn't know precisely what to do next. For a moment it looked like he was going to offer an apology. He paused. He thought. Then he shrugged a goofy kind of shrug, turned and ambled away, down the alley out of which he'd come.

Ginger watched him for a bit then continued on her way home to get some sleep.

I don't remember precisely when this story came to me, but it wasn't immediately; Ginger didn't feel it required that sort of attention. Maybe a couple of days, maybe a week later, she mentioned it to Rick when they were passing by that same lovely little alley; and Rick pointed the spot out to me sometime later when we were going by that way.

It was a particularly idyllic location for such an event. From Rick's description, before we'd reached the spot, I had already pictured it clearly, even the flowers. And, because I knew her, I could hear Ginger's calm but scolding manner—as if she expected more from all of us. I could see her standing there with her hands on her hips as she looked the poor misguided youth right straight, directly and unflinchingly, in the eye. "Haven't you got anything better to do?"
It was a good question.

I have no idea what I'd do if someone jumped out of an alley and climbed on my back and started dry-humping me as the rising sun filtered down through a lovely leafy-green willow tree, in the languid residential morning streets of Richmond. That's why I admired Ginger. Her response was eloquent and dignified. Also, I think it allowed the kid the opportunity to re-think his attitude concerning women, without embarrassing himself too much.

Ginger handled that peculiar event perfectly.

MY AFFAIR WITH A DRUG DEALER'S WIFE (1968)

Somehow one year—and this is the way things happened in those days—in the Spring, all the wives of mid-level drug dealers in our little district emerged from their freshly painted, fully renovated, antebellum houses with matching Afghan hounds on the ends of long fine leather leashes. Of the three that I recognized two were also pushing baby carriages... well, top of the line, European baby carriages with overly large spoke wheels and finely tooled brass fittings.

So, I don't know, count backward and you discover that there was some real activity in the mid-level drug dealer bedrooms of Richmond's Fan District the previous summer... and perhaps some carelessness.

Of course it was nice to see that the mid-level drug dealers were prospering. They all had fine wives. These fine, trim, elegant beings were perfectly suited for the matching Afghan hounds which trotted like peculiar-looking ponies in front of them. The word noble comes to mind. Any one of those fine wives might have fit in comfortably, and purposefully unnoticed, Opening Night at the Met. Each looked as though she'd just stepped out of the pages of some glossy New York City fashion magazine ...but casually, of course... decked out impeccably, merely by chance. The dealers themselves—in those very few times I got a glimpse of one—must have had a morning ritual, rubbing the finest grade sand paper over every inch of their face and hands. Whatever the process, it produced that unmistakable upper-class Aristocratic glow. That look appears in people who had accumulated their wealth by more socially acceptable means as well. They also had that innate smugness. But, their wives, Oh, those drug dealers' wives, they were something else. They were completely off limits for one thing.
They were certainly nice to look at from a distance however.

So, all during that Spring and Summer, you might, from time to time, observe one of these graceful creatures strolling under the sheltering trees of Grove Avenue or down the ancient brick sidewalks of Park Avenue, looking like a goddess, pulled through the dappled sunlight by her devoted, goofy-looking, hound (breathe here), and you might wonder, 'Why now?', 'Why Afghans?' But, then of course, you'd realize, 'Why not?'

One day, (now we're getting somewhere) I saw two of these women standing on the corner of Park and Harrison with their hounds and baby carriages and I realized something. I realized that, if they weren't sisters, they may as well have been. It was very much as if only one of them was standing there in front of a full-length mirror. This was without question the largest gathering of drug dealers' wives since the 26 inning, softball battle royale between the Checkered Demons and the sub-culture rock band, Titfield Thunderbolt, the previous summer. That was an event which I observed, but in which I did not partake. (I think the final score was something like: Checkered Demons 304, Thunderbolt 27.)

When this gathering of wives and dogs and baby carriages took place I was in the park across the street, sitting on a bench, arm's length away from a smelly old wino friend.
"Look at that," I said.
"Yeah, yeah," he said.
"What do you think of those dogs?" I asked.
"Puh..." he replied.
"Those are pretty expensive dogs..."
He rolled his eyes about and spit.
"What do you think of those young women?" I asked.
He looked. He pondered. "Too skinny."
"Really? You think they're too skinny? I like 'em," I said.
He looked again. He gave it some thought. "Too much trouble."
"What kind of dogs are those... do you know?" I asked.

198

"A dog's a dog," he said and spit again. "They're too much trouble too."

So, I was wondering what kind of dogs those were, and inspired by *the spirit of inquisity* (in those days I had that), I got up and made my way across the street with every intent of approaching the drug dealers' wives and asking, "Say…what kind of strange looking animals are those?" But, as I was approaching, whetting my lips in prep—a young woman stopped near them and asked with ringing bell-like effervescence, "Those are Afghans, aren't they?" The drug dealers' wives confirmed, in a cheerful but overly-dignified manner, that they were indeed.

Later on, that same week, I was carrying a painting somewhere, walking down Grove Avenue, under the trees, and the most beautiful of all the beautiful drug dealers' wives stepped out of one of the several houses her hubby owned on that street (common knowledge), led by one of these big stupid-looking dogs. Although I have always been shy—and by shy I mean socially awkward—she just looked so lovely that I could not help but smile as our approach to each other narrowed. And, she caught that. And she smiled at me.

I must have blushed (though I hate to admit it). I blushed even more deeply when that dog stopped in front of me and stuck his nose directly into my crotch. She laughed in a remarkably feminine way, placing one hand over her mouth, and said, "Oh, I'm so sorry", as I took the animal's snout in my hand and, with some authority, removed it from my crotch.

Then, me and the drug dealer's wife just looked into each other's sparkling eyes for an unreasonable (and by that I mean possibly dangerous) few seconds.
I think we both blushed and bowed our heads while still laughing quietly.

When we bobbed up again, we explored each other's eyes for a
while more, until I finally came up with something to say.
I said, "That's an Afghan isn't it?"
She said, "No, actually he's a Borzoi."

But she said it in such a way that I was pretty sure she really
meant, "Why don't you and I just run off together? We could
have a really good time."

That was pretty much our entire affair.
It lasted 47 seconds.

My hope is that when my life flashes before my eyes, just before
I make that eternal leap, I'll re-live that moment.
I've come pretty close just now, by telling it.

SPENCER III AGAIN (1969)

After Amy had departed I was approached a second time by the go-between, Spencer Something or other III. I hadn't seen him for maybe a year, but suddenly, one day, there he was.
"May I sit down?" he asked.
After settling in and ordering a cup of tea over his shoulder, as if he might be French royalty and this little college town café the royal court, he said, "It's such a shame that Amy left." I agreed.
"I bet you miss her dearly." I admitted it.
"She's a nice kid," I said. I was thinking, Now what?
"Yes," he said, "and we wish her well in all that she may do. But that leaves you... you know... kind of..." he leaned across the table toward me and said, "without someone to ——————."
I winced.

"You know," I said, "I don't want to talk about that."
"Well, OK," he said quickly, "but I know someone else who *might* want to *talk about it*. I mean if you don't want to find yourself suddenly high and dry."
I gulped my coffee and studied this guy carefully.
"Who?" I asked, just out of curiosity.

The churning in my gut told me that I had consciously stepped over the line. Whatever innocence there was in my affair with Amy could not be extended to cover what I was tempted to do.
"Well, what do you think of Carol-Ann?" he asked tilting his head and batting his eyes.
"Carol-Ann...? I don't even know anyone named Carol-Ann."
"Well, that's funny because she knows you. She's in your drawing class."
I thought about it. There was a girl in my drawing class named Carol-Ann.
"In my drawing class? Wears a beret once in a while?"

"Well…" he said, smacking his lips, "She said she simply hates to see you all sad over Amy's leaving, and all lonely like. She'd like to step in and help you out."

"She told you this?"

"Isn't it wonderful how well connected I am with girls who are interested in your happiness?"

"I don't believe it."

"Well, OK," he said, "it's your loss," and he started to get up.

"Wait. Wait," I said, extending a hand. "What exactly did Carol-Ann say?"

"Oh, she told me that she wished you weren't so sad and that she knew how to make you forget all about Amy, and that she would _____."

I think that was what I wanted to hear. "Those are her exact words?" I asked.

It went on… and on until, eventually, a time was set and I was to meet Carol-Ann at Spencer's place.

When I got there, Spencer, dressed in a Japanese robe of some sort, opened the door, invited me in, and directed me into a little bedroom fitted out like a movie-set harem. He told me that Carol-Ann would be in, in a few moments. In the meanwhile he made suggestions which were foreign to my nature and, for someone with a bit of residual innocence still remaining, more than a little frightening.

He said, "I could get things rolling, and when Carol-Ann comes in she can take over." He batted his heavily made-up eyes at me and shrugged coquettishly.

I was immediately and completely freaked out by this.

"Carol-Ann doesn't mind," he said. But that failed somehow to comfort me.

"I do," I said. "I mind."

"Well, how about if Carol-Ann gets you started and then I take over just for a little bit and then Carol-Ann finishes what she started?"

This triggered something in me which had me outside myself, frantically asking, 'Where's Carol-Ann? and alternately, 'When's Carol-Ann going to get here?' I probably asked each of those questions a dozen times with increasing concern before Spencer was driven from the room.

After a very long time, Carol-Ann came in dressed in practically nothing, smiling and said, "Hi. I'm glad you decided to accept our invitation." I didn't like the word "our" in that statement. Spencer sat down beside me, patted the back of my hand and said, "He's a bit skittish."

Carol-Ann pouted, "Are you? Are you skittish?" She lied down beside me and said, "Don't you think it would be fun for the three of us...?"

That had the same effect on me as the shot from a starting gun has on an Olympic sprinter.

"Oh no. NO no-no-no, NO. No, we cannot…." I squealed.

She said, "It's just the same. If anything, Spencer is even better than I am."

Spencer said, "Oh, Carol-Ann I am not…well, maybe a wee bit."

They finished that debate without me, because I was on my way out the door. "You must be out of your minds!" I was saying to myself as I RAN from that house. "You must be out of your goddamned minds."

My guess is, Spenser and Carol-Ann thought I was.

And, I could hardly argue… I was certainly very close.

As I stumbled out into the bright afternoon light, I immediately came upon an old black man sitting in the cab of an ancient flatbed delivery truck, with the door open. His feet were resting on the running board and his head was in his hands.

When he looked up, I could see that he was every bit as
frightened as I was. He was shaking, maybe he was in tears.

It was an old Dodge—1930's, with the headlights still attached
to the side of the radiator grillwork. The cowling was folded
back and the engine was right there in plain sight. I was amazed
at how much space there was in that engine compartment; you
could have crawled in there with it. There was just the block and
a few small wires, nothing more. You could look down and see
the paving stones on N. Harvie Street below.
"What happened?" I asked stepping into the street.
He looked up and investigated me as though I might have
descended from the sky.
"What happened?" I repeated. "Did it conk out on you?"
"Suh?"
"Did it just quit on you... can't you get it started?"
"Suh?"
"Maybe I can help you get it going again."

He looked at me all eyes, as if to say, You DO know that this is
Richmond, Virginia, don't you? You DO know that Richmond is
still the Capital of the Confederacy? Surely you DO know that
I'm black and that you are white... don't you?
"Suh," he said quietly, "I don't know what I'm gonna do, she
just cain't turn over."

I don't recall the circumstances but one time—not too much
earlier—my father gave me a little lecture on what to look for IF
my car wouldn't start. It required air, a spark, and gas—but not
too much gas. I leaned in and removed the big-as-a-barn air
cleaner. "Do you have a spark?" I asked the man who now stood
behind me. He was watching cautiously as a stranger worked
under the hood of his truck. "OK, climb in and try to turn it over
when I tell you."

204

I disconnected one of the sparkplug wires and propped it up near the block and backed off. I've never known enough about electricity to be comfortable around it, and I have always been pretty sure that if I did, it would soon give me all the reason I needed to reclaim my previous caution.

When he bumped the starter a spark flew between the end of the wire and the block, so I replaced that. Then—I don't know what it had to do with, but I remembered my father inserting a pencil into the throat of the carburetor one time and opening the butterfly valve in there. So, I pulled a paint brush out of my back pocket and inserted it into the carburetor, and went around to the gentleman. "What I would like you to do is to push the accelerator all the way to the floor and hold it. DO NOT let it up. DO NOT pump it. Just hold it to the floor."
"Suh? You mean the gas pedal when you say 'celerator?'"
"Yes. Hold it down and DO NOT let it up. DO NOT pump the gas. Just turn it over; let's see what happens."
"Don't pump it?"
"Don't pump it; keep it floored."
"'Bout the choke?'
"Leave the choke in."
"She needs choke to turn over."
"Leave the choke in, please. Let's just try that first."

I went back to the engine and pushed the butterfly as far open as it would go and shouted, "OK, give it a try!" When the thing tried to turn over a little puff of smoke came out of the carburetor. "Stop. STOP." I shouted.
I removed the paint brush. From my brief experience I thought we were on the right track; this old truck was about to start, I knew it. I felt like a million dollars. "OK." I shouted, "OK, let's try it one more time, just keep turning it over and don't quit. When it starts take your foot off the gas immediately."

The old man looked at me completely bewildered. How could a young hippie know so much about this old truck?

I opened the butterfly valve again and when he cranked the starter—when it sounded like it was ready and the smell of gas had dissipated—I withdrew the brush and sure enough that engine kicked over. The driver took his foot off the gas immediately and the thing was sitting there just ticking away like an old sewing machine.
"Ha-ha!" I laughed
As I replaced the giant air filter he was right by my side. After looking around a bit at his engine, he folded the cowling down gently and latched it to the fender.
"Cool, huh?" I asked.
The delight in the old man's eyes agreed, it was not only cool, for him, it was some kind of miracle. All I was doing, of course, was imitating something I'd seen my father do.
"There you go," I said, "You're on your way."
"Suh, thank you, Suh," he said humbly. He climbed back in behind the wheel, slammed the door shut, put it in gear, and whirred off toward Park Avenue. As he putted around the corner, he was still looking at me as though I was something he had never seen before or, perhaps, something he never expected to see again.
I felt like I kinda broke even that afternoon.

When I had my head under there, I'd noticed a dull mustard colored cylinder of some sort with a jet black wire leading out of one end. I was thinking about that as I started to walk away. I liked the way that sooty black line sat against that mustard color. Maybe I could do something with that.

THE GOOD MISTER (1980)

When I was living on Clement Street, a thousand years ago, the nearly ancient Russian lady, Marie, somehow repeatedly got herself locked outside, stranded on our shared, fourth-floor, fire escape. She shared a small apartment across the hall with 3 other Russians and the Shah of Iran's ski instructor. And, of those others, I was convinced it was the Shah of Iran's ski instructor who was somehow getting Marie out onto that fire escape and then locking her out. Although I could not figure out why he would do such a thing, believe me, I *knew* it was him. (The bastard.)

One time he showed me some photographs with him on skis, standing beside the Shah of Iran and his wife, all leering like puppet royalty into the camera. There were pictures of kids also. Their arrogance was such that they looked down upon anyone who had the audacity to gaze upon them, even in a faded old photograph. I pretended I wasn't impressed, because I knew that ski instructor guy wanted me to be, and, honestly, I really just instinctually did not like the man.
Smarmy is an interesting word.

So, we—me and whatever woman I happened to be living with at the time—would be doing whatever normal healthy people might be doing in a bedroom at whatever hour normal healthy people might be doing such a thing with the curtains drawn, and there would be a little tap tap tap upon the window. And, I knew that, when I got up, walked over, and took a look, Marie would be out there on the fire escape, with contrition written all over her lovely old face.
Through the window I could read her lips as she pleaded, "Mister. Mister." She clenched her hands in prayer and bowed her head and pleaded, "Mister. Mister."

So then I'd open the window and assist her inside with great care on my part, and some difficulty on hers. When she was safely inside she always bowed and said, "Thank you too much, Mister. Thank you too much."
(Which was a beautifully succinct description of events.)
Then I would lead her through our place and out into the hallway, and I watched after her as she entered her apartment.

You know, sometimes she'd end up out on the fire escape again just a few minutes later.
It was like a comedy routine.

So, whenever we met in the hallway Marie would take my hand in hers and pat me on the hand saying, "Good Mister. Good Mister." She always said it with tears gathering in her ancient eyes. "Good Mister."
Tears in her eyes.

"For god's sake," I thought, "what kind of mister would I be to abandon you to your fate out there on the fire escape?"

GOOD NIGHT (2010)

One of the Chinese maids seems to think that "good night" is a greeting. When she sees me coming she smiles nicely and says "Good night!" in a cheery little voice. I smile back and say, "How are you?"

Every time I enter the kitchen, she smiles and says, "Good night!" and I ask her how things are with her.

If I enter that kitchen four times that evening, she smiles and says, "Good night!" four times. Sometimes, out of the deep well of my irrepressible kindness (you can snort all you want), I respond charmingly, "Good night."

That is the extent of our communication, but there's something really very nice about it.

MARY 'n' ME (1992-1998)

After I'd been thrown out of the house in Encinitas, for mowing the lawn regularly, fixing washing machines when they needed fixing, shopping for and preparing dinner almost every night, doing the dishes as necessary, taking out the garbage before we all drowned in the damned stuff, and responding to her cries for help when she found herself in trouble, the woman who'd asked me to leave offered no apology.
Apparently, she was glad to see me go.

If anything, my departure was herald for better things to come. After all, her precious 29 year old, unemployed son—who did none of those awful things I did—remained behind. He was sure to entertain her with raucous tales of repeated drunken forays into Tijuana, and comfort her by calling occasionally from a hospital bed to brag about driving the car, which she'd bought him for his birthday, over the edge of a very high cliff and surviving. Those were the things he did. He was just wonderful. Nonetheless, I was confused.

I remain confused today, and about many things—as anyone who knows me might testify—but particularly about that woman's choice in that particular matter. Why would you toss out a perfectly good and amiable dishwasher in order to keep an egotistical, ego-centric, lay-about who, in return for his dear unshakable presence, demanded constant doting and eternal servitude? Honestly, when I told her, "There are too many people living in this house," the last thing I expected was for her to say, "You're right; you gotta go."

It's been explained to me, and by several people, but I still don't get it. The essence seems to be that blood, diluted by heavy drink, steroids, monumental, unassailable selfishness, irrepressible arrogance, and mind-boggling stupidity, is thicker than water, and perhaps especially in southern California.

It hardly matters. I moved into Steve and Margaret's garage and made a kind of home of it, with a futon, a FAX machine, a computer, a bicycle, a lovely little Sony CD player, and my ukulele. I'd taken the opportunity to quit my job at the beachfront motel at that brave hour as well, so then began to keep a very close eye on my money. After careful accounting, it really looked like I had enough to last a little more than two years; so experience told me that I might be able to last one... with strict attendance and the kind of luck I've never had. But, to my surprise, luck was about to come, by way of a FAX from London. In order to understand that FAX, we'll need to backtrack a little.

While I worked at a beach front motel in Del Mar, a woman named Mary arrived, the same time each year, for a three or four month stay. She was British, but not merely British; she was remarkably, undeniably, quintessentially British. She was an upright, dignified, somewhat timid woman; she was about 12 years my elder, and much more prim and a hundred times more proper than any person I had ever met before.

Eventually, somewhere about her fourth year with us, she revealed that she'd been coming to Del Mar to 'study' esoteric thought of some contrived sort, at an esoteric school of some contrived sort, as taught by a well-known charlatan with a huge devoted following of women who had so much time and money they had no qualms about wasting a little of both on celebrated phonies like him. During that stay, after her daily class with that idiot, she would make a point of stopping in at the front desk in order to gush about her growing insight into the loftiest of all lofty matters... contrived meta-physical bullshit.

And, I don't really know how these things happen—how we manage to establish our position in relation to each individual we deal with (some we're under, some we're over, some become our friends, some we cannot stand from the moment we first meet)—but, with Mary I soon took on a cold, critical, and somewhat snide persona, and though it is not like me at all, I found myself being, perhaps, just a little cruel. And… she LOVED IT.

Whenever she came into the office to ask my opinion, I was careful to cast my observations in a pseudo-intellectualized, somewhat oblique, clearly superior manner, so that my jackass-ness was the perfect balance for her eager gullibility. I was always busy with better things to do of course, but that never deterred her. She'd wait. Then, when she'd mention her 'spiritual journey', I'd snort theatrically. She would follow up with some ridiculous dictum, and I would make a snide comment. She'd assure me, "I'm quite serious you know…" and I'd laugh heartily while shaking my head as if what she had said might be the most absurd thing I'd ever heard… and, believe me, many times it was. (This was many years before the madness.)

She came in every evening and spoke with me for forty minutes, an hour, two hours; and, despite my massive indifference, she couldn't tear herself away. No matter how viciously I attacked her thinking, no matter how raucous my horse-laugh, I could not get rid of that very dear woman. She was fascinated by my near-dead response to every chirpy little joyous thought that drifted from her mouth. She couldn't get enough of my derision. As said, I have no idea whatsoever how this came about, I am not a cruel person by nature and I have never treated anyone like that, either before or since. I have considered the matter however, and can only conclude that I was being unbearable out of some weird kindness. It seemed to be what that dear poor woman wanted. She enjoyed it immensely, and told me as much, in almost as many words—so, I suppose she saw right through my act.

She welcomed the scathing criticism, and that allowed me to take it as far as I could... and I got quite good at it.

Apparently, my non-analytical, reckless, shotgun approach to destroying her every idiotic thought intrigued her. On occasion she'd giggle at some sarcastic statement I'd made, and, after searching my eyes for a moment, she'd say, "I really enjoy your mind. You really do have a way of making me think."
"I have no idea what makes you say that," I'd say.
"But, I'm being quite sincere," she'd say, "you really do have a way of making me consider things in a new light..."
"What goddamned nonsense, Mary," I'd say cutting her off.
She would titter and blush and say, "I never really know if you're playing with me or not."
"I'm not," I'd say coldly, and she'd study my face for a moment. Then she'd smile and say, "Well, good night then," and she'd leave, skipping out the office door like a school girl.
Mary truly is one of the innocents of this world.

The fact that she was taking these day-long seminars from some guru moron and returning to the motel every evening freshly enlightened, irritated me. One time I asked her, "You're actually paying that charlatan good money for those so-called classes in metaphysical self-deception?"
She replied, "Oh yes, and they are quite worth every penny."
I told her, "Look, I'll make a deal with you: pay me 10% of whatever you're paying that swindler and I'll fill your head with twice the nonsense in half the time. We'll meet in the morning, I'll fill your head with nonsense, and you'll have the entire afternoon off to wander around aimlessly on the beach, thinking swell thoughts."
"You really have quite a remarkable way about you," she said.
"If you mean that I have a way of staying in relative proximity to planet Earth, then I guess I do. But the offer's still good.

Abandon that idiot, and I'll fill your head with twice the nonsense in half the time."
I thought I was offering her a pretty good deal.

Mary was not staying with us at the time when Princess Diana died (August 31, 1997) and she didn't return until several months later. When she finally showed up, it was for a short stay; she was on her way to China. I asked her where she'd been and what she'd been up to, and she looked at me for a very long time before she whispered, "I wish to trust you... I wish to tell you something." Then, she explained that she was not just some wacky old British dame travelling around seeking spiritual advice from any self-appointed esoteric entrepreneur who was willing to take her money, she was actually a fairly 'distinguished' old British dame travelling around seeking spiritual advice from any self-appointed esoteric entrepreneur who was willing to take her money. I asked her to, if she could, get to the point, and she told me that she was Princess Diana's aunt. Well, so, that was a game changer. I was awash in shame.

I offered the poor dear woman my sincerest condolences, and somehow that lead to me telling her that I was extraordinarily sorry about how badly I'd treated her for all the times that she'd stayed with us. And she laughed and said, "Oh, no no no-no, no. No. I've truly enjoyed our conversations. You've given me a lot to think about. I have always looked forward, with some anticipation, not to mention some trepidation, to what you might have to say."
"Wow," I said. I was humbled. "So, you're off to China?"
"Yes."
"And what are you going to do in China?"
"Oh, travel about."
"Yeah, and then what?"
"I don't really know actually. We'll start with China."
Then I told her that I'd be moving on too.

I told her that I'd given the motel three weeks' notice and I didn't know what I'd be doing."
And she said, "What would you like to do?"

So, how do you explain Reality to a person like Mary?
"What I would *like* to do has never really been an option for me," I said.
"But if it were?" she asked.
"It's not. I assure you," I said.
"But, if it were'"" she insisted. "What would you do if you could do anything?"
She quizzed me about what I'd done before in life, and then, suddenly she said, "If you're here tomorrow, I'd like to talk to you." Then, she skipped out the door.

The following day she came in and told me that she owned several properties in London and they needed renovation and, if I wished to, I could move to London and we could form a company together. She would buy and own the properties, and I would oversee the renovations and, after a bit, I could buy a property of my own and form my own company.
I said, "What?!" She explained it again and I said, "Are you serious?"
And she said, "Oh yes, quite serious. You could live anywhere you like in Europe—you wouldn't have to live in London. Europe is quite small and you can get around there very easily. Please consider where you might like to live. I think you might like Amsterdam. You could live in Amsterdam, or anywhere else of your choosing, and come into London to keep an eye on things. How does that sound to you?"
"That sounds great, but, really, Mary, I haven't got a cent... I mean I may have enough to survive for a year, but..."
"Give the matter some thought..." she said, and left the office.

So, I gave the matter some thought, and Mary left Del Mar the next day, on her way to China, with my phone and FAX number in her pocket. For several days the FAXs were flying between Encinitas and wherever Mary happened to be at the moment. And things were firming up. Mary was encouraging me to get a passport and let her know when I had it in hand. She would then send me a ticket to London. As said, at that time I was living in Steve and Margaret's garage, and once a day—sometimes twice—a FAX would come in from Mary and she'd be telling me that I should think about where I wanted to live, and begin to make arrangements to fly to London.

So, with no other prospects at all, I did that. I thought about where I would like to live in Europe and I called around and discovered where I could get a passport. I decided that I would drive up to Los Angeles and get the passport thing settled on the following day.

That night, in the middle of the night, my FAX machine started churning out paper, and I got up and turned on the light and found a FAX, not from Mary, but from her son. There was a coat of arms at the top of the FAX with scrolls and dancing lions on either side of a shield, and a motto in Latin. In that FAX Mary's son introduced himself and, directly after, forbade me to ever have any further contact, by any means, with his mother. "I'm sure you understand," he said. "It's a matter of peerage," he explained.

From that minute on, no FAX, no phone call, no letter I sent, ever got any response. Mary's son would allow his mother to be taken by some celebrity swindler in Del Mar, but he could not stand idly by and watch as she offered a leg up to anyone of a lesser class.

This, quite naturally, I understood.

216

SCHEMATIC FOR A WIFE (2010 or so)

When asked what I was looking for in a wife—something which
I was asked frequently by my friends through the years—I
always said, "First, she must be intelligent. Then, she must be a
pleasure to look at…" That was followed by a long list of
additional requirements, always ending with, "and it wouldn't
hurt at all if she were French."

Where I got that French idea, I do not know. To my knowledge
—other than my grandmother—I'd only met one French woman
in my entire life, the mother of a strange little jug-eared kid in
my fifth grade class. And although I liked his mother a great
deal—she was a proper, trim, lovely, cultured creature—she
didn't like me at all. I gathered that from the fact that, after my
first visit to their nicely kept home to play with her jug-eared
son, he was instructed to never invite me there again.

I don't know what I could have done to offend her. I thought
about that for a long time and, once in a while, I think about it
still. In those days I rarely spoke in the presence of an adult, and
I couldn't imagine looking one in the eye. I was as meek as a
mouse. But I managed to offend her anyway. Knowing the
French as I do now, I'd have to guess it had something to do
with courtesy—I probably didn't say Bonjour with enough
effervescence upon arrival, or spend enough time chatting
mindlessly before actually walking out the door, when I left.

Nonetheless, my very dear wife could not be more perfect had
she been taken directly from my own blue prints. In fact, she
goes far beyond my schematic dreams. Here is but one reason:
We were coming out of a grocery store with one bag of
groceries—forty dollars—and, because we used a discount card I
asked her casually, "Did we save anything?"

"Yes," she said, "we saved $1.29 on the juice and 29¢ on the beans." (I eat beans.)

"Wow," I said, "we saved a dollar sixty on forty dollars. You know," I added, "if you were Debbie, we'd be hauling out TWELVE bags of groceries and we'd have something like $5.72 cash clutched in our sweaty fists."

My dear wife then turned to me and said, "Perhaps you should have given that matter more thought before we were wed."

Debbie, as my very dear wife knows, is the exact opposite of her in almost every aspect; she is loud and vulgar and slovenly, a poorly educated heavy smoker, who frequently drinks too much and is, in those moments, a public embarrassment, if you're the type who believes in dignity of any sort. BUT, Debbie can, by methods I've never understood—though I've witnessed it first-hand several times—use coupons to fill shopping carts with hundreds of dollar worth of stuff I'd never even consider eating, and either pays almost nothing for it or, as I have seen with my own eyes, is actually given cash back, after the tonnage is all tabulated. Let me say here quickly—though I fear not quickly enough—that Debbie is also a remarkable parent.

She is understanding and caring and patient, and she expects her kids to possess both honesty and character—which they do. It's for them that she spends hours on Wednesdays and Sundays clipping coupons and filing them away in a big folder. So, this dedication to clipping coupons is an honorable process.

Let's review: After my wife informed me that we had saved $1.29 on the juice and 29¢ on the beans. I said, mockingly, "If you were Debbie, we'd be hauling out TWELVE bags of groceries and we'd have something like $5.72 cash clutched in our sweaty little fists."

My excellent wife then told me, "Perhaps you should have given that matter more thought before we were wed."

In fact I hadn't given much thought at all to the matter of marriage before I met my wife, since I had little hope of attaining the wife of my own design. Add into that mix the fact that I never harbored any real desire to become a married man, and the chances became even slimmer. Certainly if I got the wife I truly deserve, Debbie would be an angel by comparison.

The wife I deserve would be massive and immobile, and probably missing her front teeth; she'd be somewhat snappish (but all those nasty looking, oozing sores might affect anyone's demeanor) and, I'm sure she would be what anyone who didn't know the details might call just a little bit demanding.

She'd have two or three dirty little future hoodlum brats from two or three previously dissolved marriages, or near marriages, or pretend marriages, and she would probably despise me every bit as much as my wife's father does now. Consequently, I'd find myself working part-time in a gas station in a permanent *I'd-rather-drink-myself-to-death-than-go-home* sort of way, and spending every spare moment peering fixedly into the never-ending darkness of my interminable future.

Of course, my miserable life would be proof, and fair warning to all, that there IS justice in this world—that we DO get what we deserve... and that no matter how much you care, or demonstrate that caring through calm reasoning, whining, complaining, threatening divorce, or cussing and slamming things around, a woman who smokes cigarettes will never even cut back, let alone quit.

But, instead, we saved a laughable $1.58 on groceries and drove away happily ever after.

A NOTE: This rant reminds me of a time when, for reasons unexplainable, I asked my wife if she would like to know the sort of thing that was going on in my ever-spinning mind in those times when I sit around unconsciously tugging on my lower lip and looking idiot-thoughtful. And, because she is kind and caring, she made the mistake of saying yes.

So, then I started out telling her what I'd been mulling over and chewing on for the last few days, weeks, months, and, I had just gotten under way when she stopped me mid-sentence (after a very short time indeed) and said nicely, "Wait. Is it too late to… uh… withdraw my request?"
"Your request?"
"…to hear all that you've been thinking."
"You don't want to hear what I've been thinking?"
"If that's all right with you," she said.
"I was just getting started…" I said.
"I sensed that," she said.

And, though it pained me deeply—because I really felt that I had a lot to say—since I love her so much, I agreed to go no further. She went back to her reading and I went back to tugging on my lower lip and thinking about things which no person I truly care about should ever be exposed to.

THE TAXI DRIVER (1983)

One day my lawyer friend called to ask if I could run down to
City Hall and file some papers. I told him I'd be glad to normally
but my truck was in the shop and I didn't want to climb on the
bus with the cold season in full swing. He said, "I need this stuff
filed before they close this afternoon, take a cab, I'll pay for it."

Let me tell you what it's like filing papers at San Francisco City
Hall. After you stand in line for forty minutes, the disgruntled
unshaven cross-eyed slovenly dressed guy, or sweaty, scowling,
slightly on the heavy side woman behind the counter looks
through your paperwork briefly then tosses it back at you saying,
"You need to fill out a 437-P2."

They say it in a manner that implies that every person on earth is
born with this knowledge, and there is no greater burden on earth
than the one they shoulder each day, continually reminding us
about which forms we should fill out. Then they look over your
head and say, "NEXT."
It's always the same.

So, you get the necessary paperwork and fill it in as best you
can, and when it's finally your turn again, you step up to the
counter, and you hold your breath. Occasionally a miracle occurs
and they pull over a rack of handstamps and flip through the
pages stamping things, seemingly indiscriminately, switching
from one stamp to another from time to time, stamping specific
pages, sometimes scrawling a signature or a date.

When that's done they instruct you to take the paperwork to
another window where another Master of the Social Graces sets
the check you've provided aside, looks over the paperwork,
accepts the check as if doing you a great favor, and smacks a few

more stamps on the papers, before handing half of them back to you without a single spoken word...
Then, looking over your head, or around you as if you no longer exist, he utters dismally, "Next."
It's such a pleasure.

So, I went into my lawyer friend's office and I picked up the paperwork and I walked over to Geary Blvd, where I flagged down a cab. So, now let me tell you this. Stick with me. Twelve years earlier, when I lived in the Fan District in Richmond, Virginia, I had been a great admirer of young women.

One of the many young women whose looks I particularly liked lived on Grove Avenue, and we crossed paths maybe twice a week. She was a lovely creature with pale skin and reddish hair and she possessed a carriage that has always just knocked me out—if you were to drop a plumb bob from the back of her lovely head, it would have fallen in a straight line directly to the back of her heels. I'm not talking about some prig who imposes that stance upon herself as a sign of her perpetual all-encompassing disapproval of passion, but a woman whose natural grace encourages her steadily toward Heaven, from which she has unfairly tumbled.

This particular woman and I never exchanged either words or glances. I'm sure she never noticed my posture. She emerged in the spring one year pushing a baby carriage, and that flipped a switch inside of me that I hadn't previously known existed. I would have difficulty explaining it, but somehow the fact that she had given birth—that she was now a mother—fascinated me. I just thought she was one of the most marvelous creatures I'd ever seen in Richmond. I don't know if 19-year-old American males are supposed to swoon, but if I ever did it was a result of having seen this woman pushing a baby carriage down Grove Avenue one spring morning.

So, on that day, twelve years later—when I was rushing down to City Hall in San Francisco to file some papers—I stepped out into traffic and hailed a cab, and this very woman was behind the wheel. She didn't know me. She hadn't known me in Richmond either, but, I recognized her immediately. I don't know if 31-year-old American males are supposed to swoon, but if I was ever going to, that would have been the time for it.

"City Hall," I said as I got in the back, and we travelled about a mile before I said anything else. Then I said casually, "You used to live in the Fan, didn't you?"
She said coldly, "I don't know what you're talking about."
I said, "Didn't you live on Grove Avenue, in Richmond, ten or twelve years ago? I used to see you pushing your baby carriage…" And she slammed on the brakes so hard I almost bit my own tongue off.

Geary Boulevard at that point is four lanes in both directions, and she was in one of the middle lanes. Cars were climbing on their brakes behind us, skidding to a stop; others were leaning on their horns as they swerved to avoid hitting us, but she was oblivious to all that. She was fixed on me in her mirror.

She did not turn in her seat to face me however, but studied me in the mirror without forgiveness. "Get out of my cab!" she sighed after a beat or two. "I don't know what you're talking about," she added.
'I'm just saying that I recogni…"
"GET OUT!" she screamed. "I have no idea what you are talking about and I just want you OUT of my cab. Right now."
"Look, I'm sorry, I didn't mean to…"
"OUT! RIGHT NOW!"
"Well, what about the fare?"
"Just get out. Please."

So, I waited for a break in the traffic and I got out in the middle of that fast moving four lane boulevard. With horns blaring at me and cars swerving in hopes of either hitting me or missing me—depending upon, I suppose, how each driver may have felt about things at the moment—I dodged and scampered, and somehow made it safely to the curb. From there I looked up to see that she had already driven off.

I flagged another cab and got to City Hall in time to file the papers, and, rather than take another cab, I walked the seven miles home. I drank alone in silence that night, feeling a peculiar emptiness. And while I drank I pondered. Naturally, I hoped that she was OK, but I had absolutely no idea what that was about.

I still have no idea what that was about.
More importantly I guess, I'm sorry it happened at all.

DAHLIA

The only one awake while driving late at night through the
Nevada desert, I was listening to the radio to stay that way.
There was a talk show on, one of those things with some phony-
baloney female psychologist giving free advice to drunks and
insomniacs. I wasn't really listening, but the rattle of human
discourse helped me to keep my eyelids from drifting closed.
I don't recall now where we were heading, but wherever it was I
was trying to get there very quickly.

In those days, if you were flying down the road at 80 miles per
hour it wasn't like sitting in your living room with the scenery
outside drifting slowly by, as it is in cars today. In those days,
when you were flying through the desert at 80 miles per hour,
the car was bouncing erratically, rocking from side to side, the
tires on the pavement sounded like pebbles on the beach grinding
together under an incoming tide, and the slightest headwind
threatened to lift the entire vehicle up and toss it over onto its
back. In those days, eighty was scary business; if you had any
sense at all, there was no doubt whatsoever that what you were
doing was both mindless and dangerous. In short: you were
risking your stupid life (not to mention the lives of those
sleeping in the back seat), and you knew it.

If you were doing that under the star-filled Nevada sky, on a
long flat stretch of deserted desert highway, with the blue-black
mountains ahead receding steadily (no matter how fast you went)
there was a sense of eternity about it; a peculiar serenity coaxed
you steadily onward toward surrender. I was of two thoughts: "If
this kills me, somehow that's OK", and "I wonder if this thing'll
do a hundred". That is the state I was in.

The AM radio doctor, tired of talking to a regular caller named
George, had given him the bum's rush, and had moved on to the

next caller. This new caller, like so many of these poor desperate people, didn't seem to understand the basics of talking to someone on the radio with a ten second delay. The doctor patiently walked the caller through all that turn-your-radio-down stuff and through this process it became clear to the doctor—an intelligent, educated, reasonably perceptive woman now reduced to talking to idiots and speed-freaks in the middle of the night— that this caller might be an innocent.

The good doctor softened her approach immediately. My ears perked up too. Innocence has always been charming to me. At that point in my life, though I'd been devastated by it before, I still had no fear of innocence.
Innocence is a lovely thing.

"What's your name, caller?" asked the doctor, softly.
"Dahlia," said a timid voice, "Dahlia _____." The producer bleeped out the last name. Such was this woman's lack of sophistication that she didn't understand that she could use a made-up name.
"Is that what you want me to call you, Dahlia?" asked the doctor.
"That's my name, yes, ma'am."
"Well...OK, 'Dahlia' what can I do for you?"

There was a long silence during which the only sound for me was pavement grinding away under my tires. I noticed that the doctor was not pushing this caller like she had previous callers; like she had poor George for example; she was gentle; she was coaxing. "Is there something...I can do for you, Dahlia?" she asked encouragingly. I found myself anxious to hear what Dahlia had to say, what she might need. I mean, I cannot explain (although, yes, I know that is my task here) how she had such immediate impact on me, but, whatever it was, it got to the good ol' doctor as well. I think we both detected an uncommon purity in this woman. It was all in her voice; in her hesitancy.

"I never called anybody before," Dahlia said painfully, "I mean, it's hard for me to..."
She pronounced the word hord...it's hord for me t'...
"Well, that's OK. Take your time; we've got the rest of the night ahead of us." I glanced at my fuel gauge.
"But, um, well, the other thing is... it's kinda personal"
She whispered the word personal.
"I mean it's very personal. Um, but I don't know what to do... elseways. I'm at the end of my rope."

The desire to protect this woman welled up warmly inside me while she gathered her thoughts. I don't know about the good doctor, but I had practically stopped breathing while awaiting her next words. My ears picked up every nuance, every variant in her tone; I thought I could detect a fluctuation in her breathing. Had Dahlia been crying? Was she crying? About to cry? To me, flying down the highway with the dark and empty universe rolling slowly overhead, it sounded like maybe she had been. I was convinced of it. The most artless being who had ever called in to a radio talk-show had been harmed by someone. OK, which one of you big stupid bastards has hurt Dahlia?!
"Take your time." The doctor and I both agreed, there was nothing more important than this, and if Dahlia needed a little time, we both wanted her to have it.

Dahlia sounded skittish when she spoke next. She whispered, "I can't talk to anyone about this... it's ver-very personal."
"You can talk to me, that's why I'm here," whispered the doctor.
"True...I don't know what to do elseways. I'm really very sorry," she whispered. "I heard you talkin' an' helpin' the others and I thought might you could help me."
"I'll do my best for you."
"Still, now I'm not so sure I can. I mean, 'haps I shou'n't, Fact is, I prolly shou'n't."
"You sound like you *want* to talk to somebody."

"Oh, I do. I do. I really need to. I just think that 'haps I shou'n't…you know? There's others involved."

"I understand. But, you can talk to me, Dahlia, OK? That's what I'm here for."

"Well…"

The world waited. And, eventually, our patience paid off.

"It's my husband…" In our hearts we urged her on. "Since I had m' last baby, my husband doesn't want to… be near me. He just doesn't seem… interested in me, since I had m' last baby."

"How many children do you and your husband have, Dahlia?"

"Four."

"And did he react this way after you'd given birth previously?"

"No, ma'am."

"And when did you have your baby?"

"It's been more than a year… fourteen months."

"I see. You know, sometimes a husband needs a little time."

"He's always been interested in me before. Times, he could hardly wait to get at me again," she pleaded. "I guess there's proof enough of that," she said almost to herself. Advocates of Dahlia everywhere laughed a little bittersweet laugh. Then we waited respectfully, in silence, for her to continue.

Throughout the dark starlit broadcast area I imagined hundreds of us tuned in, leaning into our radios; the more dedicated among us brushing aside our own loved ones, shushing them or running them out of the room— "Can't you please shut those goddamned kids up, I'm trying to listen to the radio!"—waiting, fretting, wringing our bony hands out of concern; heartsick for poor Dahlia. What after all could be more important? (Nothing.)

"He never turned his back on me before."

"Well, have you tried to talk to him about this?"

"He won't talk."

"Have you *tried* to talk to him?"

228

"He won't talk." Dahlia began to sob. "When I go to talk to him, he gets up and walks out the door."
Dahlia seemed to gather herself, to steel herself; this was the part that really hurt. It came out in spurts.
"He acts like… he finds me… disgusting."

By this time my jaded heart had become fully engaged. Maybe it was the lack of sleep; maybe it was the cold expanse of night sky engulfing me, but, I could no longer deny my love for Dahlia. I loved this woman. I loved her purely. There was nothing but purity in it. Go ahead, search the corners. Purity; nothin' but.
"Mom, Dad, this is Dahlia. Oh, and these are her four kids." The guy out there squealin' his tires and driving wildly around the block with his horn blaring—that's her husband. But, he don't want her no more, so you can just ignore him. I'm sure he'll soon tire of such childish antics and go on back to the desert."

Suddenly, as the little kids say with wide eyes, I was filled with the desire to find Dahlia wherever she was, and take her in my arms; to protect her and comfort her. I wanted to tell her, "It's OK, forget about that big stupid bastard moron husband of yours."

"I'm sorry, Dahlia," said the doctor, "but we're going to have to take a break for a couple minutes right here. But, will you stay on the line? We'll talk a little during the break, off the air."
"I don't think I should be talkin' at all…'bout this. 'Haps I shou'n't. 'Haps this is a mistake…"
"Dahlia, please, promise me you'll stay on the line so we can talk. I want to speak with you a bit off-air. Ok?"
A thousand years passed before Dahlia whispered, "I will."

During the commercials I was thinking about how to go about finding her. Maybe the radio station would give me her number. If I could talk to her a bit over the phone, that would be a good beginning. Then, I'd drive up to her trailer; I'd knock on that hollow-core tin door; she'd open it slowly, in tears, shaken. I'd say, "I heard what you were saying on the radio, my poor dear darlin' lady, and now I'm here to rescue you."

Naturally she'd just collapse into my arms. Enfold is a nice word. I'd enfold her in my arms. Caress is a nice word. I'd caress her. She'd sob a bit and I'd cradle her head and hold her tightly until she stopped shaking. I'd comfort her meanwhile by saying, "There-there." Or, maybe, "Now-now." I couldn't decide which. "Now-now, Dahlia, now-now. Dear, sweet, lovely, Dahlia. I know it's hord."

Flying through the desert, in the middle of the night, now with tears in my eyes (that always helps), I was busy composing my introduction. Keep it simple, I instructed myself. I'd announce, "Don't worry, Dahlia. I'll take you away from here; I'll take care of you! No one will ever harm you again." I thought that would be a good beginning. At that moment, rolling along blindly headlong into the endless western expanse, I was willing, eager, anxious, maybe even a little desperate, to make this meeting happen. But, if it was to happen at all, it had to happen soon, while I was still awash in human compassion (that never seems to last very long with me.)

The time was right, Dahlia was in touch with her need, I was in touch with Fate itself. Heroically, I'd scrap all my selfish little schemes (of which I had none at the time, that I can recall), my dopey dreams (of which I had many), in order to first find and then comfort my dear Dahlia. This was the opportunity I'd been yearning for; the chance for which I'd been aching, the reason for my being here on this big dumb clumsy planet. I didn't know how it was going to happen, but I had a feeling that it was Destiny itself speaking to me through that radio, and I was all ears and, due to a good upbringing, honor bound.

There may also have been some hormones involved… you know how that is.

"There-there, Dahlia; forget him. Forget that bastard. He comes back here again, I'll kick his ass." This is what I was thinking while the radio was hawking Babbo cleanser.

After the commercial break, when the doctor returned, my heart raced/leapt, cavorted in joyful anticipation. I could not wait to hear Dahlia's lovely voice again. I'd missed her. My thoughts had been on nothing else. Then, it turned terrible. I mean it took a terrible turn. There's no way to put it without employing that word. There may be better ways to phrase it—I'm sure there are dozens—but, really, there is no better word for it. It was just plain, boot in the crotch, stick in the eye, terrible; judo chop to the larynx, bite your own tongue off terrible.
"Our last caller, Dahlia," said the doctor, "had to go. So, we'll be taking another caller now."

My heart sank. I felt sick to my stomach. I gasped. I was wounded. This can't be. This ain't right. I'd been betrayed. We'd all been betrayed. How could you do this to us? How could you have let her go, you idiot? You goddamned idiot! I had plans. Big plans. Important plans. WE had plans; Me and Dahlia; Dahlia and me; kids, goats, gold flecked turquoise counter tops, linoleum floor, cold beer. I probably could have learned to enjoy pro wrestling! I could have developed a fondness for rodeo. I could take up smoking. I could drive a Ford pick-up. Whatever it might take to make it work, I was willing. Cowboy boots.

That's how late it was; that's how tired I was. At that moment, I really thought it could work. I believed I was being, actually, sorta, really kinda reasonably realistic about things. There was more to life than college… which was where I was headin'… where I'd end up again… if Dahlia and I didn't hit it off.

I pictured us sitting under the striped awning of our new-to-us Airstream trailer, sipping something cold and soothing with the endless, dry and utterly useless desert all around, just sand and hopelessly withered greyish vegetation as far as the weary dust-filled eye could squint. Are those crickets I hear, or something very much like crickets; the desert version of crickets? It's not anything dangerous is it? Let's not get picky. Let's not get too hung up on detail. Dahlia and me, that's what I'm getting at. "Dahlia, please, please please, pretty please allow me buy you some new house slippers…you can't keep shufflin' around here in those old worn out pink mules; think of the kids."

But she wasn't coming back to me. I'd been cut off, cast out, alone. And, without Dahlia, I needed to face certain undeniable facts. I had to face the callous indifference of Life (that's one); the crushing impassivity that surrounds us all (which is sorta like the first one as well), and the deep emptiness within (that's two). Weep with me here, if but briefly. Concentrate on that *deep emptiness within* thing. I'd like to stick the word 'hollow' in there somewhere too, but it doesn't want to go. That aside, I felt helpless; I felt lost, I felt staggered. Good lord, I was tired.

Realizing that I could do nothing whatsoever to help that good woman, I turned off the radio. It was over. I'd have to return to RPI after all. Still, it had been kind of a nice dream, Dahlia and me, sittin' in a tree, somethin' somethin' I. N. G.

Just one more thing and then, no more Dahlia, I promise. You'll find this revealing though. That night, I found a cheap motel for us to sleep in. Something with a huge green neon cactus flickering out front. Nothing says "Come on in. Get a good night's sleep!" like a big prickly saguaro.
There were cheaply framed pictures of cowboys on horseback hanging precariously on the pine-paneled walls, and, for some

reason I could not fathom then and cannot fathom even now, cheap plastic long horns stuck out above the bathroom doorway. I slept like a baby.

When I woke up the next day, I had been refreshed. I felt unusually pleased with everything, and I had the energy of a tiger. It was a remarkable feeling. I SPRANG out of bed and stretched like the young animal I was. I went outside hungry for life and took in a bushel of air. The air was sharp and cool and clean, the perfect environment for the way I was feeling. I shielded my eyes from the afternoon sun, and nodded appreciatively at the blue mountains all around. I greeted them, "So that's what you guys look like in the daylight." They were as far away as they'd been three hundred miles ago, and every bit as smug.

While waiting for Rick and Ginger to gather all their stuff, I tossed my bag with alacrity into the back seat and discovered that the car had a flat tire (driver's side, rear). So, naturally, all that tiger energy, the joy, the hunger for life, all that crap, just drained right out of me. All that soured, and I reverted to my normal sniveling self. I stomped around to the trunk to look for a jack. For god's sake, did I really think I could replace Dahlia's salt-of-the-earth husband?

Was I going to drag my weary ass out of bed each morning at dawn and drive my rattling old pick-up truck 37 bumpy miles to the shop in order to spend 10 hours on my back dismantling bellhousings and transmissions, or welding broken leaf springs? What a farce! I probably couldn't make it through one miserable grease monkey minute let alone a lifetime with a perpetually pregnant—wonderful as she might be—wife. I wasn't fooling anyone, Dahlia deserved better than me.

As I stomped around in that motel parking lot, cussing and slamming car doors, I was very much in the moment, as they say, and the moment was a pain in the ass. This is what happens when you're brought up to believe the world is your oyster.

"What's wrong with you?" Ginger asked as I struck out wildly at the fender of the car with the tire iron.
It took two good, solid whacks for me to vent my ire.

So that you might continue to believe there is some justice in this world, I offer you this token: I bruised the palm of my hand during that childish fit; and, for a couple of days, I thought I'd actually broken my little finger.

CELIA STALKER (1968)

I don't know when, precisely, Celia decided that she could not live without me, but by anyone's standards it was really, truly, much much much too soon. I think it had something to do with her father though. Her father had had some kind of "event" and she'd taken off to see him in the hospital; when she returned she knew I was the one for her. (This very same series of events would set me up for my second stalker 20 years down the road.)

But if I were asked to guess why Celia was so solidly hooked on me, I would have to say maybe it was because I had been willing to do something for her that I had never done for anyone else before—something I had rarely done even for myself—take notes.

Celia had missed a class when her father had his 'event' and I took notes for her. But, her view—if indeed that was her view—that this was an act of undying love, was misinformed. If my notes were an indication of anything, they were an indication of how utterly useless my notes were. I didn't even understand my own notes (though I may have understood them for an instant while I furiously scribbled them down); I couldn't imagine how they could be of any help whatsoever to anyone.

Here, make sense of this if you can:
Henry Bilthrop/1674 (17 ? 70 ?) long years to find source (look up dep. date)/at what latitude?/previously failed attempts/wife connection Scientific Comm./disc. Hoax?/was it a thumb/was it a tailbone?/joke's on us (them S.C.)...[he says this is important] later known for mixture specimen Re preserved PRE—-Bilthrop's mixture or B's fix? (which) Was B Biltrop or billings(look up pg 334 not 343)What did then? See charge hem? a dye/universally used. th'other useless used less (find out which) /rights stolen by partner's partner's SON (partner's partner? That's the real

question. Would mak a good play.) surviving son/1902 award
(IMPORTANT: relates back to that childhood being thrown from
the pony thing!!) Just like MY brother up a tree.

It started off simply enough, she asked me if I wanted to come to
her apartment and study history. I went; we studied; I left. As I
recall, we did this twice, Unfortunately, by the time I left her
place the second time she had convinced herself that I was the
one for her and she was the one for me; that nothing would ever
come between us, and that it would last forever.

I didn't even know any of this was going on. It had never even
occurred to me. Maybe she thought we had a better chance to
make it together, to the end of time, if I was kept somewhat in
the dark when it came to the details.

There is—at this point in my life—nothing very special about
me. And, though fifty years younger, there was even less special
about me then. By that, I mean now I can play an awkward
contrived blues on the ukulele, and, if beaten thoroughly enough,
I manage to shave every day—in those days I did neither. With
average height, average build, average looks, I have always
(regrettably) laid proud claim to a less than average mind and,
due to damnable Fate, a perpetually lower than average income.
In those days I was excruciatingly shy (my skin had just begun to
clear up after many years of crippling humiliation) and I worked
in the university cafeteria for something like $3.23 per hour
(maybe less, I don't recall).

I've been told that I can be charming—I guess that's true for
most of us—but if I had actually been so at any time in Celia's
presence it had been inadvertent. If I had said anything enticing,
seductive or suggestive in her presence, I was unaware of it.
Furthermore, my extreme shyness in those days caused me to put

up defenses that most people read as either pure arrogance or uncut stupidity, both of which I understand to be repulsive traits.

About that, let me only say this (quickly), I'm not arrogant. Socially awkward is the phrase I think which probably best described me then, and comes pretty close to describing me today in my 70s. So, I cannot even guess why Celia decided I was the guy for her. I cannot even guess.

I had no idea that Celia "came from money." Had I known, it would not have changed anything, because I can tell you this: it gets pretty goddamned tiresome hearing someone you hardly know tell you how deeply they love you and how they can NOT live without you, no matter how much money they have. And it soon turns creepy, and becomes even a little frightening when you bump into that person everywhere you go… by accident… or wait, can it be FATE?

It could only be Fate, for I never touched her, never kissed her, never addressed her by her name that I can recall. Knowing me back then, I never even looked her directly in the eye. So, quite naturally then, she found herself irresistibly attracted to me. Maybe she thought I was unaware of all that she was going through; or indifferent. How could anyone be so blind, so cruel?

Celia–finding herself incapable of living without me— decided that I would not be allowed to live without her. She started showing up wherever I went. I'd be in a bar—Oh, look, there's Celia. I'd be in the library—What a surprise to bump into you, Celia. At breakfast—Isn't that that Celia chick, staring at us?

She showed up at my dorm and waited downstairs until I came down to declare, once again, her undying love. She pounced upon me in the hall as soon as I emerged from my classes. She gave me that sick-cow look so often in history class that I stopped going. One day, on the street, when she saw me speaking with another girl, she stepped in between us, begging me and pleading with me to come back to her.

In stark contrast to the simple fact that I had never been with her, the fact that I had never left her seemed moot. Clearly, Celia was insane, and I found little comfort in that.

One time I spied Celia from a distance, talking animatedly to an acquaintance of mine, a girl by chance, in front of the college bookstore. There was far too much wild gesticulation going on for it to be a friendly conversation. From that moment on that poor girl avoided me like the plague. When I eventually managed to corner her and asked why, she looked around nervously and mouthed one word, "Celia…"

Celia, wherever you are—I will never forget you. We were just kids. These things happen.

I'm sure your house has been re-built by now, and I'm sure you have a smug, good looking husband, who is perfectly comfortable, standing at your side in a nicely-fitted Italian wool blend suit, riding to hounds, or simply strolling about amid life's continual banquet, basking in the ever-warm embrace of society.

HENRY (1972)

After college I scooted up to New Hampshire (God alone knows why) and stayed the winter there (God alone knows why). And I have never since been able to understand why anyone would put themselves through that more than once.
I only stayed because I couldn't dig myself out.

The locals take a certain pride in the horrors of associated with a New Hampshire winter though, and feel a constant necessity to deny that it might be crueler yet over there in what they call VER-mont. In Ver-mont they've taken up the challenge, declaring that New Hampshire folk couldn't last a Ver-mont winter; and, for reasons known only to themselves, State of Mainers have jumped into the fray with this tale:
Seems that one day the Wid-uh Hawkins spied some men surveyin' right outside her dooryard. After a while, one of 'em come up and knocked on the Wid-uh's door. "I'm sorry to tell you this Wid-uh," says he, "but it seems you don't live in VER-mont at all. From what we can determine, you live in New Hampshire." "Well, thank God for that," said the Wid-uh. "I don't think I could have stood another one of them nasty VER-mont wint-uhs."

So, one day, when Spring finally rolled around, I noticed an absolutely lovely young woman sitting in the park, on the lawn, like a flower, and I paid a local kid five bucks to let me take his truly cute little puppy for a walk. The flower I picked in that park that day was Kerry. She was one of the most delightful people I'd ever met. She even liked the rented puppy idea. So, you know, things being what they are… very shortly after arriving in San Francisco, Kerry and I discovered that the money we had set aside to cover six months was good for about one month, out there. I think we could have lived for a year in New Hampshire on that same money.

Still, we were smart enough to move out of the weekly-rate, sleaze-bag hotel in the Tenderloin, up the hill to a much *much* nicer, monthly-rate, apartment, in a *much* nicer neighborhood, near Union Square, as soon as our first week was up. At 555 Taylor there was no indifferent 'desk clerk' picking his teeth behind a 4-inch-thick glass, no old men sitting around in their pajamas and slippers fixed on an old black 'n' white TV twenty-four hours a day, no pimps, no whores, no bodies of questionable vitality lying in clumps of soiled clothing in the hallway. The new place was just plain nicer in every way.

We sat on the empty floor in the empty living room and ate carrots, canned 'meat-product', tortillas and oranges, for the first couple of months, while we sought work. Late at night, we'd sometimes take a cold quart of beer and walk up to a small park at the very top of Taylor Street, and sit on a bench, and just gaze down upon the lights of Broadway and the Bay Bridge for hours. What a wonderful time we had.
GOD, we were happy.

Across the street from us, at our level (fourth floor), there lived an old woman who would, each evening when the sun went down, throw open her window, lean out over the traffic crawling slowly up Taylor Street, and with desperation, in heart-breaking, pleading tones, yell, "Henry, please come home!" She would wait for a while as if anticipating a response from the street below, then, more quietly, with sad resignation, she'd yell, "Henry please… please come home." Then she would withdraw. She did this every night, at sunset.

Kerry and I would sit there on the floor of our empty apartment, staring into each other's eyes, crunching on carrots in silence, and grimacing. Our concern, compassion, helplessness, bewilderment, was occasionally broken by nervous laughter. Such was our innocence.

THE ONE I CAN'T FORGET

I once wrote a little tune called: The One I Can't Remember, Is the One I Can't Forget. It begins like this:

Though I've known a lot of women
And each one without regret
The one I can't remember
Is the one I can't forget

Many years earlier—while still new to college—I was invited into a nice young woman's apartment late one night, and when she left the room I started quickly ripping off my clothes. When she returned, she glanced at me, smiled a lovely little crooked smile and, eyes nicely averted, with measured nonchalance, asked, "What are you doing naked?"
I said, "Oh, uh, I thought it was… uh, you know… time."
"It's not," she said.

Although I cannot recall that wonderful woman's name, I will never forget the masterful way she handled that situation.

But, I can't say that I really learned anything from her example.

Five years later, when her roommate walked in completely naked while Kerry was at work, I didn't handle it so well. I nearly tore the door off its hinges getting out of there.

HEALTH CARE in AMERICA,
as I know it

OATMEAL

The secret of fine French cuisine, if you don't know already, is butter. Butter is the first thing in the pan and the last thing in the pan. Whatever is being prepared is first braised in butter, then placed into an oven in a pool of butter until it reaches the required state of doneness, then it's in the pan again with a bit more butter to put the final touch on it. After it's plated, some form of butter—a butter based sauce or some other buttery accent—may be dolloped or poured on top, and then dribbled all around. It's served with good French bread, which anyone who knows what he's doing slathers with good, unsalted, French or Danish butter. This approach to cooking naturally leads to universal praise, great admiration, world-wide recognition, and skyrocket-high cholesterol. After eating in one of the best French restaurants in San Francisco every evening for 5 years straight, mine was over 290.

The doctor offered me two alternatives; take some drug which, as likely as not, will later prove to cause heart attack, bleeding ulcers and dementia, or eat a cup and a half of oatmeal each and every day for six months. Then, he assured me IF, after six months, the test results were good, I'd only have to keep it up for the rest of my life.

I honestly thought eating oatmeal every day would be a breeze. I have always enjoyed the taste of oatmeal. My idea of a real cookie—other than fresh-out-of-the-oven chocolate chip with walnuts (of course)—is a nice big oatmeal cookie with a sprinkling of raisins. And, if I were the type to either be up or awake at some socially acceptable hour, I think a big bowl of oatmeal, a little pure maple syrup and a little butter, would be a great way to start any day. Even without the butter it would be more than OK.

But, if you can eat a cup and a half of oatmeal every day for six months you're a better man than I am. And apparently you're better than my brother as well since, after a similar oatmeal experiment, he gladly began taking cholesterol lowering pharmaceuticals rather than face another bowl of oats.
But, I may have just gotten ahead of myself.

I started out simply, making my oatmeal with water. Then, after a month or so, I started adding low fat milk. Soon, it started becoming something of a chore. One night, just by chance, my wife took a shot at it, and the results were just incredible. It was the most delicious oatmeal I'd ever eaten; both creamy and, at the same time, slightly crunchy. The taste was remarkable. What a difference. Now THAT's oatmeal! I asked her what she had done to create such a fantastic dish and she said, "I followed the instructions on the box."
It had never really occurred to me.

Some days later I was discussing this with my brother—who at that time was still on the oatmeal diet—and he told me he'd gone through the same progression including, ultimately, his own dear wife obtaining the very same remarkable results by the very same process: following the directions. More than high cholesterol runs in our family; we also have good instincts when it comes to picking excellent wives.

Somewhere in late March I hit the wall. Suddenly, without warning, the very thought of oatmeal made me want to retch. I didn't want to see the stuff; I didn't want to smell it; the last thing on earth I wanted to do was to eat it. Worse yet, even the word *oatmeal* caused a crank in my stomach to begin a slow churn. Unfortunately, in discussing this development with my wife, that awful word came up again and again. I pleaded with her, "Please, can we talk about… this subject… without saying that word?" What was I going to do?

I had three more months ahead of me, and, then—if my cholesterol had dropped to an acceptable level—I'd still be expected to keep it up throughout eternity.

I took a few days off and gave the matter some heavy thought. Then, I girded my loins and, holding my nose, charged head-long back into the kitchen. I added fruit to the oatmeal and that seemed to help. I mixed in nuts. I tried it uncooked with yogurt and that went fine. I added oatmeal in other forms to my diet— granola, woven oatmeal cereals, oatmeal mixes with raisins or cranberries or nuts. Before long I was back on the good ol' oatmeal wagon again.

Although I have no doubts that my 290+ cholesterol level can be reasonably traced back to my wife's family-owned French restaurant, I've never said so. It would be a waste of breath. My in-laws would simply refuse to believe it—and no people on earth have greater denial skills than the French. I've been told that the slogan, "It's not my fault", is actually subliminally implanted in the French flag.

"Why do they not eat in our own restaurant?" Monsieur wails.
"They are afraid of cholesterol," Madame chides.
They shake their heads in derision as they cut into their steaks.
"Pah! I have eaten this way my entire life," Monsieur declares proudly, "… and I have NO cholesterol! What are they eating now, hay?"
My dear, occasionally fair minded, always delightful mother-in-law responds meekly "They say that his cholesterol has dropped 112 points since they have stopped eating in our restaurant."
"Well, that is something," Monsieur admits. "Yes, but to eat with full appreciation; to experience the great joy and the rich…

(it just goes on).

SHINGLES (June, 2009)

I think anyone would have to agree that, in the on-going battle to prove who cares least about their customers the airlines or the banks, the health care professionals win hands down.

Of course, it's not surprising that anyone might find it difficult continually tending to a never-ending deluge of miserable, whining, sickly, possibly contagious, strangers—I sure as hell wouldn't want to do it—but, in general, these people don't even seem to care for themselves. Judging by their carelessness in matters of personal hygiene you'd reasonably think they're in the food preparation business, not health care.

It just doesn't really help much—no matter how sick we may be—to observe health care folk, in grubby soiled garments, shuffling along the hallways like refugees escaping a war zone, or stuffing their faces with puffy cheese snacks and shamelessly glugging down orange soda in the hospital cafeteria. And, it's disheartening to see how many of them take every opportunity to quickly slip out into the alley to desperately take in that first good hit of tobacco. Going to such people for your health, is like asking a butcher to baby-sit your favorite pot-bellied piglet.

Yet, like the banks and the airlines, healthcare people continually tell us how much they care, and ...
I probably don't even need to finish that thought.

So, let me now tell you what I know about shingles.

One time a man within earshot of me shrugged and declared that he'd once had 'a mild case of the shingles' and, immediately I knew that man to be a liar.

If by 'a mild case' he meant that he had uncountable red, encrusted, puss-producing welts which ran rampant from his sternum, around one side of his body and ended only at the center of his back; and that every single pore in each of those uncountable welts responded to the slightest touch like an exposed nerve during a root canal, it leaves me to wonder what a bad case would be like. For me, my case felt like that entire segment of my body was continually roasting in a fiery hell.

When my very dear wife asked me to describe it to her, this is what I came up with: It was as if someone had taken a dozen knitting needles plucked fresh from an open fire and, using those welts as targets, plunged those red-hot needles directly into the meat of my body, driving them in about four inches deep.

It was by far the most painful thing I had ever experienced in life… and as a child I'd been forced to watch I Love Lucy.

Initially that pain lasted six seemingly endless hours each night and, during that time, I found myself screaming and in tears.

Seventeen days later, although the welts were slowly drying up, and going back to Hell from whence they'd come, the pain had become continual (and by continual, I mean relentless). I was no longer crippled by the pain, but every movement forced me to reflect on what a regrettable mistake my birth had been. (Admittedly, I deserve no better.) And let me add quickly, though probably not quickly enough for some people, that YES, I do realize there are people in this world suffering greater tragedies than a bout of shingles. Nonetheless, as they say…

Nonetheless, I feel compelled to say something about Kaiser Permanente and their system-wide total inability to EVER answer any direct question, no matter how simply put, with a direct answer.

Though, their tendency toward inaction is worse, of course.

My father-in-law—with whom my wife and I work—had shingles, and because I was as close to 60 years old as a man can be without leaving it behind, my wife called Kaiser and asked if I could get a shot which would prevent that occurrence in me. "No, not until after his 60th birthday," she was told.

My wife, who loves me far beyond what anyone who knows me might consider reasonable, said, "Yes, but my husband is being exposed to this contagious malady even as we speak." "Not ONE DAY before his 60th birthday!" she was told with the usual uncalled for brusqueness.

Of course any time an idiot is randomly assigned authority, and that idiot comes into contact with a gentle, courteous, clear-thinking, logically minded and soft-spoken lady of pleasant demeanor, there is bound to be conflict. Beyond that however, I would think that anyone in the health care business, upon hearing about someone being exposed to a contagious disease, would—if not take action of any sort—at least not deny that person a shot that could protect him against having to go through that dread disease. But, I'd be wrong.
Keep that thought in mind; it gets worse.

My wife was born in France and had received no immunization shot against chicken pox as a child, nor has she had chicken pox. Since the two diseases—shingles and chicken pox—are so inextricably entwined, she was highly, if not very highly, susceptible to getting shingles, both from lack of immunity as well as from being around her father. But, the good folks at Kaiser could not believe, and WOULD not believe, that she had never had chicken pox. And, it was impossible for them to accept the fact that she had never had an immunization shot for that virus.

She TOLD THEM SO.

She told them so, repeatedly. They simply refused to believe it.
They suggested that she have a blood test to see if she was, for
what reason I cannot imagine, lying to them.
"Maybe you had chicken pox and have forgotten," they said.
"Maybe you had a shot but don't remember."
"My mother says that I never had this shot," said my dear wife in
her normal dulcet tones.
"Well maybe your mother doesn't remember," came the
snappish reply.

What pleasure! What caring!

So, my wife took a test to prove to the delightful, ever-caring
folk at Kaiser that she had never had either chicken pox or the
immunization shot. And that test proved that my wife was not a
liar. The results came back about the time my father-in-law had
stopped being contagious.

A few very short days before my 60th birthday, I came down
with shingles, thus putting my wife in even greater danger.

Concerned about my dear wife's welfare, I asked the doctor who
'treated' me what we needed to do to protect my vulnerable wife.
She—my doctor—said, "Have her contact her doctor."
I said, "Well, in the meanwhile what would you suggest?"
"Have her call her doctor," she said.
"No—please listen to me—what should we *be doing* to keep my
wife from getting chicken pox?"
"Have her call her doctor," she said. "I can't speak specifically
because I don't know about her case."
"Yes, you do," I said with remarkable restraint, "I just told you.
She has never had the chicken pox and she has not had an
immunization shot and we are in close, continual contact with

each other. So, in the most general sense, knowing what I've just told you, what should we be doing to protect her?"
"Have her call her doctor."

So, you know, that brings up the question: IF I had, at that moment, completely rational but in an uncontrollable rage, strangled that person—I'm sorry... that Doctor, as she sat there looking at me hollow-eyed and smugly indifferent, would I be allowed, in a court of law, to tell my whole story and, more importantly I suppose, would I be capable of telling it in such a way that the judge and jury, both, might understand that I'd been driven to it? Would they understand why I had done what I had done? At the time, I guessed not, and therefore did not.

My wife spent two hours on the phone explaining her situation, in a remarkably controlled and courteous manner—as is her way—to not just one but several consecutive healthcare idiots, each and ALL of whom expressed their inability to believe that she was telling them the truth, and ALL of whom suggested that she take a blood test—to determine if what she was telling them was the truth. When she explained to them that she had done that once already, they had a suggestion for her. They suggested that she talk to her doctor.

I stood by during all of this, listening to my wife as she was being tortured by these humans for as long as any man could, before I went into another room and picked up the phone. It took two calls to get anyone to hear or understand what I was saying which was, in essence... well you know... that I was contagious, my wife was susceptible—she has already had the blood test to prove that she is not a liar—and could she PLEASE get a shot to prevent her from contracting chicken pox?

OK, so now, it's your turn. Guess what they said.
They told me, "She should talk to her doctor."

250

"Why?" I asked.

"Because she's the patient."

"She is not the patient YET," I explained, with a constraint that amazed even me, "and what we are trying to do here is to prevent her from becoming the patient." I took a breath. "You know," I said, "I know that you people are really very busy creating TV commercials telling everybody how much you care, and printing up posters touting patients' rights, and making brochures available which encourage us to ask questions and become involved in our own health, but neither my wife nor I have EVER, in all of our dealings with you, EVER managed to get ANYONE from your organization to answer a simple question with a simple direct answer."

And the person on the other line said this, "I see they have you on such-n-such for pain, have you noticed any change in your demeanor since taking it?"

I said, "You know, I *have* noticed a change in my demeanor, but it has nothing to do with that drug. It has everything to do with your organization's policy to NEVER EVER, under any goddamned circumstance, give anybody a direct answer to a direct question."

To which she replied, "You should have your wife call her doctor."

You'd think I might have developed an admiration for the skill required to maintain such a high level of indifference while dealing with any man expressing his silly concerns about the welfare of his wife, but I never did.

Some people seem to appreciate it though.

The Economist, speaking of health plans, held up Kaiser Permanente as an example of just how wonderful, how quick, clean, neat and efficient health care could be.

In an article on that subject they started out one paragraph by saying: "Kaiser, which is arguably the best..."
I nearly choked when I saw those words.

During our tribulations—and I don't know which was more painful shingles or dealing with idiots—I kept myself in a separate room, and lived alone with only occasional glimpses of my caring wife. And during that time I renewed my appreciation for courtly love, loving her all the more dearly, though at a distance, with each passing moment.

Still, it was a hell of a price to pay for something I already understood fully.

MALE TROUBLE, without apology (2016)

I had a pain in a part of the body that many males feel somewhat possessive and overly protective about and, after putting it off as long as any American male could, without being driven stark raving mad, I made an appointment.

The doctor came in, asked me what the problem was, and I described the pain. He smiled and said, "Well, sounds like you picked something up." He winked.
"I'm a married man," I said.
"Ha-ha," he laughed, "most of the men I treat for STD are married men."
"Yes, perhaps," I said, "but I'm married willingly. I don't have a sexually transmitted disease."
He smiled knowingly. "Just relax, this is pretty common." he said. "After we find out what it is exactly, we'll take care of it and your wife won't ever have to know."
"This is not a venereal disease," I said, "I've injured myself."
He looked me in the eye to determine if I was pulling his leg, then snorted conspiratorially.
"Yeah, I know," he said, "Most of the men who come in because they've *injured themselves* are married men. Your wife will never have to know about it."
"Listen to me," I said, "I have had nothing to do with any woman other than my wife."
"Just take this to the lab," he said, ignoring me completely, "when you're done we'll see what further tests we'll have to do."
The stupid bastard winked at me again.

For some reason I felt like I wasn't getting my point across.
"Listen," I said, "I have not been with any other person. I have been with my wife and only with my wife for as long as we've been married."

He snorted again and said, "OK. But, we'll just give you a little test anyway, to determine what you have. When it comes back we'll talk about what to do about it." He smiled knowingly.

The guy was some kind of a fuckin' idiot.
[Note: When my wife looked at this piece, she made a little note in the margin: 'Do not be vulgar'. Out of respect for her, I gave it additional thought. However, though I've struggled with it for quite a while, I've been unable to come up with a more perfect description of that man.]

Anyway, they gave me a little test, and it was determined that I had NOT contracted a venereal disease; that I had, in fact, injured myself—which is pretty much what I had told the guy going in. *How*, was to remain a mystery.

When next I sat before this guy, this doctor—one half hour later—he said, "Well, there are no signs of STD, but you *have* hurt yourself; I'll prescribe something to help you heal."
He offered no apology for having offended me or my wife, or for slandering our marriage. I waited, the apology never came. After making a few notes on the computer, he simply got up and left the room. I was surprised, but I don't know why; I had fallen into that very same trap before.

Late one night, years before, I woke up suddenly with a tremendous pain in my chest. Harkening back to the continual, relentless onslaught of fear inducing commercials, I had my girlfriend at the time drive me to the emergency room. That is what the commercials encouraged us to do. Don't be silly, they said. First sign of such pain, get yourself to a hospital!
So, I did that.

And the doctor came in—casually—and checked a few things under the hood, and told me, "There's nothing wrong with you;

it's stress. You should learn to relax, instead of coming in here in the middle of the night and wasting our resources."
(That's a direct quote.)

I said, "Is there anything I should do?"
He said, "Try not to get hit by a truck when crossing the street," and left the room shaking his head.

They should probably put that in their commercials, so we won't be going in there in the middle of the night and wasting their resources. It could be a little tag at the end. "But, try to be sensible. Remember, unless you are absolutely sure it's a heart attack, these guys have better things to do than to mess around with someone who doesn't have the common sense to know the difference between stress and something worthy of their time. Oh, and meanwhile, be careful when crossing the street!"

So, with those experiences behind me you might see why it becomes a toss-up between going to a quack who simply, without pretense, reaches into his pocket and dishes up the sample drugs, or going to another health care professional who, without knowing anything about me, accuses me of cheating on my wife… OR rushing in to the hospital in fear for my life—at the medical-chemical community's constant urging— only to be horse-laughed out of the place, or—thoughtfully wishing not to waste their resources—simply dying in bed.

A MORE CARING CARE (2008)

One time when my wife was checking into the hospital; as they were preparing her for a minor operation, the brute nurse had inserted a needle so badly into her that her wrist had swollen to three times its normal size. When my, always quiet, always courteous, always reasonable and very dear wife asked the nurse about it, the brute dismissed her concerns, saying basically, "Don't be such a baby!"

My wife, still frightened, asked a passing stretcher-bearer if it seemed quite correct to him. He became quickly concerned and immediately ran off to get a doctor. Meanwhile, I'd already run off and returned with a doctor in tow.
"What's the problem here?" asked the doctor.
The nurse responded, "The problem, Doctor, is that this patient doesn't seem to understand her position here."
(That is a direct quote.)

Apparently our position, as patients, is to shut up and do what we're told to do. But my dear wife is not a sheep. And she's quite observant too. For example, concerning that event, she observed that some medical people act more like prison guards than health care professionals. From what I've seen, that's a pretty good description. Without being anywhere near as crude about it as might be fair and reasonable, and accurate, I'd have to say that the medical community is …well, forget that. Let's just say that my personal experiences have not left me with the very best impression of these people or their organizations, no matter how giddy the patients always appear in their posters, or how often their commercials tell us they care.
But then, I am not a good patient.

I don't enjoy being talked down to, and to complicate matters, I don't take orders well.

Worse still, when it's expected most from me, I refuse to bow and scrape. For example, I never tremble when my superiors enter the room exuding boredom and stale tobacco smoke.

To make things worse, I ask questions; something that goes against the grain of the entire health care system. Whatever they may say, there's nothing more inappropriate or unacceptable than a patient asking questions. Whenever I do, the umbrage fills the room so immediately that the air is driven completely out and only a chilly vacuum remains. The unspoken message seems to be: "Is it somehow unclear to you that I AM a DOCTOR? You just sit there and keep your mouth shut."
Sometimes, they feel, that message needs to be made explicitly.

One time my doctor had just given me some advice and she looked at me to see if I was listening. I assured her that I had heard what she'd said by saying, "Most of the best advice I receive I get from a woman, so I hear you."
The doctor stood up and looked at me sternly, and declared (kinda shrilly I seem to recall), "I am NOT a woman, I AM A DOCTOR!"
So there you have it.
(not a woman, a doctor)

Comforting as that event was, I remain unconvinced that these people care about anyone's health. They do seem to care a great deal about their image however.

Despite all the self-satisfied self-promotion, the inbred arrogance that fills their place of work is offensive to anyone with any degree of self-worth or sensitivity, and their individual and combined indifference to any patient with real concerns or genuine fears, is frightening.

But—you must ask—what is the alternative?

My Wife's Father's Doctor (2012, maybe)

When I'd suffered long enough with the ear infection and
thought it was long past time to take action, I picked up the
phone, and after taking a deep breath, held it long enough for
fate to intervene should she so choose, before beginning to dial.
In the midst of this my very dear caring and perpetually
wonderful wife came in and, on fate's behalf, asked me what I
was doing. I told her that I had suffered long enough—a
conclusion she'd arrived at many days earlier—and that I was on
my way to the hospital.

She suggested that I simply call her father's personal physician,
Dr. Codger—it would save time and money and I'd get the very
same results... pills.
"But, he's *your father's* physician," I whined.
"Yes, but he'll see you without an appointment; he will charge
you little if not less; and," she added, "he's just around the
corner; you won't have to take the long ride out to the hospital."

I was convinced—mainly because of the shortness of the trip—
and soon after found myself in the old physician's office, where I
sat filling out forms. Smoke?—No. Drink?—No. Diphtheria? –
No. Walk with a limp?—No. Speak with a lisp?—No. In a very
few brief moments I was whisked on into the doctor's office.

Dr. Codger was a frail old man, with wisps of white hair floating
away from his head on either side in small tufts, and a crazed
look in his eye; he looked like a demented duckling in a lab coat.
He began grilling me about the financial state of things at the
hotel as soon as I entered the room. His questions were all non-
specific, and my answers all evasive. I didn't know what he
knew or what he should know or why he should be asking me
questions about business that was none of either of ours.

258

He took my blood pressure (normal) and my temperature (normal) and weighed me (just fine) and asked me to sit on a padded table of some sort while he held each wrist in one hand and looked intently into my face (which gave me the creeps).

Then he looked into each eye with some device which projected light. Then he looked down my throat and shoved a dry wooden paddle into my mouth and asked me to gag—which I did. Then he took a device and stuck it first into my right ear, then into my right nostril, then into my left nostril and then into my left ear, in that order, without hesitation (and by that I mean without taking the time for any sort of cleansing between ear and nose, nose and ear.) Of course I've seen chefs do that sort of thing before, but I expected more from a doctor.

"Gosh," I thought. Admittedly I know nothing at all about medicine, but I do know something about hygiene. (Hygiene is that thing which people in the restaurant business always lack.)

During all this, while he was observing me, I was keeping a very cautious eye on Dr. Codger. He reached into his lab coat pocket, extended his open palm before my eyes, offered me a choice of a wide variety of sample pills. "Which one would you like?"
"There are so many... I don't know what any of them do."
"Let me narrow it down for you then," he said and re-pocketed all but two bottles. Then he held them up for me to look at.
"Well," I said hesitantly, "what's the difference between them?"
"These are made by one pharmaceutical company," he said, "and these by their competitors; they both do the same thing. I think either would work well in your case."
I selected a bottle. He commended me on my wise choice, then gave me instructions. Though I might feel well before the pills were all taken, I should take them all. If I needed more I could just give him a call.

This all seemed very strange to me, but he was strolling through it pretty casually, which gave me a queasy kind of hope.

Then it suddenly seemed as though the appointment was over. We shook hands and, when we shook, it became evident to him that there was something wrong. Specifically, (and this is my take on it) I have a torn tendon in one finger; the sheath of that tendon has detached itself and gathered in a kind of unseemly clump near the base of that finger. It prevents me from extending my little finger in a way that might be desirable, while, say, holding my wife near and smothering her in the kisses her hugability demands from time to eager time. It doesn't, however, prevent me from playing the cello badly.
Dr. Codger said, "What's this?"

He turned my palm upward and looked at the lump. "Viking heritage," he said.
I said, "What?"
He said, "You have Viking heritage. Those damned redheads all have this tendon problem."
"Really?" (I am not a redhead, never have been.)
"Oh yes; it's typical."
"Ah," I said, "What do I owe you?"
"Nah," he said waving it away. "Tell you father-in-law he should come in; I have more pills for him."
I said, "I won't do that."
He looked at me startled, and then dismissed it. "Oh, OK, I'll have the receptionist call him."
"That might be a better idea."

Of course, I *could have* gone to a "real" doctor, or to the organization which insures our health, but I hesitate to go there because they have no catch and release policy. Going there is like taking your car in for one of those free inspections: of course they are going to find something wrong, and of course it is going to be expensive. Put aside for the moment—as I refuse to—the fact that those people have called both my wife and me liars on one occasion or another.

When I returned to the hotel, my wife asked me what had happened at Dr. Codger's office. I told her, "It's amazing to me that your father is still alive after seeing that quack."
"He's been seeing him for years," my dear wife said.
"All the more amazing," I said, and told her of my wonderland experience.

A couple of days later I was in our little rooms, sacred cello bow in hand, immersed deeply in the music—my fingering was flawless, my bowing far beyond any skill that I could honestly claim—and the warm fragrance of the sound was drifting slowly up, engulfing me, gently caressing and comforting my feverish mind. I was at peace…when the phone rang.
"Yes!" I barked. "What?" I whined.
"Mr. Mansfield?"
"What?" I sighed.
"Mr. Mansfield?"
"Yes." I softened further.
"This is, Shamequa, Doctor Codger's receptionist. I have to tell you something."
"Yes?" I said quizzically. Could the quack have discovered anything at all in his weird cursory inspection of my corpus gros? "Yes?" I said using my most charming irritated mode.
"I just wanted to tell you that, when you walked in the other day I thought you looked like someone."
"I looked like someone?"
"When you walked in, I thought you looked like someone, but I could not figure out who it was."
"I… I'm sorry," I said, "what?"
I was completely confused. The good doctor's secretary (sorry, receptionist) was calling me to say what exactly...?

"When you came in for the first time the other day, I kept looking at you because I thought you reminded me of someone, and I just couldn't put my finger on who."

"Uh… OK… what can I do for you?"

"It's Peter Lawford," she squealed breathily. "You look like Peter Lawford!"

Apparently this discovery brought her school-girl delight.

"Oh," I said. "Anything else?"

"No, but, you really do look like Peter Lawford," she whispered.

"Thank you," I said, "Dr. Codger thinks I have Viking heritage."

"What…?"

"Codger told me I have a Viking heritage."

"The doctor told you that?"

"Yes, he said I have a Viking heritage. Perhaps Peter Lawford had a Viking heritage." I said, "What do you think?"

"I guess that's possible," she said, and I could hear her enthusiasm deflating.

At that moment I think she realized that talking to me wasn't anything at all like talking to Peter Lawford. Even over the phone, I think she could sense that I wasn't standing around posed nicely in a dark, snug-fitting Italian wool suit, smoking a cigarette, holding a fine crystal highball glass with scotch and soda in one tastefully bejeweled, nicely manicured hand, and smiling in that suave, married-into-the-Kennedy-clan way that Lawford had.

"If you need to make another appointment anytime, feel free to call," she said with a hint of disappointment.

I had no idea what kind of response she had expected, but it was clear the conversation hadn't worked out the way she'd dreamed it would.

"Thank you. I will," I said, putting down the phone and picking up the cello bow.

262

After toying with the bow for a minute—admiring its lines and balance, rubbing the fine wood under my thumb—I put it down, stood up, and went over to look in the mirror.

I didn't look anything at all like Peter Lawford.

WHILE MY MOTHER SLEPT

My mother—84 at the time—fell down and broke her hip, her leg in several places, and perhaps a bone or two in her foot, if stitches tell no lies. But, she was handling it well. I mean she was certainly handling it better than I would. Of course, she'd had more experience than I've had when it comes to medical tragedy and, strangely, it is her innocence that has buoyed her against the relentless, ever-emerging maelstroms of her life. So, in a way, Life had prepared her.
However nothing had prepared her for two Percocet.
And, nothing had prepared us either.

From the moment those pills kicked in she was obstinate; the answer to everything was 'NO'. For several hours, she flatly refused to leave her wheelchair for the comforts of bed, and it appeared to be nothing more than sheer belligerence. She admitted to being tired; she complained about suffering greatly from sitting so many hours in that wheelchair, but absolutely refused to go to bed. It took the combined efforts of my father, myself, and more than one kindly (long-suffering) staff person, to eventually persuade her.

Meanwhile it went on like this, for hours:
"Do you want us to call someone and have them help you back into bed?"
"No."
"Didn't you just say that you're tired?"
"No."
"Didn't you just tell us that you were sore from sitting in that wheelchair all day long?"
"No."
"Yes, you did. You told us you were sore…"
"No, I did not."

"Yes, you did. So, why don't you let us help you get into bed, where you can relax a little?"

"No."

It was the Percocet speaking.

After several hours of this (honestly, several hours) she finally gave in. Under protest she was hoisted out of the chair, back into bed, and went immediately to sleep. Did she remember any of this once the Percocet had worn off?

No.

And, when we told her about it, she thought we were joking, though why we would conspire to joke about a thing like that I cannot imagine. But, when she fell asleep again, we talked.

In the midst of one of my father's tales, my mother re-surfaced—though she was still under the influence of the double dose of Percocet—and my father—who has a dry throat on occasion—got up to retrieve a piece of hard candy from the pocket of his jacket.

"Where are YOU going?" asked my mother.

"I'm going to get a piece of hard candy."

"Well, what are you going to do when you get to Heaven?"

"What am I going to do when I get to Heaven?"

"Yeah, just what exactly are you going to do when you get to Heaven?"

"I have no idea what you mean."

"I mean that in Heaven there *is* no hard candy. So, what are you gonna do, then?"

"How do you know that in Heaven they have no hard candy?"

"THEY are tellin' me that," said my mother, pointing lackadaisically in the direction of the ceiling, and rolling her eyes Heaven-ward.

"Who is telling you that?"

"THEY…" Here, again she made a Heaven-ward gesture with fluttering hands, "They…"

"Really?" said my father good-naturedly, "What else are they tellin' you?"

"No hard candy for the white guy!" she blurted out.

We all laughed… including my wonderful mother.

"Is that what they're saying?"

My mother laughed, "Yep. 'No hard candy for the white guy!'" She laughed and winked at me, and then she fell instantly back into sleep.

I don't think either my father or I had much to say after that, for a very long time.

"Seems they have some pretty strict rules in heaven," I observed.

"Apparently," said my father.

While my mother slept, I held her hand, and found myself singing 'Old Man River' to her; after six days of 12-hour shifts sitting at her bedside, I'd run out of things to say while she dreamed. My father—who had been snoozing in the corner—became quite animated at that point and said, "Do you remember our trip in that houseboat on Lake Powell?" I said I did. "You sang that same song one night, after you had about three beers in you."

"Huh…" I said, "Did I do a good job of it?"

"Well, we were all pretty surprised by it, but I think everybody enjoyed it."

"I'm better with only two beers in me," I said.

"Maybe it WAS only two beers," he mused.

Until that moment I had no idea that Old Man River was my go-to song for showing people how much I love them. My very dear wife seems to prefer '500 Miles'.

Here's something nearly heart-breaking in its loveliness, which my father told me, while my mother slept.

Before going off to war, he'd fallen so deeply in love with my mother that he was forced to tell her, "I really want to marry you, but I don't want to make you my 17 year-old widow."

And my mother replied, "I would rather be your 17 year-old widow than never to have married you at all."

When he returned after the war—after experiencing what my father tells me was an almost endless string of miracles—they married almost immediately.

While my mother slept, several other things surfaced as well.

Since my father—an engineer—prefers a direct answer to a direct question, I've always felt a sense of relief whenever an engineer stands before me, waiting to check-in at the hotel. I know that if that engineer asks me for a brochure, I can simply hand him a brochure, and that'll be the end of the transaction. I also take comfort knowing that if he asks a simple yes-or-no question and I answer in a mono-syllable, he won't stomp out of the office in an aristocratic huff, run directly to the owner, and whine about how rudely he's been treated.

When I told my father that, he laughed. He shook his head, snorted derisively, and said: "If two engineers meet in a hallway, and the only thing they have to do is say 'good morning', at least one of them is going to fuck it up."
I laughed so hard I could hardly breathe.

"Not only that," he continued, "but engineers have no sense of humor. If you told an engineer what I just told you, they'd just look at you blankly. It wouldn't mean a goddamned thing to him." In a single sentence he completely destroyed my life-long belief in engineers—I'd always thought they were like him. (And by that I mean great human beings.)

I was a bit embarrassed because I had never heard my father use the word 'fuck' before, under any circumstances; and when I admitted that, he laughed and said, "I can't hear that word without thinking of Dr. Maurice Stacy."

Dr. Stacy was a Harvard professor, greatly honored, highly noted author of articles and books, who held every advanced degree attainable; the recognized, leading expert in his field. But, according to my father, "If Stacy uttered a sentence of seven words, *four* of those words would begin with 'fuck'".

The very first time he found himself in the presence of Dr. Stacy (my guess, early 1950's), they were on a train with a vice president from Universal Atlas Cement. "A Vice President!" my father repeated (just as if that title meant something to either one of us). Then he went on to explain, "In those days there were only about three or four vice presidents for every working man."

So, this vice president and Dr. Stacy and my father were going somewhere to look over some land the company was interested in leasing for its mineral rights, and the VP casually asked Dr. Stacy, "Tell me doctor, how do you go about determining if there *are* minerals under the surface on a piece of property?"

Rather than launch into a discourse on topological formations, escarpment analysis and eluviation, Dr. Stacy, Harvard professor, with every advanced degree attainable in any aspect of Geology, greatly honored, highly noted author of every article ever written on the matter and several, exhaustive, definitive books on the subject, looked at the VP for a bit, then said this: "Ya' drill a fuckin' hole."

If my father's imitation of the good doctor's response does it any justice, Dr. Stacy said that snappishly, and with remarkable force ... as if talking to an idiot.

Both my father and the VP were, naturally, completely embarrassed, because everybody in that railway car overheard that statement and were standing up, craning their necks to see who had used *that word* so openly in the dignity of a public railway car. My father told me he wanted desperately to act as though he wasn't with that guy, but—in a passenger car, on a fast-moving train—there was nowhere to hide.

Later on, during that same trip, while walking around on the land the company was considering, the vice president was inevitably forced to ask Dr. Stacy another question. Apparently, with some hesitancy he quietly asked Dr. Stacy if he thought the company *should* purchase the rights to that land. Stacy replied, "If ya' did, you'd be steppin' on your own fuckin' dick."
The VP, confused by that answer, humbly asked, "I'm sorry, Dr. but, I don't understand."
Dr. Stacy snapped, "It'd be fuckin' painful for *you*, and *no one* would benefit from it."

My father was a wonderful human being, and great story teller.

While my mother slept, we slipped away to go get something to eat. And on the way there my father told me this tale:
"One time, a vice president handed me a letter from the President of American Bridge to the President of US Steel, saying, 'Read this and tell me how you would respond.' So, I looked at the letter, and it said something like this…
Dear Jimmy,
My boys are telling me that your boys are raising a ruckus, saying we don't have enough steel on the ground at the upstate site. My boys tell me they have 5000 tons of steel on the ground, including:
Braces
Beams
Posts

Girders
Flanges
Trusses and Channel.
Maybe you can tell your boys to back off and get to work.
Signed, Paddy"

(My father continued, saying…) So, I sat down and wrote this:
Dear Paddy,
Your boys are correct; they do have 5000 tons of steel on the
ground upstate, including:
Braces
Beams
Posts
Girders
Flanges
Trusses and Channel.
But, since we can't build this structure in the air, hang it from a
cloud, and slide the baseplate and columns underneath later, our
boys cannot get to work.

Maybe you can tell your boys that our boys will back off when
your boys supply them with the goddamned baseplate and
columns they need in order to do that work.
signed, Jimmy."

Next time they met, my father handed his written response to the
VP, and the VP said, "Good heavens, I would never send a letter
like that to the President of American Bridge."
My father said, "I know *you* wouldn't. You asked me how **I**
would respond. And that is how I would respond.'

While sitting around in that hospital room, watching my mother
sleep, he also offered me this bit of wisdom concerning
accountants, drawn from many years of his personal experience.

270

"Stick two of them in a room together, with nothing to do, and in three days they'll both be working overtime."
I said, "I think that's the way government works, isn't it?"

From the glint in his eye I could tell he was proud of me.

After all this talk, when the nurse came in, my father, a wonderful combination of common sense, endless caring, and keen wit, immediately instructed the nurse to *never again* give his wife more than one Percocet.

She understood.

BREAKING NEWS (2012)

The days of me tromping around on the stage of Life bellowing toward the heavens, "Give me a break!" are over. On Sunday last I not only got the break I've been demanding for so many years, I got two breaks. As Life would have it, they came about totally unexpectedly.

My truly wonderful wife and I were walking the pretty-damned wonderful dog in the late evening and we decided, since it was a cold clear night, to go a few extra blocks. Near the center of the block, on our side, the sidewalk disappeared and I suggested, "Let's go across the street, it's probably safer over there."

As we approached the sidewalk, on the other side, my foot landed on the mist-slickened surface of a manhole cover and the long bone of my left leg turned inward, to the right, and my left foot collapsed to the left, and I came crashing to the pavement. Somehow I knew immediately that I had broken my ankle. What I didn't know was that I had broken it in two places.

When my startled wife saw me sitting in the street holding my dangling, unresponsive foot in one hand, I told her, "I think I've broken my ankle." As she reports it, and as I remember it, I was perfectly calm when I said, "I've just broken my ankle; see if you can get some help, please."
It was the one time in my life when my normal high-strung, near-hysterical approach to every tiny inconvenience might have made some sense and, instead, I'm sitting there on the pavement, an idle duck casually adrift upon a placid pond.

By chance a Chinese woman was coming out of her house and she lent my worried wife her cell phone to call an ambulance. A young man stopped his car to see why an old man was sitting in the middle of the street. He got out, asked a couple questions, then went back to his car to get me a blanket. Tossing it at me, he said, "Keep it." Then, like the Lone Ranger, he was gone.

When the ambulance arrived it was being handled by two kids of the Justin and Jason generation, though one of them—as I recall—was named Josh. They seemed relatively indifferent to my pain, and showed even less interest in my concerns about how my wife and the dog were to get home. They gave me orders, and demanded answers to a variety of questions before they stuck me in the back. I pleaded one more time that my wife and the dog could get a lift in a homeward direction, but no dice; my wife and the dog would have to fend for themselves.

Locked in back with Justin or Jason (or Josh) I had no choice but to listen while he told me, with a peculiar kind of arrogance-laced humility, about each of the many glorious skateboarding injuries he had sustained. He'd broken his ankle four times; this rib, that elbow. He was quite proud of his own stupidity. I'm sure his adoring mother was quite proud of her little man as well. And, at some point during the trip he called me a tough guy.

Before I left the hospital five hours later, with my leg in a cast, two doctors, some unspecified clipboard-bearing male, and a nurse had all looked at me at one time or another and declared me a tough guy. It was a nom de guerre which carried over to the doctor who re-set my ankle and put a permanent cast on it, two days later. He called me a tough guy too… at which point I tried to get a look at my chart to see if someone had written those words on it in bold print somewhere.

Just for the record, I'm not a tough guy; I just don't take all the pills doctors broadcast so casually and—upon my grandfather's advice—I don't surrender to the knife if still conscious or living.

Day Two: I had already called everyone I could think of to say that Christmas gifts would be delayed, due to this broken ankle thing, when my dear caring wife turned to me and said, "If blind women can weave baskets you can certainly wrap a few gifts."

We are a gift giving people, and nothing short of death will prevent us from doing our duty in this utterly meaningless exercise. An aside: One time many years ago, I made a futile attempt to convince people whose lives were already full of useless junk that the exchange of more useless junk with other people whose lives were also completely full of useless junk was idiotic. I stood in the business district handing out flyers which stated my case. (I was young at the time.) What I was doing caught the attention of a Chronicle reporter (Dwight Chapin) who then interviewed me and wrote a fairly representative, but still kindly, article about my idiocy.
(This was long before I met my wife.)

So, in reference to that—I forget how the matter surfaced, again—my dear wife said to me, "I can't believe you launched a campaign in an attempt to destroy Christmas."
I, tough guy though I be, explained, "I didn't launch a campaign in an attempt to destroy Christmas. I simply tried to convince a few people who already have too much useless crap in their lives that giving more useless crap to others, who then feel compelled to give them useless crap in return, is silly."
"Well, you know what my view is on that," she said.
"Yes, I know what your view is on that. Your view is that people should be able to accumulate as much useless crap as they might ever want, and exchange it with others should they so desire, without criticism or interference of any sort from miserable people like me."
To which my very dear wife replied, "Precisely."

That's why I love, not just my wife, but our marriage. Other wives, in other marriages, would have taken that opportunity to mess with their poor broken- ankled husband in one completely unnecessary way or another; but, not my wife. In our marriage we are often entertained by the other's weird, somewhat misguided, point of view on matters in which we maintain our own unique clarity. And, I don't think the honeymoon is entirely over, because she continues to wait on me, with a concerned look in her lovely eyes, but I think we're both pretty tired of this broken ankle thing already.

Day Three: I can't do a thing but sit around with my foot up, writhe in continual, relentless pain, and look on helplessly as I slowly begin to understand why the houses of invalids are always in such an embarrassing mess.

My nightstand, which usually holds a framed photograph of my dear wife and her adoring husband, a little needlepoint she did for me in a similar frame, and a peculiar little bronze lamp with an embroidered lily-shaped Victorian shade, now holds all of that as well as a letter from I cannot recall whom, a telephone, two remote controls, several small scraps of paper covered in awkwardly scrawled undeniable but indecipherable pith, some pills my delightful mother-in-law gave me which I refuse to take (cause I'm a tough guy), an unopened bill of some sort—which I mean to get to—and the spoon that I used last night to eat yogurt. Next to me on the bed, is, curled up nicely, a cat, and the case for my ukulele, upon which now rests an address book, a case for my reading glasses, two good books (one by E.B. White, the other by Admiral Lord Cochrane), an empty plastic water bottle, a used paper napkin, a cup with a used fork in it, and something which, because of the light, I cannot determine the nature of, though I'm sure it has a reason for being there. We have 6 weeks to go, and already I have the pallor of a poet.

A few days have passed and now it's Christmas. I wandered out on my crutches to the office to sit for a while with my good wife and to employ the skills I've developed over the last few days, wrapping gifts with only one useful ankle.

I've gotten pretty good at it and managed to wrap one nicely framed opera poster, one small cast iron pig and a glazed white ceramic bowl with a pewter pill box resting inside upon a bed of freshly shucked walnuts, all without causing myself any further injury. I have rejected my friend Bruce's advice—he saw this as an opportunity for me to sit around in cafes with my crutches, a cup of coffee, and three days' growth, scowling at people as they go by. (I didn't really understand where the crutched fit in.) Although, it is true that this fractured ankle has not turned me into a sweetheart.

The few guests I've come into contact with all seem surprised to discover that a broken ankle hasn't rendered me more amiable and a great deal more chatty. I've noticed that people who have never spoken to me before now suddenly want to hang around and talk about my injury for hours; they smile sweetly as they prod me for details. I know the response they're expecting; I'm supposed to shrug it all off with wit and charm—but I can't. Or won't. With each passing day, I find myself liking Bruce's suggestion more.

Nonetheless, this event has given me some time, at last, to think epic thoughts...

...not that I will.

POVERTY in AMERICA,
as I know it

WALTER, ONE SATURDAY MORNING

I'm standing on the front step of the hotel with a homeless guy at serious arm's length. I've known him for years. We're talking quietly. I'm saying, "I don't know if me giving you money every day is really helping you, Walter."

He says, "Yeah, you're right. I really need to do something about that."

"Well, what are you going to do?" I ask.

He whines, "I don't know, Richard, I'm a wreck. I'm dirty and I'm smelly and some guy keeps beating me up." He ponders. He sees the book in my hand. "Hey," he says, "have you ever read much Maupassant?"

"No, I guess I should," I admit.

"Should!? Man, you **gotta** read Maupassant! Him an' Gogol. You ever read much Gogol?"

"No. I read 'The Nose', but that's about it. He's on the list though."

"Man, you gotta read Nikolai! Gogol, and Maupassant and Montaigne; you **gotta** read him, man!"

"Yeah. I've read some of his work. Montaigne's one of those guys who I somehow agree with everything he says."

"Yeah? Like who else?"

"Emerson... I don't know... maybe one of two others."

He pauses and thinks. "By diverse means we arrive at the same ends. Man, you gotta read more Montaigne."

Walter's eyes are bright with enthusiasm for this subject.

I muse out loud—I have a tendency to do that with Walter—. "More laughable than the list of things I haven't read is the fact that I don't retain a damned thing. I've read Hobbes; can't quote two consecutive words from the man... well, nasty, brutish and short, of course, but all the rest is lost."

"If I am a man of some reading, I am a man of no retentiveness," Walter quotes off hand.

"That's Hobbes?"

"Montaigne, Richard. He's always right about everything, man. You GOTTA read MORE Montaigne." He cranes his neck to get a look at the book I'm holding. "What are you reading?"

"It's Dumas, La Reine Margot." I show Walter the cover.

"In ENGLISH?!" Walter slaps his thigh and goes into a fit of uncontrollable laughter. "In ENGLISH?! You're reading Dumas **in English**? I thought your wife was French."

"She is…"

"I thought you went to college or something…"

"I did."

"HA! Some education! Reading Dumas in English..." He's laughing so hard he almost falls down. When he recovers he's still shaking his head and laughing. "I'm sorry, Richard," he says… "but, man, Dumas, in ENGLISH!"

He turns and, as he begins to walk away, he's still laughing like a hyena. From a distance he shouts "You're missing everything..!"

I look at the spine of the book, hang my head in shame, and go back inside. "I'm missing everything," I'm saying to myself. My very dear wife, standing in the hotel office doorway, welcomes me back with a smile. She's arranging some flowers in a vase for the lobby.

"I'm really getting the hang of this, Mon Ange," she says.

"… though I still don't like doing it."

"Am I missing everything, Sabine? Walter says I'm missing everything when I read Dumas in English."

"Well, you may be missing something but not so much as you would reading Gérard de Nerval, for example."

She disappears down the hallway, while I ponder.

"If I'm missing everything I want to know it."

Several minutes later, she appears in the office doorway with a book in her hand. "Chapter 14" she announces. "Let's see what you're missing... Oh yes." She begins reading out loud while I flip through my book looking for the place. "*A ces mots, Marguerite se leva avec une grace toute voluptueuse, et laissant flotter entrouverte sa robe de nuit, dont les manches courtes laissaient á nu son bras d'un modèle si pur, et sa main veritablement royale, elle approcha un flambeau de cire rosée du lit, et, relevant le rideau, elle montra du doigt, en souriant á sa mère, le profil fier, les cheveux noirs et la bouche entrouverte du roi de Navarre, qui semblait, sur la couche en désordre, reposer du plus calme et du plus profond sommeil.*" She looks at me. "What does yours say?"

"Let's see... *Margot got up, went over to the bed, tore the curtains back and there was Navarre, lying around like he owned the joint...*"

She laughs in a particularly feminine way, and her eyes sparkle. "You may be missing something," she says, and departs to return her book to our room.

I'm left thinking about what a lovely laugh my dear wife has, and how magnificent her eyes are when she looks at me fondly. And I'm thinking about Walter; how could a man like that—with such knowledge and such an accepting attitude—end up on the scrap heap of our society?

A peculiar little footnote:
I mentioned Walter to my old friend, Bruce, and he told me that he'd been giving money, and things, to a guy named Walter for years. After listening to the details—has a brother in Alameda who wants nothing to do with him, has a degree in psychology from (I forget where), speaks French; has a remarkable, extensive literary knowledge—we decided that his Walter and my Walter are one and the same.

We also agreed that neither of us had ever heard our friend Walter complain about his situation.

PHYLLIS (1969)

One night, seeing Slim down there, I went across to the park and sat down on the bench next to the one he sat on. We just looked up at the moon for a while. Then he said quietly, "Mind if I talk?" and offered me a swig from the bottle he held in a bag.

"No thanks."

"Tempted?"

"No."

"Scared t' ?"

"No."

He thought for a bit. "I'm not drunk...You believe me?"

"No."

"Didn't think you would. I admit it. I might cry, though."

"It's OK to cry."

"Grown man."

"It's OK," I said.

He repeated, "I'm not drunk" and offered me the bottle again.

"Want some?"

"No thanks."

"Look at that old moon will you? Solid as a rock. There she is."

"There she is," I agreed.

He thought for a bit more.

"I left my wife in Carolina," he said. "That was 16 years ago. August 11. I guess it's all for the best. What do you think?"

"I don't know." I said, "Heck, I don't know anything, Slim."

"Nah, you know stuff. I seen it."

"Yeah, sure. I know a little about visual perception... and that's absolutely useless."

"I had to leave her," he said. "I suppose you could have guessed that. I had to; so, I did. I'm not drunk though, you know that don't you?"

"Sure."

"Just up and left her." He snapped his fingers weakly. "Like that."

We sat for a while.

"Which Carolina?" I finally asked, with what I thought was appropriate solemnity.

He looked at me with a look that seemed to demand apology. "Sorry," I said.

"You should be," he said. "Is that the bes' you can come up with? Which Carolina? Does it make any difference in the matter?"

"I'm sorry," I said again, but he just shook his head in disgust. We sat in silence for a bit more.

"I tried to write," he said. "I tried to explain a thing. I just stood there outside the door and listened to her cry. I couldn't move. I couldn't speak. After a bit, I just left."

"Slim…" I started.

"This is the stuff that hurts," he said. He looked at me briefly. "I don't want you to ever understand any of it."

"I'd like to… "

"You can't," he said, cutting me off, "and I hope you never do. Don't you have any answers though? They teach you anything about such in that school? This is the stuff a man needs to know!"

"I don't have any answers for you," I admitted.

"Her name was Phyllis," he said.

ABOUT SLIM (1968)

The first time I met Slim I was so impressive was the weirdness
of that meeting that I ran back to my room afterwards and,
typing furiously, recorded all that I could recall of what the man
had said. What I remembered became the opening scene of a
play (An Appeal For Shorter Doors): Summer. In the small city
park there are two benches lined up end to end. Behind them—a
hedge. In front of them—a statue of a Confederate War hero. A
wino sits on one of the benches. Between his legs he holds a
bottle in a paper bag. He holds it with both hands, as if it might
otherwise escape.

While my clothes were in the Laundro-Mat, I decided to go
across the street to the park and catch some sun. On one of the
benches an old wino sat, mumbling to himself.
"Look at all them fine people," he said. "So fine, so good, so
pure, so sure of themselves."
I was not so sure of myself, though. I was then, as I have been
throughout my life, socially awkward. I thought this might be a
good opportunity for me to develop some social skills; after all I
had very little to lose. I decided to try my hand at conversation.
I cleared my throat and quietly croaked, "I'm just waiting for my
wash to get done. Over there, you know, in the Laundro-Mat."
"Why here?" snapped the wino. "You oughta know better than
that! You got yourself a college dee-gree."

I didn't have a college degree—I'd only been in school for a
semester or two—but it didn't seem a point worth arguing.
"That won't help," he said contradicting himself. "You should
know that by now."
I nodded agreeably, despite the fact that I had no idea what the
old guy was talking about. "Glad to see your education is doing
you some good," he said and, without looking at me, smiled a
crooked smile.

When his cold grey eyes fixed on me, I quickly looked to the statue in front of me.

"Do you mean..?" I stammered.

The guy exploded with anger. "Course I mean!"

He calmed down as quickly as he'd exploded; suddenly we were buddies. "They're all expectin' somethin' to happen." "Not me an' not you though," he said quietly, confidentially. "Me- too old, too tired, too bullheaded. YOU- too well educated. You know better. Just waitin' to shove your clothes in a pillow case and trudge on home. Isn't that it?"

"Well, yes."

"Nothin' complicated in that."

I was finding this guy a little scary. My instincts were telling me to get up and get out of there. But, my humanity—in those days it still spoke to me—told me to stay and work on my social skills, here in the park, at no cost, and maybe emerge a fully adjusted social butterfly.

(In those days I still harbored that hope.)

"PERFECT!" he suddenly shouted. "But just look at THEM though. Oh, THEY JUST KNOW somethin' is goina happen. Don't want to miss it." He laughed to himself. "Want to be part of it. They think they got a better chance in their cars. Drivin' all over...up 'n' down." He pondered. "It's always happening in the nex' block though. Dog chasin' his own tail. Cars!" he sneered.

"I guess I'm out of it then," I said, "I don't even own a car."

"Wasn't accusin' you anyway," he said, almost to himself.

"I didn't think you were," I said, matching his tone.

"Can't catch it. Too elusive. Me, I..."

He forgot what he was saying.

After a while he assured me, "Good education's th' answer. What you studying anyway?"

"Art History. Painting. Print making." I said.

He sat up properly and straightened his grimy old silk tie. "You don't say?"

I laughed. "I guess it won't do me much good, you know, without a car…"

"Sadly, I reckon not. Without a car, you are nothing! Drive all night, up in the morning, start all over. God bless America." He paused, he stood half-way up, he saluted smartly, he wavered, he sat. "Stick to it, by gid or by gad. Be CONSCIENTIOUS- you won't miss a thing. YOUR big fat face on the flickering screen. THAT'S what THEY think! HA!" He covered his ears with his hands and shook his head. "I don't want to hear it anymore."

The old guy was insane as far as I could tell. I stood up.

"Well. I gotta go put my stuff in the dryer," I said.

"Sit down," he said, "This is gonna take a while."

"Gotta go," I said.

"Go on then," he said and dismissed me with a broad swipe of his hand. "What do I know? It was only hypothetical anyway."

"Pardon me?"

 "Pardon me?" he said mockingly. "You're too anxious to join 'em, that's what I said." He looked me in the eye and his chin was quivering with rage. "And you heard me too. So, go join 'em."

"See you later," I said, "OK?"

"It ain't OK. Maybe *I* don't want to see *you* later. Maybe I don't want to see you ever again. MY clothes will never get dry. I defended this goddamned country!"

I stopped and looked down at the poor guy. "Free advice," he said, in disbelief, "… he don't even want none."

He took a drink from his precious paper bag.

While folding my wash, I thought about that entire exchange and, after shoving it into a bag, I headed back to the park for further abuse.

When he saw me coming across the street he purposefully, dramatically, slid to the center of the bench and turned his back on me. I took a seat on the edge of the next bench over and, closing my eyes, raised my face to the sun. "Nice day," I said. After practicing the words a dozen times in my mind, I added, "Feel that sun."

"Oh? THAT?" He fiddled with the bag for a while. Then sighing, he said, "You're not the victim. I don't know why I always treat you that way."

"I'm not?"

"Neither the cause nor the cure." He offered the bag to me. "Want some?"

"No thanks. I don't drink."

"I wish I could say that," he chuckled, and took a slug. He pondered a bit, then took another slug. "It don't make any sense," he said. "I'm outside today; can't seem to get anything done. The people stop to talk. Yes, they all want to talk to Slim all right. 'Hey Slim', they say. The time just goes by that way."

"I know what you mean," I said.

Suddenly he turned vicious again. "No you don't." As suddenly he was kindly again. "Want some?"

"No thanks. I don't drink."

"A horse on me then. Look down that way and see if you see any cops." While I looked, he gulped at the bag.

"What does that mean 'a horse on you'?"

"Do you see any cops?" he snarled.

"Nope, don't see any," I said.

"Keep lookin'," he said, and for the entire time I looked I could hear him gulping desperately from the bottle. Then he put it quickly under his coat. "See that car?"

"The Chevy?"

"Right on schedule. Yes sir, right on schedule."

"You think that's a cop?"

"Ha! Do you think you're you?"

"I don't think that was a cop," I said.

"You been studyin' that in your school have you?"

"Well, no, but…"

"Every day, this time, headin' in that direction. Or the other, maybe. They're not as clever as they think though." He shook his head and stared down at the bottle. He removed it from the bag, lifted it above his head to see how much was left, and then put it back in the bag. "You ever see a wino do that before?"

"What?"

"Lift the bottle like that?"

"No."

"Never see it again either," he said smugly, and he took what was clearly the final swig. "Want some?"

"No thanks, I have to go." When I stood up to go, he stood up with me.

"It can't get along without ya?"

"What?"

"Your laundry."

"No, I just… better go."

"Hey, let me tell you somethin'," he said confidentially. "A lot of people don't like you college kids, because they think you're kiddin' yourselves." He snorted at the absurdity of that. "But I like you, 'cause I *know* you're kiddin' yourselves." He smiled. "'Course," he said, "I don't know if there's any comfort in that. Prolly very little."

"Well I gotta go," I said. "Take it easy, OK?"

He shook his head dramatically and snarled, "You think it's easy? You think it's EASY? After all I just taught you, you still think it's easy?" He looked down at the empty bottle in one hand, the empty bag in the other as if surprised at the discovery. Then he mumbled, "For someone who don't drink, you sure managed to make me drink your share."

Lessons learned—ZERO.
Social skills developed—NONE.

GOODBYE, SLIM (1971)

One afternoon I was sitting in the park pawing through a stack of books which my parents had bought for me. It was the Vision and Value series; a hard to come by, expensive compilation of work by various authorities in the field of visual perception, and one of the few possessions I ever physically ached to possess. When a shadow fell across the page I looked up and there was Slim, standing there with a suitcase in his hand. I smiled, squinted, and shielded my eyes with a salute.

"I guess I'll be headin' down to Florida. I got a sister there," he said.

"You look good, Slim," I found myself saying.

"Welp, they treat you good in the veteran's hospital."

"I'd forgotten that you were a veteran..." I said, like an idiot.

If there was anything evident about Slim it was his service to this country. "We all were," he said. "Whole generation. Big flock, brainless sheep. Save the world. 'Course it had to be done. None of us were what you would call deep thinkers, though. We did what we were told; we did what we had to do. Otherwise, they called you a Nazi."

"I get called a communist a lot."

"It goes on. How did you think I knew so much about that hollow guy?" he said, referring to the statue of a Civil War hero that stood in the center of that park. "Maybe we were forgotten on the same island. That coulda been MY statue. 'Stead, I got this raspberry for a nose. That's my medal."

"I don't think it looks so bad. Are you gonna sit down?"

"I wear it with shame. But..." He turned up his suitcase on end and sat on it. "I sure as hell earned it," he said.

After a while he said, "You don't want to end up like this, son. Course, you don't want to end up like that either" he said pointing to the Civil War hero. "It's a tightrope all the way."

"I know what you mean," I said.

"I'm afraid you prolly do."

"I do," I said trying to sound convincing.

"Well good then. I'll tell you something else too."

"What's that, Slim?"

"There is no truth in the bottom of that bottle. Don't waste your time looking for it there. I already tried it. It's a goose chase for sure."

"I don't drink, Slim," I lied. At that point I was drinking regularly, steadily, sometimes heavily, mostly beer.

"Good. Don't start. I told that redneck wino to stay away from you. He didn't like it, but, who knows what he'll do. It's up to you."

"I know."

"I believe you do," he said wearily, while looking me in the eye. "'Bout your art: ignore what people say. Paint your pictures. You know what's good and what's not. They'll try to tell you that what you're up to is silly. They're all jealous. Jus' ignore 'em."

He stood up and fiddled with the edge of his suitcase. "Look up at that old moon when you can. It's as solid as a rock. Latch on to something big like that. I seen you waltzing by here with a girl the other day. Find one you like, grab hold on t' her, don't ever cross her. It doesn't matter what she looks like, no matter what they say, that don't matter. There's more value in a good wife than anything else on this globe. You like my new haircut?"

"Looks good."

"Compliments of the United States government. All it cost was my innocence. The nose came with the deal. No extras charge. Goes well with the suit don't you think?"

"You look like you just stepped out of Gentleman's Quarterly."

"All I need is a boutonnière and a casket to lie down in."

"No. You look good, Slim."

He did. And healthy too; I hardly recognized the man.

"Your tax dollar at work," he said. "Only way my sister will recognize me is the nose. I hear you'll be heading up to Pennsylvania."

"Christmas vacation. Visit the folks. You know…" I said.

"Looks like we're heading in different directions then. I sure hope so. I like you a whole lot, kid."

I stood up and Slim pulled me in and gave me a hug.

(And, unless you were there, it's impossible to convey how rare such a thing was in those days.)

"I gotta be down to the Greyhound. Don't want them to hold the bus just for me."

I started to speak but he gestured that it was not required.

"You sit back down. Enjoy the sun." He picked up his suitcase. "Look at this bag will you? Not a thing in it. Part of the act though."

Then Slim began to walk out of my life.

"Thanks, Slim!" I shouted.

"That's what we're here for!" he shouted back.

3 TWO-DOLLAR BILLS (2013)

One morning I went out to walk the dog, and while the dog was occupied sniffing around the front door, a young man was coming up the street toward us. He was shabbily dressed like a derelict and acting particularly strangely; waving his arms around wildly, talking to himself (though these days it's impossible to tell) and rolling his head around in a peculiar manner—as if to dislodge an insect from one ear.

He approached me and asked if I could help him out with some spare change, saying, "I'm not really having the best luck right now," or something of the sort. And, though I don't usually carry any money, on that day I happened to have 3 two-dollar bills on me; someone had given them to me, saying they would bring me good luck. So, I gave those 3 two-dollar bills to the young man, saying, "Maybe this'll help change your luck…"

So, the day went on—walked the dog, prepared and ate lunch, that sort of thing—and went outside in the afternoon to look at the weather. And as I was walking up the street I saw that same young man heading my way. But, this time he was reasonably dressed, clean shaven, with neatly combed hair, and walking in the normal way of normally adjusted people.

He noticed me at about the same time I'd marked him, and as we approached each other he stopped, took out his wallet, and extracted some bills from it. As our paths crossed I smiled and said, "It looks like you've had a change of luck."

Without saying a word, he handed me 3 two-dollar bills, and continued on his way.

HOMELESSNESS is FOREVER, apparently (1974-2021)

When I hung around Upper Grant Street, because I lived nearby (starting about 1974), there was this drunk couple, who were always sitting on the sidewalk, begging for spare change. They were almost always drinking, and usually squabbling, and it was not unusual to see one of them—usually the male—stand up in a fury, point a finger at the other, issue an ultimatum or threat, and go stumbling off in disgust.
They both had faces the color of ripened raspberries.

They could be found on that street, in that state, day or night, for as long as I lived there. They were there when I left, and, when I moved back into that neighborhood again, after being trapped in southern California for 9 years, those two were still there; still sitting on the sidewalk; still begging, still perpetually drunk, still squabbling, still red-faced, and most amazingly, still alive.

So, I have no idea how that works. I can only suppose that the on-going massive consumption of alcohol, in conjunction with an unbreakable commitment to an insufferable relationship, had somehow sustained them throughout all those years.

When I used to hang around Clement Street, because I lived nearby (beginning around 1976), there was this young, grey-haired Japanese guy—always wearing an iridescent trench coat —who would appear, from time to time, and glide through the streets of that neighborhood, in silence, like a ghost.
He was fairly obviously homeless.

He never spoke to anyone, never looked anyone in the eye, and never put a hand out for help. He had a remarkable presence about him, and my conclusion then was that he had taken some kind of spiritual vow.

One time, out of who knows what foolish idea, I approached him offering a few bills of cash. He shrieked, as if I'd jabbed him with a red hot branding iron, and ran off.

Yesterday—June 19, 2021—while walking on Bush Street, I saw that same Japanese guy walking toward me. He looked a little older—but didn't seem to have aged as much as I have in that time. He still wore that, now tattered and torn, old iridescent trench coat. Clearly, without a doubt, he is still homeless; and still gliding ghost-like, in silence, through these streets.

He did not look at me as we passed each other—though I admit that I fixed on his face, in the selfish hope that he would. He still has a remarkable presence about him, and I cannot help but feel that the spiritual vow he's taken has sustained him throughout all these years.

The GOOD MISTER LEARNS A LESSON

I lived out on Clement Street in San Francisco for something like 10 or 12 years. And where I lived, because of the steady climb of the landscape, you could look off to the west and see Clement as it ran all the way up to the Palace of the Legion of Honor. That's about 30 city blocks.

So, one day I walked out onto the street and a tiny little old lady approached me. She was dressed in a manner that pegged her somewhere between previously well off and currently insane, but she had a gentle way about her.
"Excuse me, sir," she said in a soft, slightly wavering voice, "but, can you look down there and tell me if you see the Clement Street bus coming?"
"Sure," I said. I was glad to help her out.
She apologized, "My eyes have gotten so bad lately."
"That's OK," I said and stepped out into the middle of the street, and casting my eagle eyes westward, I waited to see if I might detect any bus-like movement headed in our direction.

I watched for a bit because I wanted to be able to offer her good news if I could, but there was not a single bus to be seen in any of those 30 blocks.

So, I stepped back to the sidewalk and I said, "I'm sorry, but I don't see any busses."
And she looked me right in the eye, and she began to tremble, and she said, "You FUCKING LIAR!", and marched off smartly down the street.

KINDNESS AT THE CROCODRE (1998)

When I found myself in San Francisco for the first time in maybe
a decade, I witnessed a simple act of kindness that followed so
closely upon the heels of an attempt on my life that it really
reached me. This combination of events assured me that I was
home again. Thanks for being yourself, San Francisco—
embarrassing as that sometimes is.

In order to fully appreciate this you'll have to place it against the
backdrop of San Francisco in 1972—when I first arrived—a time
when cars stopped for pedestrians. In those halcyon days that
was pretty much the norm in this town. Visitors from other parts
of the known world were always surprised, but that was the way
it was done out here; you stepped off the curb, cars stopped. It
was a simple arrangement, if not brilliant in its humanity at least
exemplary in its civility.

But, I'd been away for a while and things had changed; the city
felt inhospitable; the town was noisier, dirtier and smellier than I
remembered, and everything seemed to be happening way too
fast. This leads us to the threat of vehicular manslaughter.

As said, I haven't been in town for several years. I've been living
all that time in a small beach town in Southern California, where
things are slower. It's raining, heavily, and I'm standing at a
fairly complicated intersection, where streams of rapidly flowing
traffic from the business district, Chinatown, North Beach and
Broadway all collide. The cars are just flying by, all horns, lights
and windshield wipers. I'm not really paying attention—my eyes
are still slightly glazed-over from looking at far too many
beautiful young naked women, in the only establishment in town
owned and operated (here's progress for you) by the female
"sex-workers" who work therein (I'm proud to say.)

When the light turns, I step out into the street, and about halfway across, I realize I've made a mistake. Suddenly from around the hidden bend comes an entire herd of stampeding vehicles. One of them is bearing down directly on me. I'm dazzled, like a deer in headlights, but, my mind is amazingly active—for some reason everything is happening slowly; the oncoming car is taking what must be minutes to arrive, and as it approaches I observe it in every detail; the make (Plymouth), the model (Valiant), the color of the thing (kind of a worn-out beige), the pelting rain rolling off its hood.
Because of this, I honestly believe that I am about to die.

What can I do?

I have no place to go. Also, because I've been living on the beach too long, I'm slow and unprepared. If I once possessed the ability to spring gazelle-like between cars, I have lost it. I can't leap in a single bound 20 feet to the safety of the curb ahead of me. Nor do I possess the skill necessary to do a back flip, followed by the series of cartwheels, necessary to attain the safety of the curb I'd just vacated. So, I took the only physical option available to me; I held up a hand in the universally recognized sign for 'please don't hit me'.

At the same time, I offered a wrinkled brow (admitting my vulnerability) and a little apologetic smile (admitting my stupidity). Everything about my posture is pleading: "I know that I really should not be in the middle of this intersection right now; I've made a mistake. It's a big mistake; a dangerous and possibly costly mistake; I admit my stupidity. .. and, I also know that you are in a hurry to get home. But, I hope you can find it in your heart to delay your progress for just a few seconds more in order to spare a stranger his life."
That's the message I'm sending.

The driver has received my message, and it only infuriates him. Apparently he's decided to simply kill me where I stand. So, now I offer the hand again, but this time with some authority. 'I'm commanding you to stop!'

Of course, this is precisely the sort of belligerence no driver should ever have to put up with, from any pedestrian. Now, I'm defying him, daring him to hit me. He's bristling at the idea that he should have to remove his foot from the accelerator and place it on the brake for an idiot like me. On the other hand (I've got this on my side), I'm not someone he knows and might actually enjoy running over. He has a micro-second to weigh his options.

His car comes rocking to a sloppy stop, inches from bashing and shattering my legs. For a moment we make a nice little frozen tableau as, through the windshield wipers and pelting rain, the driver and I lock eyes. On his face, I can see that it was a tough decision for him, and that he regrets his choice. Then, as if a starting gun has been fired, he's screaming obscenities at me.

On the passenger side of the car, a woman frantically rolls down her window and sticks her head out—so that she might make more direct contact—and she's screeching at me. She's snapping and snarling and barking out obscenities. In the backseat is a third person, tugging desperately upon the back of her seat, he wants to claw his way into the action. The driver is still yelling, but I'm barely aware of him; the guy in the backseat has a few foul words to add, but he's a lackey; I'm fascinated by this vile woman. I've decided to face that real demon directly.

I'm on her side of the car now, and we're looking each other in the eye. We're maybe four feet apart, and all the city, traffic, and weather noises have disappeared completely. The only thing I hear are the truly foul and vicious words spewing out of her garishly painted mouth.

I'm amazed at how long she manages to string the scathing invective together. There's a poetic sense to it, as if she's been planning this for a very long time, and she doesn't want to let the opportunity pass.

For reasons which I cannot explain, I am perfectly calm—perhaps for the first time in my life, I am perfectly calm. I'm even feeling a little playful. "My god, Lady," I tell her, "relax."

But, this only seems to offend her further; so, she escalates. Now, the stuff coming out of her mouth is so disturbingly sordid as to be an embarrassment to me, to her, to all womankind, to society, and perhaps to humanity itself. "I'm the one who almost got run over," I explain, "I'm the one who should be upset."

I'm the one who should be snapping and snarling, but—being contrary by nature—since she's decided to make this the most catastrophic event in history, I've decided to simplify it. I point at their car, smile broadly, and say, "That's why they put brakes in those things, Lady!" And I go sauntering off, on my way.

I found myself safely (at last) on the other side of the street, feeling kind of lost. I'd forgotten where I was going and what I was doing. In my muddled mind I considered the idea that I had come very close to being run over by a car—and I was stunned by the thought. It would have been a shame to be run over and killed by a carload of such stupid bastards. If I'm to die like that I want it to be an accident, not an act of entitlement.

Shaken, I walked up the hill a bit and leaned against something; it may have been a mailbox, or a post of some sort or a parked vehicle, and became absorbed in rethinking what had just happened.

Mostly, I was struggling to understand the driver of that car. Why did he think that removing his foot from the accelerator was such an unfair demand that he was willing to kill another human being rather than grant it? I was also thinking: Maybe I've been away too long; this doesn't feel like the San Francisco I used to know and love.

I was leaning against whatever it was I was leaning against, still disoriented, when a woman emerged from the alley-side door of a night club called The Crocodre. I observed her casually as she stood at the curb attempting to get the attention of someone across the street, by frantically waving during the gap between cars as they go flying by. When that proved futile, she started to step off the curb just as a bus appeared, coming up the hill full speed. She stepped back just in time.
"Maybe it should wait," I suggested.

She turned, evaluated me briefly and then smiled.
"It can't," she said, "I've got a lot of things to do before we open tonight." She was the first person in this town, in my two days here, to offer me her eyes in kindness.

She was tall and trim, in denim jeans and a white cotton shirt; simple, honest, neat, a heroine from an early Hollywood adventure film. If she had just emerged from a café in Bombay or a bar in Santa Rosa, Costa Rica, she would have seemed a natural fit. Her brown hair fell loosely to her shoulders, brushed back behind one ear and falling untended, on the other side. She was a pleasant, intelligent looking working woman, your basic clean-cut, uncluttered American beauty—a look that has become all too rare these days—broad smooth forehead, a dignified nose, mouth slightly larger than necessary, eyes that sparkled with an appreciation for life.

When the bus huffed away in a cloud of smoke and mayhem, she finally got the attention of a homeless guy squatting beside the pornographic theatre across the street. He stood up, a mass of old overcoats with a kindly comical weather-worn face, and she gesticulated broadly waving him over. Much wiser than me, he *looked* before picking his way skillfully through traffic.

These two—the wino and the America beauty—huddled at the curb a few feet from me. He was bending toward her, in order to hear her through the traffic noise; she had placed a hand on his shoulder.

I was curious—nosy –though still recovering a bit from my near-death confrontation, and I zeroed in on what she was saying. "Do you want to do a little work for me?" she shouted. "I'll pay you what I would have paid the other guy, but I need it done right away." He nodded 'yes; vigorously. He told her 'thank you'. She asked him to walk up the alley with her, to look at what needed to be cleaned up. Then she told him to come inside for whatever tools he might need to accomplish the task. "Can you do this right now?" she asked.
"Yes. Thank you," he said. "I'll do a good job," he said.
And she said, "I know you will."

That nearly broke my heart the way she said that. "I know you will." Such remarkable kindness wrapped in so few words. It filled me with warmth. It brought tears to my eyes. It did. It brought tears to my eyes. "I know you will."

What she said next nearly brought me to my knees. She said, "And, when you're done, come inside and have a good meal."

Now THAT'S the San Francisco I know.

SUCCESS in AMERICA,
 as I've seen it

SUCCESS RICK McCANN STYLE (1968 I think)

When we finally ended up in San Francisco, after four days and nights on the road, Rick said, "I want to go over to *Rolling Stone* and see if I can get Jann Wenner to assign me a piece."
I laughed raucously. Even then Rolling Stone—which was just getting started—was a huge phenomenon and an impossible dream for writers to attempt. But then, I didn't know Rick as well as I eventually would.

As I recall, we went down Third Street to the old brick building where Rolling Stone was situated, and Rick found a parking spot right in front—an impossible task even then. We went inside together, and Rick asked the security guy what floor Rolling Stone was on. We went up in the elevator, and when we got off Rick went over to the girl behind the desk and spoke with her quietly. There were smiles. She picked up a phone, spoke, nodded and pointed toward a set of huge wooden doors. Rick went right in. I started to follow him, but she stopped me.
"I'm with him," I whined.
"Have a seat," she said sternly. I sat.
I waited for what seemed like a very long time.

When Rick came out, forty minutes later, he told me he'd be writing a piece for Rolling Stone.
It's really that simple.

I remember being a surprised that Jann Wenner didn't personally carry Rick out in his arms.

WEANER (I don't know... maybe 1976 or so)

Sometime after midnight, after the TV proved itself to be utterly useless once again—we didn't really need anything for $19.95, let alone two—I leaned back and tugged on my lower lip, lost in idiotic thought. My wife was stretched out beside me, lovely, at peace, book in hand, cat in lap, irretrievably immersed in the South Pacific musings of some guy named Horwitz. I don't know what made me think of him, but I found myself saying out loud, "I wonder whatever happened to Weaner."
My lovely wife, drawn to the surface by this statement, asked softly, "Who?"
"Weaner; Peter's cousin. I never told you about Weaner before?"

She looked up from the book. Good wife that she is, she preferred my mindless musings to the award-winning nautical prose of Horwitz. The cat looked at me disapprovingly; he demanded an explanation for this completely uncalled-for disturbance. I ignored him (if an exaggerated sneer qualifies as ignoring someone).

"Weaner showed up out here from Wisconsin a couple years after Peter moved out..." I began.
"Why do you call him Weaner?" she asked.
"*They* called him Weaner. I don't know if I ever called him anything. If I did it was probably by his name, which I forget. Jerry, I think. Anyway, I seem to recall Peter telling me that a weaner is the runt in a litter of pigs. The little guy's a weaner. I'm sure there's more to it than that."
"But, a wiener is a sausage, isn't it?"

My wife is French, well educated, well-traveled, well read, and impressively informed on a wide range of topics. In stark contrast I provide the dismal background by which her brilliance is all the more keenly revealed. But, when opportunity presents itself we add to each other's universality. For example, I know something about the price of common lumber (specifically soft woods) in the mid-1980s in the San Francisco Bay Area; and my expertise concerning the flattest bicycle route between the 5700 block of Geary Boulevard and Golden Gate Park cannot be challenged.

So, she dove into an explanation on the derivation of the word "wiener" which encompassed, as I recall it; Vienna, veal, and vandalism in its purest puerile form—and, in this case the apparent intentional bastardized pronunciation of the Germanic tongues...

"Well, but..." I interrupted, "I don't think Weaner being called weaner has anything to do with sausage directly. I think Weaner was called Weaner because he was so small. You know, Peter comes from a family of giants. Standing on a crate, Weaner might get a good view of the underside of Peter's jaw."

She closed the book (which I considered a compliment), but kept her thumb in place (a slight which I did not overlook); the cat continued to stare at me, awaiting an end to the disruption.
From experience I knew I had, maybe, three minutes.
So, I summarized.
"Weaner came out here, raised on a milk farm in Wisconsin, and declared to all that he was going to go into the real estate business and make a lot of money. Peter, with genuine affection for his young cousin, laughed at such naiveté and said, 'How are you going to get into real estate?'
Weaner didn't have a penny that anyone knew of; he didn't know anybody out here, he knew absolutely nothing about business, and even less about real estate, but—he seemed convinced—that wouldn't stop him.

'Couple months later, we're all invited over to Weaner's place in Oakland for some kind of Sunday brunch, and I'm thinking,

'Poor Weaner, man, prolly livin' in some old run down slum in the sleaziest part of Oakland.' But when we get to the place it's in a nice part of town. VERY nice. And good old Weaner is living on the top floor of this big apartment building.

When we pull in the driveway Peter comes dashing out to the truck, leans into the window and says, "This is Weaner's place!"
I say, "It looks like Weaner found himself a nice place."
Peter says "No. Weaner OWNS this place. He owns this entire building!" Peter's got a big grin on his face like he's just been slapped silly.
"Weaner **OWNS** this place?" I say.
Without lookin' in the mirror, I'm pretty sure that I look like someone who's just been slapped silly.
I look at Mary, and *she* looks like… (you know.)

Maybe a year later—not more—and NOW Weaner owns several buildings in Oakland. He's driving whatever car he wants—and apparently he wants a big flashy one—he's putting in about three hours each day in his thirty-third floor downtown office; he has gold rings on every finger, he's wearing fine Italian wool suits, his shoes are custom made. Somewhere along in there he's also married an ice-cold, reasonably foreboding, semi-unattractive foreign chick.

In the blink of an eye they have a kid and they're working on another. That's the last I ever heard of Weaner."
My wife returned quietly to her book, and the cat returned quietly to licking his whiskers, and I got up and walked out of the room.

When I returned, after tearing off a little 20 minute, ad-lib, bathtub style blues on my ukulele, my wife looked up and said, "Maybe the wife had something to do with it."

"Something?!" I exclaimed. "She had EVERYTHING to do with it. As far as I can figure it, Weaner married into the mob."

But, you know it really doesn't matter; however he did it, you gotta give good old Weaner credit. He came out here, saying he was going to get rich in the real estate business, and he did.

Me, I always wanted to write a bunch of books that nobody would ever read and, so far, I'm still on track.

HOW to make a little EXTRA CASH in the PIZZA Business
(1982)

George owned the pizza place I swept and mopped every day,
seven days a week, for seven years. I did some yard work one
day for his mother. She had a really nice place down on the
Marina, overlooking the yacht club.

On that morning, George said to me, "Would you like to make a
little extra cash?"
And I thought, 'Actually I would, because the guy I'm working
for doesn't pay me very well', so I said, "Sure, I could use a little
extra cash, George."
George said, "Soon as you're finished here, I'll take you over to
my mother's house, you can yank some weeds in the back yard,
and she'll pay you cash."
I said, "How much are we talking?" and he named the same rate
I was getting from him. So, I said, "Usually gardeners get paid A
LOT better than that, George."
He said, "Do you want the job or not?"
And I thought, 'What is it that makes rich bastards so stingy?'
Then, realizing the answer was embedded in the question, I said,
"Sure, I could use a little extra cash."

So, we arrive at her extraordinarily nice place down at the
Marina, overlooking the yacht club, and we go up the steps and
we go inside. George says to me, "Wait here," and leaves me
standing in the hallway.

I look around at the heavily ornate, deeply carved and gilded,
furniture. It's all covered in clear plastic. The couch, the chairs,
the lampshades, the tables; they're all covered in thick clear
plastic. After waiting for George for a very long time, I step into
the room and perch tenderly, cautiously, upon the very edge of
the seat of one of these plastic covered, ornately carved chairs.

George comes out after a bit and lets out a yelp. He rushes over to me and whispers, "What are you doing?! Mother of God. Get up, get up; get out of there. If my mother comes in and sees you sitting on that chair... Ma-rone."

I think he said Ma-rone. I don't even know what Ma-rone means, if in fact he did say Ma-rone. If he didn't say Marone, I have no idea what he actually said, but It sounded like Ma-rone. Whatever he said, I certainly understood the message; I stood up immediately. To this day, if I'm sitting down and someone walks in and says Marone, I pop right up to my feet.

"She wants to meet you," he said and. after carefully readjusting the nap on the carpet wherever my footsteps remained, he lead me down a carpeted hallway and into a dining room with similarly ornate chairs, tables, and cabinets holding crystal and porcelain of every conceivable vulgar stupid sort (cupids and swans, and strangely draped, semi-nude women with their palms raised as if startled by the voice of god.) There, with her back to me, sat his mother.

The table she sat before was stacked with cash and restaurant receipts—some in stacks with rubber bands around them, some free, some in fresh new, unused pads—accounting books, coins, checks, an adding machine, and—to my great surprise—a cash register. It looked just like the one George had in his restaurant.

While George and I waited in silence, she looked through a stack of receipts, extracted one, picked up a book of blank receipts, flipped through it until she came to one that she liked, held it up next to the other, and after entering some numbers into the adding machine, started writing upon the receipt. After that was done, she tore up one of the receipts and dropped it into a paper bag, placed the other one on top of a stack of receipts, and rung up the cash register.

When she turned in her chair and looked at me, I got the idea that she didn't really like what she was seeing. She questioned George in Italian and, from his tone, I deduced that he was apologizing for my unfortunate presence in their lives. She smiled a genuine phony smile, nodded at me and waved us both away with a back-handed kind of regal disgust.

George took me out back onto a small porch overlooking the backyard, from high above. "She wants you to tear out all these weeds," he said, making a sweeping motion. "Just the weeds; she wants it to look nice back here. I'll be back in about an hour or so." George then disappeared.

So, I went down and started tearing out weeds wherever I found them. Some of them were pretty gangly and tough and sorta reedy and just plain ugly. The ugliest ones were also the hardest to pull because they were all intertwined. This particular weed had gone completely wild back there. It filled up an entire corner of the yard, but I managed to get most of it yanked and tossed into a big pile by the time George's mother appeared, like the Pope, on the porch above me.

By that time, I must have had a pile of weeds about 6 feet in diameter and two or three feet deep. As she looked down upon my good work I stood there smiling up at her with one foot on that pile of weeds, sweaty and proud. I waved a gloved hand, gesturing at my accomplishment. She gazed down upon me with lofty disdain for a while, then her eyes bugged out, her mouth dropped open, and she screamed, "My God, he tore up the oregano!"

She screamed again, "My God, he tore up the oregano!" She screamed a third time—but this time in Italian—and George appeared instantly at her side.

"My God, he tore up all my oregano!" she screamed at George. Then she pointed down at me—the only person around—and said, "I want him fired.

George spoke calmingly to her in Italian and followed her back into the house, where I could hear additional argument and screaming. It went on for quite a while.

On the way back to his restaurant, George and I got into a little argument ourselves, over whether or not he was going to pay me for pulling up all his mother's oregano. And it ended, 40 minutes later, with him pulling a huge wad of cash out of his front pocket, peeling off a couple bills and throwing them at me.
He said, "Don't EVER tell ANYBODY I paid you."

I said, "Who'm I gonna tell, George?"

RELATIVE SUCCESS (2000)

By anyone's standards my wife's father is a success. He came
here from France, a humble school teacher, and ended up the
owner of a fine hotel in one of the most coveted cities in the
world. By contrast I guess you might say that I am un-successful.

By the time he was 50, my wife's father owned a hotel. By the
time I was 50, I worked for a man who owned a hotel.

He worked THIRTY years to get where he is today. It was not
easy; he worked long and hard and put in his time. Of course,
during those same years I worked as well. I worked long and I
worked hard, and I put in my time. It's not as if during those
thirty years—while my wife's father was working to attain his
success—I was laying around on an old couch in my underwear,
with a cat at rest on my belly, eating Doritos, drinking beer,
belching, and dozing intermittently while watching daytime soap
operas.
(Though, admittedly, some time was spent in that manner.)

So, while my wife's father was busy working and slaving away,
I too was busy working and slaving away.
I just took a different path.

While my wife's father was fixing the wiring in a room, in the
hotel which he did not yet own, I was busy fixing broken
windows in apartment buildings that I would never own.

Later on, while my wife's father was being asked if he might be
interested in managing the hotel which he did not yet own, I was
being asked if I could fix more broken windows in apartment
houses which I would never own.

And when the owner of the hotel, which my wife's father would inevitably own, died and left the building to a careless drunk of a son who had no interest whatsoever in running a hotel, that careless drunk asked my wife's father if he would like to buy the place. Meanwhile, on the other side of town, the guy I was working for did not die, he continued living. And, when the time came, he planned to pass his property on to a son who was not a drunk and who was very much interested in retaining all his property; a guy who would, in turn, ask me if I was still in the business of fixing broken windows. And, I probably would be; I'd have to do something with the time I was wasting not buying unwanted hotels.

Sure, I should probably have owned a hotel at some point in my life, and I would have too had I not squandered all those years working for a man whose son wished to possess property instead of a man whose son wished only to rid himself of it.
Looking back now, I can see that was my mistake.
(Though admittedly, it was difficult to see that at the moment.)

All that aside, my wife's parents not only managed to turn a run-down old residential hotel into a lovely, inviting, and unique little place to stay, they also managed to do something that perhaps every hourly wage earner on earth has dreamed of doing—something rarely attained by anyone other than in the movies—after working in that hotel for many years, they bought the place.

By anyone's standards, that's success.

HOWARD and the BICYCLE (1969 or so)

A reasonable percentage of our little college-based community was, quite naturally, or so I thought back then, drug dealers. In fact, I can't honestly really recall anyone who didn't deal in drugs on one level or another, at one time or another, advertently or otherwise.

To find someone who hadn't handled drugs in our district would be like trying to find an American male who had never driven drunk... or a tap-dancing dodo who could sing Suwanee River backwards. But, let me quickly state unequivocally here that any drug dealer named LeVeau who may have owned a building on the corner of Grove Avenue and Harrison Street in 1968, along with other buildings throughout the Fan District, and who had a truly lovely wife named Evelyn, who walked a borzoi under the sheltering trees that year, and the following year pushed a baby carriage along that same idyllic daily route, is strictly a figment of my imagination. Amid all the weighty truth that occupies these pages, this character alone is pure invention; he's made up entirely; he never existed.

However, let us pretend that someone named Dealer did exist and he lived like a millionaire, which I suppose, if he did exist, he would have. And, let us pretend that I went to his house—an antebellum palace in the highly respectable Monument Avenue neighborhood, with a great little carriage house out back—one time. You'd probably think that every room in that house was replete with fine stuff; elegant stuff, expensive stuff, all gilded, hand-carved exotic hardwood, marble or crystal, or cast bronze. And you'd be right,

I did actually go to such a carriage house one time, by way of the alley, to drop something off. And it was there that I realized how very much some drug dealers love their possessions.

That was immediately clear, even to the casual, untrained, disinterested, somewhat nervous eye. There was no doubt about it. Opulence is the word I suppose.

Furniture, paintings, statuary of every size, shape and medium, and every electronic device known to man were on display in that place. Oh, did I mention handguns? The man also seemed to have a fondness for handguns. They were laying around on occasional surfaces—tables, mantels, shelves—wherever the wandering eye might wander. For me—who had neither possessions nor guns of any sort, and had no desire for either—all of this seemed very strange. As a college kid, who had to save for a week in order to buy himself a carrot to gnaw on, the carelessness with cash also struck me as a bit peculiar.

In those days I always knew, as I do today, almost precisely how much, or how little, money I had on me. From looking around this man's place I could see that he had NO idea how much cash he had. Piles of it were everywhere. For a guy whose regular acquaintances stole waitresses' tips in the 24 hour diner at 3 AM, in order to treat themselves to an order of toast—this disregard for money was incomprehensible. The thought, "Why don't you just take some?" stumbled around a bit giddily in my mind before I rejected the thought.
"Go ahead, just grab a fistful! He'll never miss it."

So, that's the (completely fictitious) guy, Dealer LeVeau. He liked his possessions; he liked his guns, he liked his women—his wife was a trim statuesque, silent, dark-eyed beauty worthy of Monaco, and his mistress (the one I slept with one Summer afternoon while he was playing softball with his lieutenants) was a pornographic fantasy come to life. He liked them both. He also liked real estate; besides his elegant home with the little carriage house where his couriers collected their goods and brought back the cash, he had several apartment buildings in the Fan District.

314

Howard rented an apartment in the one across the street from where I lived. So, now we've come full circle.

On a nice crisp fall day, with leaves from overhanging trees falling gently to the cobblestone street below, I walked outside, and there, in the middle of Grove Avenue was Howard, whom I knew, and Dealer LeVeau, whom I knew of, but had never met. Between them was what anyone would recognize as a bicycle. It had the shape of a bicycle, however, it was unlike any bicycle I'd ever seen. The frame of the thing was much thinner than what you might expect, the tires looked like they'd been extruded from the same device that makes erasers for the ends of pencils, the seat was like a straight razor enshrouded in old leather, and the handlebars consisted of a single straight tube wrapped in shiny white fabric.

I like bicycles. I love bicycles. I think bicycles are one of the cleverest and just plain wonderful things that man has ever invented. They're fun too; a good bicycle will introduce its rider to flight. So, naturally, I was drawn to these two guys standing around in the middle of the street with this peculiar-looking, emaciated machine.
"Wow, that's a pretty nice bike, Howard."
"It's Dealer's."
"You just get it?" I asked LeVeau.
"Cost six thousand dollars," said LeVeau with indifference.
I gulped. "Six THOUSAND DOLLARS?"

In those days I was making something like…well we've been through that already. Telling me that bike cost six thousand dollars was about the same as saying it had cost six million, or six trillion. Six thousand dollars was about what it cost me to go to school for the year; food housing, tuition, supplies, books, all in. Howard said, "Lift it." I did.
"Wow. It must only weigh ten pounds," I said with admiration.

"Seven," said LeVeau, and muttered the precise equivalent in kilograms.

"Wow."

"Bring it by when you're done screwin' around with it, Howard," said LeVeau as he turned, and walked off. He went straight into the building on the corner, just as if he owned the damned place—which he did.

"Watch this," said Howard and he mounted the bike and gave the sprocket half a crank.

Howard took off, floating rapidly down Grove Avenue. He drifted sweetly, smoothly, swiftly for two long, tree-covered blocks. Then, he put his feet down and dragged them along the pavement. He turned the bike around got situated, gave the thing another half crank and it came gliding toward me like downhill on ice. It was lovely to witness. Howard was grinning like a maniac as he started dragging his feet, soles flat and yelling, "Stop me. Stop me. Get in front of me!"

"Use the brakes! Use the brakes!" I yelled.

When I threw myself in front of him to keep him from going into the intersection, the impact almost knocked me down.

"Why didn't you brake? What wrong with the brakes?"

"It has no brakes."

"No brakes? Six thousand dollars and it has no brakes?"

"It's a track bike, it doesn't need brakes. It's made to go; it's not made to stop."

I hadn't noticed that it had no brakes. I HAD noticed that the tires were tiny. And I HAD noticed that the seat looked painful. I couldn't get over it. "No brakes?" I said. "It cost SIX THOUsand dollars and it's got no brakes?"

"It's not made to stop," Howard repeated, "it's made to go."

"Where are the shifters?"

"It only has one gear," said Howard proudly.

"No brakes, one speed… This thing is absurd."

"You want to try it?"

"ABSO-lutely!" I climbed right on.

"OK. Listen," cautioned Howard, "Don't give it more than one half crank or you won't be able to stop. I'm serious; one half crank."

"OK," I promised.

That razor sharp seat was every bit as uncomfortable as it looked, but I was anxious to see what a six thousand dollar track bike with one gear and no brakes could do. Howard let loose of the handlebars and I smiled an evil smile. "So-long, Howard," I said and cranked that goddamned pedal smartly.

Instantly, I found myself in a dream world with the parked cars and trees and buildings on Grove Avenue slipping quietly behind me. There goes a dog. There go some passersby. The only sound I could hear was the wind in my ears and the high-pitched whirr of the spokes. It was like riding something shot out of a cannon.

Rapidly approaching the intersection at Lombardi—where there was bound to be cross traffic—I started emergency stopping measures. Now I knew why Howard started dragging his feet so soon; the damned thing didn't want to stop. You'd think that a machine weighing seven pounds would be easy to stop, but it was tricky simply because it was so light. The damned thing was skittish. Anything less than perfectly-balanced resistance applied equally on both sides and that bike took off in a new direction. I started swooping in large switchbacks to control this tendency, but that only seemed to make it take on speed; the thing was built to take turns practically lying down. In essence, I was riding on a six thousand dollar gyroscope. It was bullheaded and high-strung and frightening. The only thing I could do, while wobbling wildly out of control, was to straddle the cross bar and thrust my feet straight out in front of me, while praying.

We came to a sudden catastrophic stop when one of my big stupid feet caught on the pavement and turned under, nearly ripping my foot off in the process. The six thousand dollar bike went flying into the air; I was heading face first toward the pavement...

The acrobatic maneuver that followed cannot be described, as I, with one hand still on the handlebar, landed flat on my back, carried the bike in a large arc over my head and somehow managed to bring it bouncing to earth, upright, without any harm. Had I practiced the maneuver every day for a thousand years I never could have duplicated that move. It was like something out of a cartoon.

I looked back down Grove Avenue, but, thankfully, Howard was nowhere in sight. Quickly I got to my feet, and while shaking from head to toe, straddled the bike just as though nothing had happened; just as though I had not almost destroyed some drug dealer's six thousand dollar track bike; just as if I hadn't almost killed myself, nearly ripped my foot off, and twisted my arm in my efforts to save the damned thing.

I stood there panting for a bit, thinking about what kind of trouble I might have been in if I had destroyed Dealer LeVeau's bike. I was gibbering out loud, trying to convince myself that everything was alright. I put on my very best phony smile, pointed the bike down the center of Grove Avenue, and I gave it a tender, gentle little crank, the slightest little crank, a nudge, nothing more, and began drifting slowly homeward.

In seconds I was back where I'd started and Howard was running beside me to keep me from coasting into cross traffic.
He was laughing hysterically. I was still pretty giddy myself. He had no idea what had just transpired.
"Where'd you go, man?"

"I just went down to Lombardi."
I got off the bike and let Howard hold it up; my knees were wobbling.
"I thought you'd decided to take it for a ride or something."
"Nope, just down to Lombardi."
"It's pretty nice, isn't it?"
"Yep."
"It's amazing isn't it?"
"Yep."
"This could be yours, Richard, if you only got off your artistic ass and started peddling smack!" Howard laughed loudly.
"Six thousand dollars, Howard," I reminded him.
"Amazing huh?"
"For six THOUSAND dollars, Howard, it ought to be amazing."
Howard was laughing as he lifted the bike and carried it away.

As he carried that thing into the building, I was thinking, "Six thousand dollars for god's sake. One speed. No brakes. Tiny little macaroni tires. A seat like a razor blade. My ass is already sore. It's belligerent, it's skittish, it's impossible to control. The damned thing is completely unpredictable and extremely dangerous and …six thousand DOLLARS!" I snorted. "For god's sake."

Still, I thought, "Flies like a bird… …worth every penny."

CLASS and WEALTH in AMERICA,
as I know it

CELIA

One rainy afternoon, near the end of September 1967, I found myself crouching behind a stone retaining wall at the corner of Harrison Street and West Franklin in Richmond, Virginia. I was a freshman in college—had been there about two months at the time. Through the drizzle I watched as a man, short and broad, in a very black, nicely made suit, carried cardboard boxes down a slippery brick pathway to the open trunk of a large old Rolls Royce. Behind him, following slowly, head down as if in mourning, was a college girl I recognized. He placed the boxes in the trunk, opened the back door for her (I expected to see a little bow, but there was none), closed the trunk as he went around, brushed his gloved hands together, slid in behind the wheel and drove off smartly.

There was something very sad about this ceremony; maybe it was the rain, the girl's demeanor, the way the huge shiny car disappeared in silence down the street.

I stood up. I didn't know quite what it all meant, but, once I was sure they were truly gone, I emboldened myself to walk around the corner and up that same slippery brick pathway to the apartment door where it lead. I knocked. A girl I'd never seen before came to the door. "Is Celia here?"
"Nope. Are you Richard?"
"Yeah..."
"This is for you."

She handed me a tasteful envelope. I tore it open and took out the tasteful note within, and read these words: "I will never forget you. I will always love you. Celia"
"She's gone?" I asked while folding the thing and shoving it into the back pocket of my jeans.

"Yeah," sighed the girl, perfectly bored. "She's rich, and now she's gone." She started to shut the door, but I put up a hand to prevent it.

"Is she coming back?" I had to ask. I had to know.

"I hope not."

"What happened?"

"Her house burned down." The girl sounded burdened but, at the same time, just a shade elated to convey the news. She put the back of one hand to her brow and tilted her head back and fluttered her eyelids like a heroine in a silent film. "Celia's tragedy," she said, "Tra-la-la-la-la."

"Her house burned down?"

"Right to the ground. Her brother's in the hospital," she said leaning one hip against the edge of the door.

"Is he OK? I mean, I don't know the guy but..."

She sighed. "I think he's OK. It's the house they're upset over."

"But, Celia—she's not coming back?" I needed to hear it again.

"Well, she took all her stuff, what does that tell you?"

"Wow," I said.

"Yeah, bummer, now they all have to fly off and live in their place in Europe somewhere until their humble mansion in Alexandria can be restored to its former glory."

"Wow," I said again.

"Yeah, wow," she said and closed the door.

Apparently, Celia came from money; although, to her credit, there had never been any blatant indicators. She simply enjoyed the pleasure of my stammering company.

SLIM AND THE ROYCES

Slim and I were standing on a grass covered hill in the shade of some hickory trees. It was a large park miles away from the little triangle park where he usually hung out. And, it was morning. So, it was unusual in that as well; Slim was a night kinda guy. There was a slight breeze and I could smell ten thousand years of grime and sweat wafting off good old Slim.
"Shhh," he commanded suddenly. "What do you hear?"
 I listened. "I don't hear anything."
"Listen again."
I listened. "All I hear is the breeze through the trees."
"Listen HARD," he urged.

I leaned forward a bit—indicating that I was listening hard—and I did hear something. I heard the soft crunch of big rubber tires rolling slowly over the hot summer pavement of the lane that curled around through the hillocks of the park.
"I hear tires," I said.
"Ha!" declared Slim with delight, and he slapped me on the shoulder. "Here come the Royces!"
I looked at him and, through all the accumulated grime, he looked like a kid... a badly shaven, smelly old kid layered in tattered overcoats.

The night before Slim had asked me, "You want to see something wonderful like you ain't never seen before?" and I'd answered yes. Then, he said, "I'll provide the transportation."

So; we'd gotten to that park, that morning, in the back of a newspaper truck. The driver, who knew Slim somehow, had given us both a hand up into the bed, where we sat with our backs propped against tall unsteady stacks of old newspapers. When we jumped out again, at the park, something maybe not quite right occurred.

Instead of us paying the driver for his services, the driver paid us; he gave Slim a dollar bill, then said, "I'll swing by to pick you up, after I dump this load… 'bout an hour or so."

So there we were, standing on that hill, under what Slim said were hickory trees. We'd been watching a bend in the road below as perfectly restored old automobiles; Packards and Hudsons, LaSalles and Desotos, Model Ts and Stanley Steamers, hove into view. They seemed to arrive in herds. And, we knew when a fresh herd was about arrive by their engine sounds, the hissing and clattering and gurgling as they chugged and belched and fffft-fffffted their way by. They were each on their way to a spot down the road where they would be carefully parked, tenderly washed, lovingly dried, gently polished, doted upon from a respectful distance, and, ultimately judged for perfection.

But, when the Royces came into view Slim asked, "You hear any engine sound?"
I leaned forward. "Nope."
"You hear any muffler?"
I cupped an ear.
"Nope." I said, though I thought I could hear a soft muffle.
Slim was grinning. "Ex-ackerly. Can't hear that engine turn over. They got a light on the dash to tell the driver when the engine has started. I love them Royces."
As a long line of Rolls Royces drifted by below and floated silently away, Slim's eyes were sparkling with childlike delight.

While we walked down the slope toward where all those vehicles were headed, Slim told me a little history of the Rolls Royce and why he, "and everyone who knew anything at all about such" called them Royces. Apparently (according to Slim) Royce was the engineer behind these magnificent machines—the guy who set the incredibly tight, almost unattainable tolerances on every aspect of the design, manufacture and assembly of the vehicles.

Royce was the guy who demanded a hand-hammered body and ensured that each part was flawless when checked by blindfolded perfectionists; he was the guy who insisted that thirty two thousand hand-rubbed coats of clear lacquer be applied on top of 640 coats of unique, custom blended, hand-mixed color; the guy who oversaw the selection and handling of perfectly matched leathers for the interior—which would then be hand-stitched by pre-pubescent virgins who'd eaten only flax seed and lamb's ear since age seven, each a direct descendant of Queen Clothilde. Rolls was only the money man.

When we entered the grove where all the cars were being placed side by side, Slim smiled and slapped me on the shoulder. "Heaven," he said; and I agreed.

What Slim didn't know is that I'd been a fan of Rolls Royce for years. I'd read a book or two, of course; but more importantly, while in high school, I once made a pilgrimage to a town some thirty miles away to look at, admire, and actually sit behind the wheel of a 1967 Corniche. So, yeah, I had to agree with Slim; it certainly had the appearance of Heaven. I loved the look of all these old cars and I liked the idea that people had gone to the effort and expense to restore and maintain them. Slim and I both began to run (each in our own way) directly toward the Royces… and he actually beat me to them.

There were maybe eight, maybe a dozen Rolls Royces of different years and models, half with red logos. Slim came to a stop in front of the first of these.
"Mr. Royce himself built this car!" he declared wide-eyed. "Look at that, Charlie.[Slim always called me Charlie, for reasons which cannot be explained.] Royce built that car! He adjusted the bolt heads on the valve covers himself."
Once again I looked at Slim and saw a little kid—a smelly, grease-encrusted little kid, with missing teeth and pink eye.

"Can we see the engine, Mister?" Slim asked the owner eagerly.

"Step back," snapped the guy, "And don't touch anything."

"Hey,…" I started to say, but Slim quickly put one hand on each of my shoulders and turned me aside. He put his finger to his lips. "Shhhh," he said, "It's OK."

The gentleman folded back the top of the engine compartment gingerly and Slim, placing his hands respectfully behind his back, leaned in to have a look. He just stood there looking at the engine for a very long time, with the owner hovering anxiously beside him, and me eyeing the owner. I was seething. Finally Slim straightened up, grinning and said, "You ever see anything quite like that before, Charlie?" He took one final look and began to lead me away with firmness.

I swung around to see the owner of the vehicle already buffing out the spot where Slim's breath might have tarnished the surface of his possession. I broke away from Slim and went back. I went right up to the guy. He was about my height, about my father's age, slightly balding, dressed like a golfer, with a Rolls Royce emblem embroidered on his pale yellow knit shirt. I looked him in the eye and I said, "You're an asshole."

He smiled smugly, as only the very rich can, snorted and said, "And that's what you think." (The rich are never appalled by their own shameful behavior, no matter how shameful.)

"Yes," I said. "That's what I think."

He smirked and, shaking his head, turned his back on me.

By this time Slim was leading me away by the elbow again and the crowd—good people who only wanted to look as some fine automobiles without the riff-raff disrupting an otherwise pleasant afternoon—parted before us like the Red Sea. We must have made quite a frightening pair, the insane old wino and the clearly deranged, sputtering hippie.

326

We walked back down the road and up over the hill where we'd watched the cars arrive earlier, to the edge of the park, to await our ride home in the back of a newspaper truck.

We sat on the edge of the curb while waiting, me sullen and still seething, Slim poking at the pavement with a twig he'd picked up. "So, what did you think?" he asked.
"I told that guy exactly what I thought," I snapped.
"What did you think of that engine?"
"Built by a genius, restored by an asshole," I smoldered.
That was precisely how I felt about that man. From this distance, I have to wonder how much my grandmother's admonition—Say what you mean and mean what you say—had to do with it.

"Charlie," said Slim, "If I didn't know you better, I'd a thought I didn't know you at all." It was a sentiment many women would later share. I was still fuming, but I laughed.
"I've never used that word before in my life," I confessed.
"An' here you've gone and used it twice in one day," he said.
"Honestly. I've never uttered that word before in my life."
"Still," he shrugged, "you delivered it like a licensed professional."

I DOUBLE (1970)

I think it must have been Rick who introduced me to the
daughter of the guy who owned the largest collection of
contemporary sculpture in the world... which was a mistake. (It
was just the first of many.)

Before she arrived, I put in a stock of White Horse scotch
because I'd been told she drank scotch. I had 3 bottles proudly
displayed, neatly lined up on my buffet when she arrived.
"What's this?"
"Scotch. For you (my love). I heard that you drink scotch."
"This? I wouldn't drink this stuff."
"Oh. Uh...What..?"
"Chivas or better," she said flatly.
 "Well, gee, I spent every penny I had on this stuff."
"I'll buy the scotch, just don't expect me to drink this." She eyed
the label with disdain.

That was my mistake.
Her mistake was telling me that she could make me the next
Larry Poons.
"It is literally within my grasp to make you famous," she assured
me. "I could do that. I could make you the next Larry Poons."
She meant it too. She rattled off the names of all the people she
knew who would have a hand in making me the next Larry
Poons: gallery owners and patrons and art critics. They were all
her friends and all positioned nicely in the Fine Art world. Oh,
and, of course she also knew the writers who regularly contrived
the overly-oblique, laughably absurd, pseudo-intellectual
justification for every act any artist of their choosing might
commit. There was no doubt about it; she was the right chick in
the right place to make all my little painterly dreams come true.
And it made me sick; sicker than she would have been had she
stooped to sip a little tin cup of White Horse.

Of course, her response to being offered cheap scotch was nothing compared to my most high umbrage at being offered a lift up into a high position in the world of contemporary Art. I was disgusted to think that, through her connections, she could make any artist she chose—in this case, me—the next big New York success story.

"I want to make it because my work speaks to the viewer," I whined.

"What?" she laughed crassly, and almost collapsed under the monumental absurdity of that statement. I can still feel her hand on my arm as she reached out to steady herself, to keep from falling down. "What are you talking about? Painting doesn't have ANYthing to do with that!" she said. She looked at me carefully to see if I was serious, and when she discovered that I was, she burst into laughter again.

"If that's the way it's done, I want nothing to do with it," I declared, chin up, eyes cast toward heaven, from which I receive my motivation, my inspiration, every kick in my teeth, my failure, my disgrace, my embarrassment.

"Fine," she said, "I'll make some other guy the next Larry Poons." It didn't really matter to her.

OK, so that was settled.

One day, about 6 months later, we—Rick and Ginger and I—found ourselves in New York City, and sleeping in this same young woman's apartment on Central Park West. I'd gotten up late and everyone else had departed for the day, leaving me alone with a guy who claimed to be a Persian Prince. He told me how his lineage went all the way back to Nebuchadnezzar, or someone like that, and how the great Assyrian lions that we see in our history books, carved deeply into the stone walls of ancient buildings in and around the Tigris-Euphrates valley, are part of his family logo and how, when he pisses it drifts, in lyrical script, slowly upward into the atmosphere until it forms an umbrella of pure crystalline droplets under which all god's creatures are protected from harm, and did I want to play a little backgammon?

I told him I didn't know anything about backgammon. He said that was OK, he could teach me. I told him I didn't really want to learn and I didn't care to play, and so the game began.

What the heck, why not? I was stuck there with this Persian prince until something better, or less arrogant, came along, and so I rolled the dice and moved some pieces about the board. The only thing of note that I can recall is that periodically he would chortle and declare, "I DOUBLE!" then he would take a cube, which sat unused in the middle of the board, and served no purpose that I could see, and turned it. Then, for a while, he would glare at me meaningfully.
But, I remained completely indifferent.

The game went like this. I rolled the dice and moved, he rolled the dice, declared loudly, "I DOUBLE!" laughed snidely, and moved. Eventually he declared himself the winner and I congratulated him and got up to go find myself a beer.

At this point the Persian prince became cantankerous, stood up, put a hand on me and demanded, "Where are you going, my friend?"
"I don't feel like playing anymore." I told him. "I think I'll go try to find something to drink."
"You are not going anywhere, my good friend," he said, "You owe me $34,000."
I laughed heartily. "What? What the heck are you talking about?"
"You have lost this game and you now owe me $34000, American."

"Yeah?" I told him. "That's funny for two reasons. The first is that I don't HAVE $34,000, and the second is, if I DID have $34,000 I wouldn't give it to you."

Even if there was more royal blood in his piss than in my entire extended family, the guy was wildly misinformed about the nature of reality and, on top of that, he was a jerk. He glared at me for a while, which I admit was pretty frightening—he had the moist dark eyes of an arrogant, young, irate Persian prince—and he told me that it was a matter of honor, and that he would pursue me to the ends of the earth until I paid off this sacred debt. "This is a matter of honor!" he said repeatedly.
And he meant it. To him the $34,000 was real; the debt was real; the game was real, the threat was real; I was real.
I had my doubts about all of it.
"I'll tell you what," I said, "if what's-her-name makes me the next Larry Poons, I'll give you one of my paintings."

I don't recall much more about this event except that when Rick and Ginger finally showed up again I grabbed Rick, took him quickly aside, and whispered, "We gotta get out of this place right now, right this minute, immediately. That Persian prince moron thinks I owe him $34,000 and it's a matter of honor."

Rick understood perfectly, and we left New York that very evening. Of course, I'd like to say that since that time I've gone on to become very very wealthy, and occasionally, in honor of that Persian prince, I take $34,000 in cash and flush it, with great ceremony, down the toilet.
That's what I'd like to say.

And if it were true, I would.

FERRARIS in DUBAI (2018)

Three guys from Dubai and I were in one of those airport shuttles, on our way into San Francisco—this one had been serviced about the same time Adam awoke with a rib missing. The gentlemen from Dubai were dressed something like 1970s tennis stars, while off the court. They told me that they were here to find out what they could in order to corner the market in cell phones back home in Dubai—which I found interesting because, with no knowledge whatsoever about either that technology or the country of Dubai, I felt like they were, just maybe, getting into the cell phone game a little late.

The driver, who spoke broken English with an accent I didn't recognize, asked the boys from Dubai where they were headed. They named a place down the hill from where I reside, and that driver erupted into effervescence. "OH, man!" he gushed, "They always got so many Ferraris and fancy cars parked there, at that hotel. Are you sheiks?"

The Dubai guys said something among themselves—which I guessed meant, "Yeah, in Dubai all us sheiks ride around in smelly old vans with rusty mufflers and bad shocks!" One of them added something which I assumed was, "I'll bet you $100,000 this kid mentions Maserati in the next 30 seconds", and they all laughed.
"What kind of car do you drive?" the driver asked no one in particular. "I bet you all drive Ferraris, no? Maserati?"
The Dubai guys said something among themselves again, and laughed heartily.

The driver turned to me. "What kind of car do you drive?"
"Well," I replied, "I have the most common car in San Francisco; in most parts of the world they're used as taxis."
The driver switched his attention back to the guys from Dubai.

"And tell me," he said with childish eagerness, while looking at them in his rearview mirror, "DO you drive a Ferrari?"

The Dubai guys laughed and one of them said, "I will tell you something, my friend; a story." And then, he said something like this: We know a man—a guy—he had just arrived in Dubai, you see. He had a new Ferrari. And he thought his new Ferrari was *very* impressive; he was very proud of this car. When he went for his first big important job interview in Dubai, he drove right up to the front door of the building in his new important Ferrari, and the doorman came running out and shouted at him to go away. He was *very* angry. "No-no, go away, go away!"
"But, I am here for my first big important interview!" he said.
"NO," said the doorman, "NO. You cannot park here. You are making a big mistake." He explained to that man, "They will not even speak to you if they see you arrive in such a car."
He told him to go around and park in back of the building.
In back, he saw all the parking spaces, in all directions,
all over, far as a man's eyes could see,
EVERY SPACE, every one of them,
was parked a Lamborghini.
Believe me, no man in Dubai—no successful business-man in Dubai—would go to an important interview in a Ferrari."

When we arrived at their hotel, the guys from Dubai jumped right out. One of them gave the driver a tip and said something, which I didn't hear but I assume was, "Here you go; buy yourself a Ferrari." Then, laughing and patting each other on the back, they headed toward the front door, where a doorman awaited them, with a smile.

They didn't even seem to notice the Ferraris parked out front.

EDUCATION in AMERICA,
as I know it

BULLYING, BOREDOM and DINOSAURS (1954)

I asked my father—who was 90 at the time—what he thought of all this talk about bullying. He laughed and said, "When I was a kid we took care of that ourselves."

"Yeah… what'd you do?" I asked.

"When I was little, just starting to go to school, I had a kid bully me…" he said.

"And what did you do?"

"I hit him with half a brick."

"You hit him with a brick?"

"No, I hit him with *half a brick*. I hit him in the back with half a brick, and that put an end to the bullying right there. He didn't want to have anything more to do with me."

"That stopped the bullying?"

"That was the end of it. They called me into the office and said, 'Keith, why did you hit so-an-so with a brick?' and I said, 'I didn't. I hit him with *half a brick*.' They said, 'OK, so why did you hit him with half a brick?' I said, 'Because I'm too little to pick up a whole brick.' And they said, 'Why did you hit him in the back?' And I said, 'I wanted to hit him in the front, but he kept running away.' But, that was the end of the bullying."

"So, you'd recommend that method to the kids today, Dad?"

"Oh, I don't know. All I can say is that it worked for me."

When my wife, at 4 or 5, was being bullied in kindergarten, her father showed her 'how to box', and I've been told that she only had to employ those lessons one time.

As for me, I've never been bullied. But, I did find school itself to be something of that sort. From the first day I set foot in my first grade classroom, until the day I graduated from high school with a B average, I felt like I was being crushed, misunderstood and stripped on my liberty. School was like prison to me.

I distinctly recall those first few hours in first grade; I found myself thinking, 'Why do you keep repeating the same things over and over again? Please, please, please can we just move on.' I also remember making the conscious decision, sometime during that first excruciating year, to drop out. From that point on I monitored all the classroom goings-on while, subsurface, I was anywhere but in that awful, boring, place.

One day the teacher said something that really caught my attention, though. She said, "Today, children, we're going to go to the library." Then she started to explain that, in the library, there were books of every sort; books that covered every subject we could imagine, and my hand shot up. She seemed startled, but called on me nonetheless.
"Do they have books on dinosaurs?" I asked.
"Yes, there are books on dinosaurs in the library."
"How many?'
She laughed, "As many as you might want—on dinosaurs or anything else you might be interested in; AND, you can take them out of the library and take them home with you, if you'd like to do that."
Oh, man, I could hardly believe it; the library sounded like Heaven to me, and I couldn't wait to get there.

Once inside that wonderful place I waited for all the other kids to finish asking the teacher for help before asking her if she would show me where I could find the dinosaur books.

They were on a shelf, under a window—and just as she said, there were many books on dinosaurs there. I started eagerly poring through them, and was totally immersed when she clapped her hands together and said, "OK, it's time to take any books you'd like to take home up to the desk to check them out." I quickly gathered up 6 or 7 big beautiful books on dinosaurs and I lugged them up toward the desk. I couldn't wait to have them.

It seemed like I'd been standing in line a thousand years when it finally came my turn. I stepped forward, and eagerly dropped all those books on the librarian's desk.

She looked at me, scowled, and demanded. "What are you doing?" I was shocked and embarrassed, and I didn't know what to say. I knew from her tone that I had done something wrong, but I had no idea what my offense could have been.

She glared at me as if I was the stupidest child she had ever had to deal with and said, "You can only take out three books at a time. Decide which three you want, and put the other ones back." I felt so humiliated. And, I knew I couldn't face that woman again, so I took them all back, placed them on the shelf, and left the library empty handed.

That was not the first time, and it would not be the last, that a teacher thought I was stupid because I was inward.

After the library incident I disliked school more with each passing year. By the time I was in junior high, it felt like prison.

EVERYTHING I REMEMBER ABOUT HIGH SCHOOL (1964-1967)

My brother was strong, good-looking, and capable of covering 100 yards in 9.8 seconds, and that created a vacuum around him which drew in admirers; my sister was pale and frail, and so soft-spoken that her vulnerability drew people closer, in their desire to protect her. Me, I was skinny, excruciatingly awkward, ugly and repulsive to all.

By the time I hit high school my skin had rebelled so hideously that it made every minute of my life hell. I started out each day looking at my horrible face in the mirror, awash in shame. Of course, going to school was torture. I truly, ardently wished to die. Throughout my high school years my most fervent prayer was, "Please, just let me die."

The single person, in school, who I felt might understand what I was going through, was a weird, dark-haired, artist-chick, who everybody laughed at or ignored. She was so used to indifference and derision that, the one time I spoke to her, she immediately brushed me off. But, I understood; I had those same feelings in me. Not too long after that, she disappeared. It was whispered that she had been found dead, with a needle in her arm, in an abandoned car, in New York City. And, I understood that, too.

The only other kid, in that entire school, who spent any time talking to me, for those years, was Jimmy Hamilton. Without his quiet friendship I would have spent every minute of my day in solitude, cowering in embarrassment.

High school was not the joy for me that it was for some kids. If I was supposed to learn something from the cruelty of my existence, I don't know what it was.

REAL EDUCATION (1963)

For a while there—when I was fourteen perhaps—my mother
was involved in real estate, and many of her clients found it
convenient, in a two-birds-one-stone way, to thank her for her
good work by giving her things they didn't want.

"How would you like this old chair, Elizabeth? I'm sure there
must be good solid, hand-carved walnut concealed here, buried
under all these layers of chipped and blistering old paint!" OR, "I
thought I noticed you admiring the organ that we've abandoned
in our basement…" My mother, out of kindness I suppose,
accepted some of these things; and she proved to have a good
eye; the chair, after some work, did prove to be hand carved
walnut, and the organ brought her many hours and years of
delight, while noodling around on the keyboard.

By this natural redistribution of the world's most cherished
possessions my mother came home one day with an old heavy,
cast iron Remington typewriter. Just as a side note: the good
folks at Remington also made guns… so, by now—having read
what you've read so far—you should have all the ammunition
you need to finish the joke.

Anyway, my mother said to me, "If you can get it out of the
trunk of the car, it's yours."
Get it out of the trunk?! Make way, woman!
For years, I'd been reading Evergreen Review, and Ramparts,
and the Village Voice, and… more shamefully, Playboy (not to
mention Jaguar and Swank) whenever I could get my hands on
my brother's stash. Naturally then, I saw this opportunity as
Providence urging me to get my career as a writer under way.
There was no stick involved. It was all carrot.

As a 14 year-old with ravaged skin, I knew Life to be cruel. I was inward and awkward, and I was ugly. I was excruciatingly shy; shame rode upon my back every minute of every day throughout the school year; embarrassment lived like a perpetual flame within me. So, the world I lived in was full of derision, imagined and otherwise. And—as if that were not enough—because of all that I was frequently thought of as stupid.

That hardly matters, though; what matters is that—thanks to that unkindly mix—I escaped school each afternoon with the welling desire to get home where I could pound out my tortured thoughts on that old typewriter.

In the solitude of my room I read and did my own version of thinking, and lost myself in the fulfilling rhythm of hammering out words. Back then, you really did need to hammer them out… I still have calluses on the tips of my fingers from pounding on those old metal keys. While that was underway, I listened to Charles Aznavour. And though I did not understand a single word warbled by the great French crooner, I was somehow convinced that Monsieur Aznavour would have understood the inner-most yearnings of this skinny, pimple-faced American recluse. So, I wrote… clip-clip-clip… clip clip clip clip… clip clip… clip clip clip… on into the night. I wrote steadily; I wrote tenaciously… doggedly too. The click-clack of that old Remington was ever present in that house, with a brave young lad at the keys. Of course, cold as this fact may be, I probably should admit that I really had nothing better to do. Nobody ever rang out doorbell saying, "Hey do you wanna go…"

At the time, my thinking, in its entirety, was this: I write, therefore, by definition, I am a writer. The blind desire that drove that process added to my conviction. And, you know, I have to confess, that even after all these years, that's still pretty much my thinking; because I write, I must be a writer.

In my defense—before we go any further—let me say that I am not the first human being to foolishly confuse his compulsion with Destiny.

At 16, one glorious day, I opened up one of the magazines I'd been pawing through, and there, prominently displayed in a photograph of Nelson Algren, was the very same model Remington typewriter I'd been pounding away at for two years. So, OK, that nailed things down pretty tightly for me. (Such is the mind of a 16 year-old.)

In the early stages of the infection, the process could probably best be described as 'pumping out piles of purely pretentious crap' and, I'm guessing I knew as much. But that didn't stop me. At that stage of the neurosis, we all glow with the fiery certitude that every word we write is precious, and that it would be both selfish and wrong (in equal parts I imagine) to deprive Posterity enduring insight into our every thought.

Though I didn't realize it, at the time I was an unwitting participant in a loosely organized global-wide effort to disprove the theory that *enough monkeys sitting at enough typewriters, given enough time,* would eventually produce something worth reading. No one, at that time, could have guessed that, forty years down the road, entire generations would voluntarily commit themselves to assiduously pumping out so much purely pretentious crap that it would destroy that theory forever. Nor could anyone have guessed that they'd do it by phone.

But, let me add here quickly that I never once removed my fingers from those keys without reality flooding in through the breach that act created. By that I mean: I never resurfaced from total immersion in my so-called writing without instantly remembering that I was stupid and ugly, and that every giggle, every derisive snort behind my back, was aimed at me.

Here's a mystery.

At some point, for no reason that I can determine—and I've given the matter some thought—I suddenly took to the vicious, noble craft of slash and burn editing. Suddenly, nothing was good enough. No single word was the correct word, no coupling of words strong enough, no phrase carried its full weight, no sentence sang as it should. Every word, phrase, sentence, paragraph, page, chapter was worrisome until it was altered; cut, cropped, throw out entirely or re-written in every available combination known to man.

Yes, THIS is how one attains martyrdom.

I remember, one shameful day, proudly, declaring, "Give me three words and I'll re-arrange them 'til the end of time!" This was in an age when, to change *then* to *than*, you'd have to re-type the entire damned page, and sometimes (by what anomaly we do not know) the next page as well… and, more inexplicably still, sometimes the previous page.

Of course, one might reasonably ask—So what?

Well, here's so what. I offer you a tale to laugh at knowingly. One particular day, suddenly inspired by who knows what (though it could have been something else entirely), I took an eight or nine inch thick stack of my scrupulously edited stuff… each page typed, single-spaced, edge to edge, top to bottom, without relief… placed it all in an old cardboard box, hauled it downstairs, and placed it in the trunk of my parents' second car (an old green Dodge with iffy shocks). Then I set out for a small college town, 30 miles away, where the offices of a literary quarterly could be found.

Once there, lugging my heavy cardboard box, I entered an old brownstone building, walked down a long hallway, and stood for a while, to catch my breath, before a door marked, Molly Toothsome, editor.

(I am so sorry I do not recall this good woman's actual name—I have tried—she was, as you'll soon see, an excellent example of the working American editor).

When I knocked, a female voice within shouted, somewhat distractedly, "Min."
I entered, went right over and dropped my box upon the woman's desk (mainly because of the weight of the damned thing), and I started to speak, but didn't—I was just too embarrassed. Then, in what is probably the most awkward move I'd made up to that point in my life, I turned and walked out.

All the way home, the phrase, "I should have said something!" and the question, "Why didn't I say something?" continually replaced each other in his mind. My dreams were crushed.
I guess it's really unnecessary to use the word, *idiot,* here. In the battle between implicit 'n' explicit, implicit wins again.
There's gotta be a story in here somewhere.
Oh, and here it is.

At about that time (I'm guessing 1964) I sent Evergreen Review my first submission, and it was rejected. HOWEVER, along with the standard rejection slip the Editor-in-Chief, Barney Rosset included a brief handwritten note encouraging me to continue writing. Quite possibly there was not a person anywhere on earth who needed that encouragement less—at that point I couldn't imagine life without writing.

Forty-six years later, I discovered Evergreen Review, still alive, on the internet. So, I sent them a copy of what I thought was my best stuff (Lambfield)… only to be rejected again. They told me it wasn't really their style. Of course I knew that going in; I also knew what their style was. So, I sat down and hammered out something *in their style*. It was about three evenings' work. This they accepted.

Barney Rosset, first to read all submissions and make the final decision about what was to see print in Evergreen Review—the guy who encouraged me to keep writing when I was a kid— published my first piece in his esteemed publication when I was 60 years old. Of course, my immediate fear, once that piece was accepted, was: If it's another 46 years before my work sees print in Evergreen again, I'll be 106. At that point, I'll probably have lost all interest in anything that isn't called chocolate pudding.

All that aside, that note, scrawled by Barney Rosset on my first rejection slip, inspired me. So, I *actually* went back to Molly Toothsome … maybe it was a month later, I don't know. I knock-knock-knocked, and when Ms. Toothsome shouted— somewhat distractedly—"'Min..." I entered, slunk over, stood before her, head down. Contrite is a nice word.

She looked up from what she was doing. She pursed her lips. She leaned back in her squeaky old solid oak chair, and thought a bit, with her eyes fixed on me. She leaned forward (squeakily) and, while drumming the rubber end of a pencil on her desk, raised both eyebrows in question, 'You again?'

The box of junk I'd abandoned there previously was sitting over against the wall, under a window. She pointed at it with her pencil, and I went over and picked it up. She pointed at her desk and I placed the box softly in front of her. She pointed at a chair, as if to say, 'Have a seat'. Then she said it. "Have a seat," she said. "This may take some time. Time I don't have," she added, with a hint of exasperation.

She picked up the first page, looked at it. She read a bit, then put it back in the box without comment. She closed her eyes for the very briefest moment before slowly taking in a deep breath. Much to her credit, she did not sigh loudly, shake her head wearily, or roll her eyes about wildly. "OK," she said, "this is what <u>you</u> need to know. BUT, briefly," she cautioned.

"From now on: double spaced throughout—we need the room for markup. Give us an inch and a half all around, at least an inch and a half. Keyword up here; your name opposite. MALPUS, slash, PAGE NUMBER. [In those days I was writing under the name John Malpus. I thought that was better than being a skinny little, pimply, outcast named Richard.] You can put the page number with the keyword if you wish. Mindless Drivel, SLASH, page two; Mindless Drivel, slash, page three. OK? Now…"

She turned the entire stack over and flipped the last page face up. Scanning it she laughed. "What's this? Your last shot is: 'He'd thought he had.' ?" She pulled the previous page and read a bit of that and laughed. "Very nice. I like a sense of humor… especially at the end; it's a nice idea. However," she said, leaning toward me, "it's **not a bad idea** to get your reader to like you from <u>*the beginning*</u>…OK? Now, exact word count, here." She tapped the paper.

I looked confused. "You see, Mr. Malpus, we have to look at it in terms of layout. In a very real way all your good work is nothing more than column inches to us. Do you know anything about specing type? Lead? Justification? *Kerning*? *Pica*... in either form? Do you recognize an elite face when you see one? Mr. Malpus," she sighed, "do you know WHY so many literary publications publish so much poetry?"
"Eating stones..?" I ventured quietly.
"Eating stones?"
"Isn't Pica when a kid eats sto…inedible stuff?"
"Well, that's a third form; if I'm not mistaken there is also a rodent, but I'm talking about measuring a line of type. Let's just go back to exact word count. OK," she smiled a little forced smile, "but briefly. Count every word, *every* word, for twenty

lines. Divide by 20, multiply times the number of lines per page, multiply times the number of pages and you have your exact word count. In your piece here, I'd estimate about 800,000 words. Name goes here. John Malpus. Malpus? What kind of a name is that? Scottish? I'm not sure I've ever… Name address and phone number, Mr. Malpus. OK?"

"NEVER send <u>anything</u> without a SASE…self-addressed, stamped, envelope. *Correct postage please.* In your case an envelope clearly would not do, send us a crate. And, BEFORE *ever   sending   anything,* it's really a very good idea to send a query letter. Don't just show up here like you did and drop your work, like you did, on the editor's desk, like you did, and expect anyone to take the time to explain the way things work, like I just did—it is not going to happen."
She cocked her head to see if I got it.

"Query letter. *Get the editor's name and title correct.* Form, simple sweet: 'Dear Miss Toothsome, I have a little piece of 800,000 *plus* words ending in 'He'd thought he had.' Would you like to take a look at it?' Four or five months later I fire back, 'Dear Mr. Malpus, we here at Briarwood Press, which has, for forty-seven years, published no single work longer than 1600 words, would be most pleased to look at your 800,000 *plus* word monstrous, single-spaced, unedited, practically unreadable, particularly ponderous tome—use a clean ribbon, next time.' So, then what do you do?"
"I send it."
"Yes. You send it. You *keep a copy*, and you send it. And how am I to discover it in amongst all…" She waved in the direction of a half dozen cardboard boxes stuffed and overflowing with bulky manila envelopes. "How—if I am interested—am I supposed to find your work in all of this?"
I shrugged.

She took an envelope and wrote 'REQUESTED MATERIAL' in one corner and underlined it twice. "Requested Material, underlined, block lettering, in red ink if you choose. OK?"
"OK."
"OK, briefly, briefly, briefly; I have to get back to work. So, I then read your 800,000 plus words, or enough of it to determine that it's not for us, and I send you one of…"

She looked around on her desk, started looking through drawers and swung around to look upon the shelves behind her, "one of…." She got up and left the room. Several long minutes later she returned with a tiny piece of paper and held it up for me to see. "…one of these. It's a rejection slip. If you've given us the SASE, with appropriate postage… it will arrive paper-clipped on top of your very good work without further comment, when it is returned to you. If you haven't given us a SASE, you MAY receive this separately. It says: thank you, we're not interested, keep up the good work. The part that concerns you, Mr. Malpus, is in the middle of that padding—we're not interested. Briefly, briefly—HOW-ever, we are more likely to show some interest IF you did *everything* in the manner I've told you here, just now. Why? It makes our task easier… it's a matter of courtesy on your part. If you choose NOT to follow the format suggestions I've offered you, **we** may use that as cause enough to reject your work without consideration. That means without looking at it. Thank you for coming in again… Mr. Malpus. (She placed one hand on my box of 800,000 plus words.) You can leave that with me. It's been a pleasure; I'm sorry I don't have more time. If nothing else, let me say, I like your ending. You may or may not hear from us… probably, being honest with you as I have been so far… not."
She looked at me.
"Don't look so sad, Mr. Malpus. Believe me when I tell you that this is far better treatment than you might reasonably expect to receive ever again."

I stood up.
"Am I wasting my time?" I asked timidly.
"I don't know. We'll take a look."
"I'm kind of… driven to do this."
"I can see that."
I stood still (and you may take that either way.)

"Don't expect too much." Molly Toothsome said. "For what it's worth, chance plays a big part in what you're up to. No matter how good you may be, there are always people out there who are *worse*—some FAR worse—who are getting into print, while your work lingers. More vexing still, some of them will make a good living at it. It may drive you CRAZY … if you let it. And, despite the common wisdom, insanity won't improve your position. Neither will alcohol. In a very real sense, what much of the publishing industry does has nothing to do with writerly talent. I offer you this good advice for free." She smiled. "Thanks for dropping in."

At the time, (circa 1965), that excellent woman had just handed me the keys to the kingdom. And, although I took her advice to heart, and applied her formatting assiduously, by the time I left high school I had acquired enough rejection slips to wallpaper every room in the Taj Mahal.

MAMA TRIOZZI (1964 or 1965)

Mama Triozzi was the toughest math teacher at East Brunswick High. When my brother asked me who I got for geometry and I told him, 'Someone named Triozzi…' his eyes popped out of his head. "Oh man, you got Mama Triozzi?! You *poor* bastard."

Anyway… for some reason, although everybody else in class seemed to understand it, I was completely lost when it came to geometry; none of it made any sense. I tried. I struggled in class and, though I went over it repeatedly at home, it just made no sense to me. Postulates and theorems were beyond my grasp. I spent most of my time in that class trying to decipher the mumbo-jumbo that spilled so freely from other kids' mouths, and the entire time thinking, in the back of my mind, that I must be an idiot. If everybody else gets it and I don't—what other conclusion can you come to—I must be an idiot.

One afternoon, after flunking yet another quiz, I went up to Mrs. Triozzi after class, in tears. I told her, "I'm sorry, Mrs. Triozzi; I'm trying, I'm really trying, but I just don't get it. None of it makes sense to me; most of the time I have no idea whatsoever what you guys are all talking about."
And that truly excellent teacher said, "Well, why don't you come by after school and we'll talk about it, you and I. Let's see if we can't help you make some sense out of it."

So, after school I went back to Mrs. Triozzi's classroom and she worked with me for a while—assuring me that understanding sometimes takes a little time—and, after the fourth or fifth such meeting, it still made no sense to me. So, I went home more distraught than ever. At home, I sat down, and I opened the damned geometry book with tears in my eyes, and I looked at it with NO hope whatsoever, and BAM!—just like that—suddenly it ALL made sense. Suddenly it all made perfect sense.

From that point on, every aspect of geometry made sense to me; there was no part of it that I did not comprehend. It came to me almost naturally, and I eagerly looked forward to class.

I was so glad that I got Mama Triozzi for geometry that year. Because of her kindness, her encouragement and patience this poor bastard got an A in that class.

HOW TO RUN A COLLEGE COURSE (as told to me in 2016)

At age 90-something, my father told me that the first five minutes of Bill Miller's engineering class, at Purdue, were etched into his mind forever. More than 70 years later he could, and did, tell me—quite possibly word for word—what that instructor had said.

Bill Miller walked into class on that first day and said this:
"I'm not taking roll today and I won't be taking it any time in the future. You've paid to take this course, and whether you attend or not is entirely up to you.
I will be giving short tests from time to time. You may take those tests or not; that's entirely up to you. If you take those tests, I'll correct them, so you'll know where you went wrong.
At the end of the course each of you will be given a problem to solve. You will each have your own problem...you may work on them together, if you wish, but you'll be responsible only for your own work; bear that in mind.
If you solve that problem by applying what you've learned in this class, you will get an A. If you fail to solve that problem, you will fail this class.
That's the way it works in the real world."

Those few words, quite possibly, encompass the most refreshing and enlightened view I've ever heard concerning advanced education. Attend or not, take the tests or not; in the end, we'll test you to see if you've learned anything. If we think you're ready, you'll be free to go out into the real world.

I really wish that was the way it worked in the real world.

It isn't.

MONEY AND DIPLOMAS (May 1971)

I'd just spent that afternoon at the comptroller's office. They wanted me to pay them $35 before I would be allowed to attend the graduation ceremony and receive my diploma.

The wide, gull-eyed woman squatting behind the desk in a muumuu was cold and precise. The matter was pretty straight forward: pay the $35 and get my diploma or don't pay it and don't get the diploma. It, clearly, made no difference to her.

I had no objection to paying for the repair of a hole in the dormitory wall, four years earlier, since I had created that hole. But, they wanted me to pay for the labor of fixing a hole that had never been fixed. More idiotic still—from my point of view—the building itself no longer existed; it had since been torn down.

"You're demanding that I pay you $35 to fix a hole in a wall of a building which no longer exists?"
"If you do not pay this fee, your diploma will be withheld and you will not graduate."
"Does that mean I will not get my degree?"
"It means that your diploma will be withheld."
"Does that mean I won't have a degree?
"You will not be allowed to attend graduation ceremonies."
"I don't care about that. Will I or will I not have a degree?"
"Your diploma will be withheld."
"I'll have a degree but I won't have the piece of paper that says I have a degree? Is that it?"
"Your diploma will be…"
"May I talk to that guy?" I said, pointing at the overly-large, nicely polished, imported hardwood door with the gold lettering saying: Office of the Comptroller.

"The Comptroller?" asked the woman in the muumuu—there was some rolling of the eyes. I could not possibly understand what I was asking.

"Yes. May I talk to him?"

She sighed and, then looked at me to determine if I was sure I wanted to do that—and, despite her naturally protective nature, she pressed a button on her desk....

After some whispering over the phone, I was escorted inside.

He had a nice office and he had a nice big desk and he was nicely dressed, but that's where the niceness ended. He was an ugly bearded guy with big pink ears, yellow skin, and massively framed eye glasses. He asked me what he could do for me with only the coldest indifference. Unfortunately, of all the functionaries at RPI, he was the one probably most aware of the kind of money my parents and I had paid that institution over the last four years.

I explained that I was being asked to pay $35 to fix a hole in a wall which had never been fixed in a building that had been torn down years ago, and that I didn't think that was either fair or reasonable and that, in fact, it seemed completely UN-fair and UN-reasonable for them to withhold my diploma because of that. He mulled.

The fingers, the beard, the eyes were all involved in this.

After some thought, he pushed a button and asked the gull-eyed woman to bring my file in to him. She did; she handed it to him. He looked it over in a strange off-hand sort of way.

"You put a hole in the wall of 935 Park Avenue the week of your first arrival here," he said, as if that was an end to it.

"Four years ago, yes." I admitted. "I was pushed by another kid and my elbow went through the wall."

"And you were told, at that time, that you would be held responsible."

"Yes, but that wall was never fixed. Two years later, I took advanced printmaking in that same building, and that hole was still there. The following year, when that building was torn down, that hole was still there. It is now an empty lot."

"I see," he said. "Unfortunately, there is nothing I can do about this. If you refuse to pay this 'fee' you will not graduate."

"I will not graduate?"

"You will not receive your degree."

"I will not receive my degree?"

"You will not receive your *diploma*," he corrected himself.

"The piece of paper?"

"The parchment."

"Does that mean I will not *have* a degree?"

"It means that you will not *have* your diploma."

"Does that matter?"

"I'm afraid I cannot answer that question."

"Well, can you answer this one then: Why am I being charged to fix a hole that was never fixed in the wall of a building that no longer exists?"

To my surprise he had an answer. "Balance..." he said. Then he gazed at me as if there was nothing more which needed to be said. But, when I stuck, he explained. "It's on our books; funds were issued on your behalf. We wish to recover those funds before you leave us."

"You know what?" I said bitterly. "You should recover those funds from the maintenance department. They're the ones who were paid to do the work and didn't do it. I'm telling you that that hole was still there a couple years later when that building had become the stone-lithographic studios, and it was still there on the day they tore that building down."

We glared at each other—well, no, I glared at him; he looked back upon me with cool aristocratic indifference. That went on for a while. Then I departed in defeat... of sorts.

So, after I finished my four year stint at Richmond Professional Institute without a diploma, due to a monetary dispute, I quickly landed a job as a part-time janitor.

The very same high level educational institution from which I'd just graduated—or not, who knows?—hired me immediately to mop their floors.

With no diploma, it seemed like a reasonable option.

CAR REPAIR and BEANIES at PURDUE (2018)

I was sitting in the office of a car repair shop in San Francisco, looking out at the damaged front end of our poor car, when I noticed the Indiana license plate on a *totaled* vehicle. I asked the kid who owned that car, if it wouldn't have been easier to have destroyed it back home, rather than driving it all the way out to California to destroy it, and he laughed. I asked him where he was from and he said, Indianapolis. I told him that my brother had been born in that town and my father had gone to Purdue.

He told me that he'd gone to Purdue too, and I asked him if freshmen are still required to wear a beanie on campus. He said he'd never heard of that. I laughed and said, "Yeah, My father may have had a hand it putting an end to that nonsense."

Then, I told the kid from Indiana this:
When Dad was a freshman at Purdue, all freshmen were required to wear a beanie while on campus. So, one morning Dad was walking across campus, on his way to an engineering course—without that stupid beanie—when an upperclassman stepped in front of him, stopped him, and demanded, "Why aren't you wearing your beanie, Frosh? How's about I teach you a lesson concerning that."
My Dad, just back from the relentless Hell of war—liberating Paris and driving the Nazis back into Germany—replied, "How about the next time you utter the word 'beanie', I rip your head off and shove it up your ass?"
According to Dad, that was pretty much the end of that discussion.

The kid from Indiana thought for a bit, and said, "Huh…"

JUSTICE in AMERICA,
as I know it

ONWARD I GO (1971)

In September 1971, or thereabouts, for some reason which cannot possibly be explained, I sold my 1957 Mercedes Benz 190 SL and bought a new motorcycle. The motorcycle was a 650 Triumph; it was a beauty. It might be of interest to note that the Mercedes Benz would be worth something between $60,000 and $120,000 these days, the 650 Triumph would be worth less, and, possibly, worthless. But, I was young and I wanted a motorcycle, and I suppose I was short-sighted (and by that I mean stupid).

About that same time, I took my four-year college education and got myself a new job as a part-time janitor. I was the only white guy on the cleaning staff. I may have been the only one there with a high school diploma. I was certainly the only one there who had four years of college and had been hired to push a mop around on the floors of classrooms in which I had once attended class. So, I was breaking down some real social barriers.

Some of the young male janitors had motorcycles; little things; the largest was maybe 250 cc. They lined them up proudly at the curb, out in front of the brick building where us janitors started and ended our shift each evening. After work these kids would climb on these little motorcycles and z-z-z-z-zip off speedily.

One pay day, instead of walking four blocks to work, I rode my 650 Triumph and parked it at the end of the line of the tiny bikes. Beside them, my bike looked like a MONSTER. So, after collecting my paycheck, I went over and climbed on my monster bike and kick started it and, after revving it a few thunderous times, took off like a bat out of hell.

My guess is that it is 80 yards to the point where Grove Avenue splits off to the left, and Park Avenue ambles off to the right. By the time I hit that fork I was already in fourth gear and going

FAST. I swerved left, saw that the light ahead at Harrison Street had changed to yellow, gunned it, ran the red light and flew down the lovely tree sheltered straight-away known as Grove Avenue.

I was moving at a pretty good clip and quite proud of my performance—I had made impressively smooth shifts. Now, long out of sight of my fellow janitors, I thought I'd better slow down. That's what I was thinking when I noticed a flashing light in my mirror. There was a cop car back there eager to pass, so I slowed down and pulled to one side of the street so he could go by... but he didn't. He didn't go by. He didn't pass me. Instead he bumped his siren a couple times and announced over a bullhorn, "Motorcycle rider, take a left turn at the next corner and pull over."

I did as I was told. I got off my bike, removed my helmet and waited. He sat inside his car doing something which I could not see, and when he got out, slowly, he stood there near his car for a while writing in a note pad. When I approached him, he did not look at me. Instead he reached inside his car, got his hat, and put it on.
"What... uh... what...?" I began humbly.
"DO NOT say a word," he instructed me.
"But..."
"DO NOT say a word." He continued to write.

When he was done writing, he handed me the pad and asked me to sign it. I did. He tore a copy of whatever it was off that pad and handed it to me.
"Did I do something wrong?" I asked in complete innocence. He squinted at me while trying to determine if I was being some kind of wise ass, but couldn't really decide.

He then said this:

"Thirty five in a 15 mph school zone, running a red light, speeding in a restricted neighborhood, crossing a double yellow line, speeding—60 mph in a 30 mph zone—reckless driving. failure to yield, failure to pull over, failure to use proper signals. In Virginia you can go to prison for reckless driving," he added. "Let me see your registration for that device."

I had it in my nervous shaking hand.
"Let me see your driver's license."
I had that too.
"Do you want Tuesday or Thursday?"
"Pardon me?"
"Do you want to face these charges in court on a Tuesday or a Thursday?"
"Thursday," I said.
He handed me my driver's license and registration back.
"Do you want 12:30 or 2:30?"
"Twelve-thirty," I said.
He smiled. "That's Judge Langdon. Langdon takes great pleasure in throwing people into prison for reckless driving. See you there."
He tore something else off of the pad and handed it to me.
He then got into his car again and, as he pulled out slowly around me, he said out the window, "Oh, and I strongly recommend that you do not exceed the speed limit anywhere within the city limits of Richmond with that device anytime between now and your court appearance. IF you do, we will confiscate that device, and you will go directly to prison. If I were you, young man, I'd park that thing and walk home."
Then he drove off, slowly.

So, you know, that was kinda what the hippies in those days called *a bummer*. I was scared to death. Judge Langdon takes great pleasure in sending people like me to jail.

The next day, when I arrived at work, I was a hero... a <u>HERO!</u> People were clapping me on the back and shaking my hand and calling me brother and just standing around, at a respectable distance, grinning widely at me, and nodding approval.

Apparently, that cop had been on my tail from the very moment I took off like a rocket that evening, and the entire cleaning crew had witnessed the event from that moment until I disappeared, out of sight under the overhanging trees of Grove Avenue. They believed that *I'd seen* the cop. They thought *I knew* he was there. In their minds *I was daring that cop to catch me.*

Suddenly the long-haired white kid was all right; more than all right. One of my fellow janitors came over, clung, drinkin' buddy fashion, to my shoulder and laughed loudly into my ear. "Man," he said, "you are one mothuhfuckin' crazy-ass son of a bitch, m' man." He seemed to speak for everybody there.

I never could have dreamed that people, who had been so indifferent to me or resentful of me, just one day earlier, could find me suddenly so irresistible.
"Man, you is alllllll-right, Richard! We were sure we were never gonna see your ass again."

They were convinced this crazy-ass white boy was on his way to jail. And, I have to tell you, this crazy-ass white boy thought so himself. But, no, I'm just too fast; TOO FAST; no lazy ass cop gonna catch THIS part-time crazy-ass janitor! At that moment, awash in weird triumph it seemed very cool to be me. I didn't know what lay ahead, and didn't care.

It wasn't so cool to be me on the agreed upon Thursday morning, when I arrived downtown at the courthouse. As soon as I walked in, the cop picked me out of the throng and made a point of

coming over, to say, "Yep, we got Judge Langdon. He's thrown thirty people into prison for reckless driving this year so far. I got a feeling you're gonna be thirty-one."
Having the opportunity to convey this information to me seemed to fill the man with tremendous delight.

I went into the courtroom and signed something and took a seat in the audience as Judge Langdon called case after case and handed down huge fines, and jail time, and even had one guy taken away immediately in handcuffs. When someone called my name I stood up and, weak in the knees, went up to the bar like a sheep to slaughter.

Judge Langdon looked down on me with cruel eyes under a stern unforgiving brow. "Let me see here," he said. "You were caught exceeding the speed limit in two separate zones; you ran a red light; you rode on the wrong side of the road; you ignored the demand of the officer. Where is the officer? OK. You'll have your turn in a minute, officer. You ignored his order to pull over, evading arrest, that's what we'll call that, for here, for now, and worse than any of this, you did it all with an overall and complete disregard for the safety of anyone else who might have been on that road at that time—we'll call that reckless driving."
He looked down at me. "What do you have to say for yourself?"
I said nothing. I kept my head down and I said nothing.

"These are pretty serious charges," he said. 'Can you tell me why you were acting in this reckless manner?"
"It was pay day, uh, Sir, uh, Your Honor."
"It was pay day…"
"And I was feeling kinda good… Uh, and, you know, uh… everybody was watchin'."
"You had just been paid and you were feeling spunky because everyone was looking at you. So, you thought you'd put on a little show for these people?"

"Yes, Your Honor. I was, you know… feeling pretty good."

He stared down at me for a long time while I cowered before him. "What kind of a motorcycle is this we're talking about?"
"A 650 Triumph, Sir."
 "Yeah. And how long have you had this motorcycle?"
"About three months I guess… sir. Not quite."
"Well, I'm sorry," he said, "The law is the law, and I'm going to have to…"

Judge Langdon raised his gavel and held it aloft for a bit.
"Oh hell," he said, "Case dismissed!" and he brought that gavel down with a clack.

With the sound of that clack my eyes filled instantly with tears; tears of joy.

And, although the people I worked with had really enjoyed my one-man motorcycle spectacular, the administration at RPI was not so pleased to hear about it.
I lost that job as quickly as I'd landed it.

JUSTICE SAN FRANCISCO STYLE (2014)

One afternoon, the phone in our room rang and it was my wife's father saying, "Quick, get your camera and come out front right away!" So, we rushed out and there, along with the Lamberts, were two young women, both talking on cell phones. Madam was standing there looking a bit lost and saying, "Oh, such a big deal over such a small matter!" M. Lambert pushed past us and ran into the hotel followed by his good wife.

That left my wife and I standing there wondering what the problem was. Usually the problem was that a delivery truck had come too close to the curb and had shattered the neon signs which hung on the front of the marquee, for the 37-thousandth time. So, we were looking around for evidence of the shattered neon when M. Lambert emerged, pushed his way past us again, and kneeling beside a car which was not his, began rubbing the fender with his handkerchief. My wife and I looked at each other in complete bewilderment.

When M. Lambert instructed his daughter to take a picture of the fender, one of the young girls quickly interposed herself between her and the car. The other approached rapidly shouting, "No pictures! NO pictures!"
"Take the photo. Take the photo!" M. Lambert commanded.
"Why?" she asked.
"Take the photo, take it!" M. Lambert ordered rapidly.
"Why?" I asked.
"They are telling us that it has been damaged by Madame's car," he moaned.
"Damaged?" I couldn't detect any damage whatsoever; not a dent, not a ding, not a scratch, not a scuff, no mark of any sort; nothing, and I have pretty good eyes.
"Where's the damage?" I asked.

"This is not your business!" hissed one of the girls and she placed herself directly in front of me.

"This is not YOUR business!" said the other from her position between my wife and the car.

By this point the guy who works next door had emerged and I welcomed him eagerly, as I escorted him over to look at the fender. "Do you see ANY damage to that fender?"

"THIS IS NOT YOUR BUSINESS!" said one of the girls loudly and stuck her nose practically upon my chin. "You stay out of this!" she said to the guy who works next door, and pointed at him in what anyone would say was a threatening manner.

"Where's the damage?" I asked. "I don't see anything."

"It's NONE of your business," she said emphatically.

Meanwhile my wife had side-stepped the other girl and managed to take a picture.

"NO pictures are to be taken of my car!" said the other stamping her foot and wheeling to face my wife. "No pictures. You cannot take pictures of my car!" she said and stood blocking our clear view of the damage that did not exist.

Of that entire gathering—M. Lambert and Mme Lambert, my wife and I, and the guy who works next door—only the accusers could detect any damage.

M. was upset and Madame was bewildered. The lead female was saying, "Just pay us and we'll forget about it."

M. Lambert said to his daughter, "They are saying it will cost $700 dollars to repair this car."

The other one said, "Why don't you just pay up, old man, and we can forget about it!"

M. Lambert then said, "But, there is no reason for this animosity. The damage has been taken care of. Why don't you and your family come to our restaurant? You can have a nice dinner in our restaurant; I am the owner, I invite you; you will be my special guests."

I told one of these girls that this was all bullshit, and I told my wife to take a picture of their license plate, before I stepped out in front of oncoming traffic. I was looking for the cop that is NEVER EVER EVER around when you need one.

As I stood in the middle of Bush Street, hoping, praying, weeping for a cop, one of these chicks came over to tell me, "This is none of your business."

"Oh yes it is," I assured her.

"IT is NONE of YOUR busINESS," she hissed.

"It IS my business," I said calmly, while looking at traffic. "I'm a witness."

"You're not a witness. You were not here. You did not see what this crazy woman has done. What are you a witness of? What are you a witness of? Tell me. Tell me please. What are you a witness of? You are a witness of nothing!"

"Exactly!" I said, "I'm witness to the fact that there is absolutely nothing wrong with that car. There is NO damage to that car, and my wife got a pretty good shot of that fact, despite your friend's interference."

"That's because he wiped the damage off," she said and left me.

"Well then it's gone isn't it? I shouted at her.

She turned to face me again. "This is none of your business!" she squealed in frustration.

Right then a cop appeared in the distance. At my furious flagging he pulled over. As soon as the cop's car stopped the leader of the scam switched gears, saying quickly to M. Lambert, "That's OK, if you apologize we'll just forget about it."

"Now, you're gonna get the justice you're looking for!" I said as the cop painfully extracted himself from his car and dragged himself toward the crowd.

My wife and I didn't stay around to explain the obvious—they wanted no photos, no witnesses… there was no damage.

This is an accurate portrayal of what transpired on that day. Things that were said directly to me are, for all intents and purposes, word for word.

My wife's father went to court, with this very transcript and several photos of the immaculate, showroom level, completely undamaged fender (which included the license plate of that car).

And, after looking carefully at this evidence, the judge ordered my wife's father to pay something close to two thousand dollars in damages to those chicks.

MINOR JUSTICE

My wife regularly buys books for me.

Although she reads three to five books per week; I read only one book in three to five months. So, typically it is a while between the time she gives me a book and the time I finally get around to reading it. Such is the case with The Pastons—a cool (involving) nicely bound (expensive) book, mostly private letters between various members of a noble English family in the 15th century.

Apparently, one of the matrons in the Paston family had put up a toll gate on the road that went through her property linking the town to whatever it was that lay beyond, and that caused some real trouble with those who wished to pass through there. So, I'm interested, I'm reading it and getting more deeply involved in the tale. I'm doing a pretty good job, setting a good pace, because I'm wondering particularly about how this toll gate thing is going to work out—I am completely on her side by the way— and when I turn page 96 I find myself suddenly on page 145.

Upon further investigation, I see that page 160 is followed directly by page 113. That ain't right, even for a casual reader like me. So, I'm concerned, and I start pawing through the thing with increasing concern only to discover that pages 97 through 112 are missing entirely.

So, I wrote a nice letter to the nicely-bound book sellers who sold the book to my wife (and who have sold many nicely-bound books to her in the past), asking them if they would please replace the faulty book with one of the same title which had a more traditional approach to page-related continuity. I told them I would gladly return the other. I explained that I was concerned because Lord Hungerford just rode past Sheringham…
but I didn't know what happened to him next.

Well, the good people at the nicely-bound book company wrote me back almost immediately, sending me a terse little note saying they would 'need proof' that I had purchased the book from them. Let me say here what I thought when I read that note. "Christ, what idiots!" That's what I thought. And I thought that more than once; in fact, every time I reread that letter, I thought it, but with increasing irritation.

But, I calmed myself before responding.

This idea of calming myself before responding to idiocy is something of an accomplishment of mine, a little trick I've taught myself after 30 or 40 years of doing it the other way around, with limited success. Of course, during those many years, I recognized the wisdom in the concept of calming myself before responding to idiocy, but I never quite learned how to apply the method. For those same years, I also recognized that there was not even the slightest glimmer of reason in responding to such things without first calming myself. So, frequently I pledged that next time, before responding to idiocy, I'd first give calming myself a try, just to see how that might work out—but never did. In the heat of the moment, calming myself never really occurred to me, or if it did I didn't feel as though I had the time for it just then; couldn't squeeze it in, before firing off a pointed response.

So, in this instance—concerning this battle over a badly bound book—I'd made some real headway as a man striving to become a better human being. Bloated with pride, I tracked down my dear wife and told her, "You might want to write this down: At age 50-something he decided to calm himself *before* responding to idiocy." But, it goes beyond just that. I also promised myself that I would maintain a good attitude throughout the ordeal, in which I was, no doubt whatsoever, about to find myself embroiled. No matter how long it took to get the thing resolved, I planned to remain calm. (I was growing by leaps and bounds.)

So, I wrote them back explaining that I had not, myself, purchased that book from them; that the book had been a gift given to me by my dear wife a long time previous to me ever picking it up, and that I wanted, out of kindness, if it was at all possible, to keep her out of the matter. Perhaps, I suggested, we could forgo making my poor wife paw through stacks of credit card and bank statements; perhaps they could determine, from their own records, whether or not my wife had purchased such a book from them OR, by that same process, determine, as they seemed to suppose, that I was perpetrating some kind of an overly complex scam to screw them out of a free, nicely bound, properly paginated, copy of The Pastons.

It was a carefully crafted letter, an appeal for decency and common sense, minor justice of a sort, and a small portion of the kind of consideration that we can no longer expect as a given in this rapidly disintegrating society. It was not a strongly worded letter, it was neither overly clever nor too chummy, it was carefully constructed (I thought) so as to keep fairly well hid what I honestly thought of their idiotic response to a perfectly reasonable request.

Can I say something about banks here?—just a single tale which comes unexpectedly to mind. One time, forty years or so ago, I deposited $300 into a Wells Fargo savings account. I was flush at the time. But, down the road a very short piece I had need of that money and I went into that bank to withdraw it. I had a little book with a stamp and a bank employee's signature saying I had given them $300. However, when I presented my little book to her, and asked for the $300, the clerk counted out $298.56.

I threw up both palms in an overly dramatic gesture which meant, "Whoa! I ain't touchin' that." I explained to the clerk, that I had deposited $300 and I expected $300 back. She, without further pleasantries (neither the eye contact nor the faux-smile *which is always expected of me* in the hotel business), printed out something that showed my account number and the figure $298.56. I then very quickly reached across the counter, recovered the little book with the stamp and the bank employee's signature stating that I had given them $300, and I showed it to her. I said, "I put $300 in this account and I want $300 out." That, to me, seemed perfectly reasonable.

I'll be brief because I know you have bank stories of your own, and probably better things to do, as Robert Frost might say, and better things to do.

So, after some quibbling, with her dug-in behind the safety of her counter, followed by a little remote quibbling with someone of a sterner sort, seated 18 feet away—who would not come out from behind her desk—I eventually ended up sitting in a comfortable chair across a much larger desk from the Branch Manager. He listened to something whispered in his ear by one of the others, eyeballed me, looked at the paperwork, including the little book with stamp and signature, before saying, "We can give you $298.56 right now and settle this, or you can come back in three days."
I said, "See you in three days," got up and walked out.

But, here's a question for you—wouldn't you, if you had been that bank manager—wouldn't you have simply reached into your pocket and pulled out a couple of dollar bills and tossed them casually upon your great big nicely polished desk? Wouldn't you then have said, "Here you go; you've been a good customer. If you ever find yourself on surer financial footing come back and see us again." Wouldn't you have done that? I would have. I probably would have changed it up a bit, shouting, "Here's your goddamned money, now get out!" He didn't though. More frightening still, I'd bet the thought never even crossed his mind.

Just to wrap things up; I returned three days later and the matter still hadn't been settled. I was told the accounting was handled in Los Angeles and it would be a few more days. (I actually wondered at the time if Wells Fargo was giving me the run-around in order to screw me out of a dollar forty.) When I returned again—couple of days later—they gave me my $300 without comment.

Who knows what GRAND banking machinations went into that excruciating decision concerning $1.44? I'm sure it involved lawyers and accountants and board meetings, finger-pointing, firings, resignations in disgrace, perhaps a suicide or two.

Bankers are such goddamned idiots. Most of 'em would screw their own grandmother out of a penny to gain a day's interest on it. As for the nicely bound, but somewhat unpredictably paginated copy of The Pastons, I think we went one more round in written form before I picked up the telephone. The implication that I was perpetrating an elaborate scam required the kind of huffiness only a stern voice over the phone can provide.

"I want to speak to someone there who is reasonable," I said nicely to the woman who answered on the other end.
"I'm sorry, what did you say?" she asked with maybe just a bit of surprise.
I said, "I would like to speak to someone there who is reasonable; you know, someone who is capable of thinking straight, and who is in the position to accomplish something."
To *my surprise* the woman then said this: "That would be me. How may I help you?"
As it turned out, she was correct. She was reasonable, she did think straight, and she did have the authority to make things happen. With very little effort on my part the thing was soon settled. I received a good copy of The Pastons a few days later in the mail.

I haven't been able to work it back into the rotation yet, but I checked, and when I turned page 96—breath held, eyes asquint—I found myself on page 97. Better still, from that point forward through the remainder of the book, the pages run in standard order.

So now I have two nicely bound copies of The Pastons, I'm thinking about giving the first one to someone as a gift just to see what happens. It is, basically, a new book; hardly been touched. My hope would be that after discovering its flaw, they'd write a letter to the nicely-bound book sellers and tell them it had been a gift from me.

(My insightful wife suggests I simply turn it into a book-safe.)

MAKEUP and JUSTICE (1981)

Holly was a real girl. She wore lots of eye makeup and very
short skirts. She was 12 years younger than me, and I think I was
32 at the time. Her moods fluctuated rapidly and unpredictably
between sullen and playful and playfully sullen (what the French
call pouty) and deep dark impenetrable silence. This last, she
liked to employ during our many lengthy, drawn out, endless
phone conversations.

At the time, wherever we went together I was treated with a very
real, almost obsequious, deference. Because I had this pouty
little leggy creature clinging to my arm, many assumed that I had
to be a rich guy. Holly's car of choice was a Triumph convertible
and we got around mostly in that and mostly with her at the
wheel, which added to the illusion. Holly was alternately a
dream and a completely unnecessary pain in the neck, and she
was vitally, at times vibrantly, aware and belligerently proud of
being both.
Only women have ever asked me why I put up with it.

So, Holly'd bought some nail polish at a cosmetic store—two
tiny bottles—and something else of a similar sort which I don't
recall. And, as was her way, only after driving away from the
store did she decide that she didn't want those two bottles of nail
polish; she kept the third item however, whatever it was. So,
martyr that I am, I stuck those two tiny bottles—still attached to
the cards they'd come on—with the receipt, in the side pocket of
my jacket. I carried them around with me for a while, until one
day I found myself in the vicinity of that cosmetic store and I
happened to have on that same jacket.
I took that as a sign from above.

I entered that cosmetic store thinking I'd be walking out of there
about $12 richer. I went to the counter and placed the two bottles

on the counter and said to the trim young male in a black sleeveless, tightly fitting knit top, "She's decided she doesn't want these."

"Oh, OK," he said, "Do you have a receipt?"

"I thought I did," I said, dragging everything out of my pocket and looking through the post office receipts, restaurant receipts, and miscellaneous notes to myself scrawled and unreadable upon various scraps of paper, "but I don't seem to." I shuffled through that stuff again nonetheless. "She bought 'em here about a week ago, I was with her."

"Well, let me see what the boss says," he said, and picking up the two bottles, he drifted in an impressively casual manner back to the back of the store where an unshaven dark kind of guy, in a black silk shirt buttoned just above the navel, was flirting with a fairly ugly girl whom no amount of make-up could help.

There was some discussion, and the young lad drifted back up front and behind the counter, where he put the bottles aside, rung up the cash register and handed me $1.20. "Here you go," he said with a barely forced smile.

The owner, passing by behind me at that moment, tossed some keys on the counter, saying, "See you Tuesday" and went out the door with the fairly ugly girl in tow.

"Bye-bye, Rodrigo!" said the young lad with great cheerfulness, "Have a nice weekend!"

I looked at the pittance and said, "What's this?"

He said, "That… is… your refund."

I said, "THAT's my refund? Let me see those bottles."

He rolled his eyes in an exaggerated way and, with the greatest herculean effort, moved the bottles from one side of the cash register all the way around to the OTHER side of the cash register, where I could see them.

"They're $5.98 each," I said.

"No, I'm sorry." he said, "But they are 59 cents each… and, you don't have a receipt."

I said nothing, but showed him the prices stamped on the label. Admittedly, they had been stamped carelessly, and the numbers ran off into the decorative border of each card.

"You're telling me that this says 59 cents?"

"That's what the boss said to pay you… and, you don't have a receipt."

"Well, whatever the boss says, those things didn't cost 59 cents. I admit it's hard to read this price but, it's not 59 cents." He said nothing, so I continued. "So, in the boss's scenario I come in here and shoplift two bottles worth 59 cents each and come back a few days later to screw him out of $1.20?"

At this point another trim young man, similarly attired, appeared out of nowhere, sighed, and said, "What seems to be the problem?"

One explained the problem to the other and they both looked at me for a bit and sighed in unison. Customers can be so tiresome at times.

"You both know that those bottles don't go for 59 cents, don't you?" I said. "Where are they? Where do these come from?"

"Over there," one said pointing, "but we're out."

"You're out? How do you know that?"

He sighed again, but remained silent while the other went over and started checking the hanging racks for the same items.

"We're out!" he shouted, and came back to their defenses behind the counter. "We're out," he repeated to me.

"Maybe it's been discontinued…" said one.

"That would explain things," said the other.

I said, "Please, listen to me. Let me say what I have to say, and then I'll go with whatever decision you make. How does that sound?"

They looked around at the empty cosmetic store, they looked at each other, they looked at me. "Oh, why not?" one of them said, rolling his eyes. The other thought this would be a good time to inspect his fingernails.

I began my appeal. "This is not a bank," I said, "and this is not an insurance company, and this is not a government agency, so I don't suppose you're required by the nature of your employment here to see all of your customers as the enemy."
They looked at each other startled, bewildered maybe, and returned their faces to me. So far, they were not convinced.

"There is not a single item in this store—I'm guessing—that goes for 59 cents, and, you guys know that." I picked up a paper nail file from the counter; it was priced $1.89. I waggled the nail file. I pointed in silence to the price tag. I raised my eyebrows. They noted the fact. "I bought three items in here with my girlfriend last week and the bill was a little more than $18. I remember that because I was complaining all the way home: 'EIGHTEEN DOLLARS?! EIGHTEEN DOLLARS for THREE stinking little bottles!' and she said, 'If my friends knew that you walked out of a cosmetic store and it'd only cost you $18, they'd think you were a genius… or a shoplifter.'"

They looked at each other in complete, and I mean COMplete, agreement. They looked at me. I felt I was making headway. I turned and took a small bottle off the closest hanging rack.
"Similar item," I pointed out, "$14.98" I pointed at the price.
"You guys both KNOW…" And I didn't know how to end it, so I just stopped.
They looked at me for a while.
"That's it," I said. I didn't know what else to say.

They both smiled and shook their heads, as if they'd never seen anything quite like me before.

Then, one of them opened the register, and handed me $12. "We're gonna get in trouble for this," he warned his friend, "I just know it."

I couldn't believe I'd won. I was dumbstruck for a bit.
"Thank you," I said.
"Oh, please. There's no need to get maudlin," said one.
"Have a nice weekend!" said the other cheerfully.

Then they both shooed me away, right out the door.

Justice for the HERMIT THRUSH

My wife and I were out walking the dog, a term which means letting him off leash in the park with the hope that we might catch him again sometime later and hold him long enough to leash him up and drag him, unwillingly, homeward. About 10 minutes after he'd disappeared I managed to track him down, far from the designated dog run area, prancing around in amongst the ivy, at the bottom of a steep ravine. I was doing what I could to coax him out of there—which meant doing everything I could *not to drive him further away*—when a gaunt, bearded guy of about my age (old but not frighteningly so), with binoculars and dressed like some kind of a cartoon bwana in khaki from head to toe, came swiftly up the path shouting, "Get that dog out of there!" If he'd have been waving a riding crop it couldn't have been better.

"Get that dog out of there!" he commanded. He was saying this with such unquestionable authority that I almost didn't laugh. Somehow, I'd stumbled into a New Yorker cartoon.

I'm always amazed at how many strangers assume they have authority over me; I'm even more amazed at anybody dumb enough to assume I have any authority whatsoever over my wife's dog.

"This is no place for dogs!" he said sternly. And he said that with such ascendancy that I nearly didn't laugh a second time.
"I'm trying to watch a Hermit Thrush!" he said snappishly. I was practically in tears. My god, W. C. Fields could have learned a thing or two from this guy.
Hermit Thrush!
Now there were tears in my eyes.

I didn't have the chart with me at the moment, so I couldn't pull it out and unfold it and point out the part where it says that a guy trying to coax his wife's dog out of the ivy supersedes the needs of anyone trying to watch a Hermit Thrush, but I'm sure that if I had, he would have simply reached into one of the many pockets that he had on his many-pocketed light tan poplin vest and pulled out his own chart and, with trembling umbrage, read aloud the part which said, "There is no act or action more vital than watching a Hermit Thrush, and especially that vile and senseless effrontery known as dog walking."

So, there you have it in a nutshell. (I'm kind of assuming you would want it that way.) We each have our priorities. We each assume others can see the undeniable value in ours. Some of us assume that, once they see things more clearly, others will dump their own stupidly held ideas, take up, at last, the banner of truth, and begin marching in lock step with us—though just slightly behind perhaps—toward a better, more reasonable world.
That is politics.

And, if there were any justice in this world, this is the way things should have played out, according to my new found friend.
My wife arrives to find me hunkering down in the bushes.
"What are you doing hiding in that shrubbery?" she asks.
"Shhhhhhhh…." I say, placing a finger upon my lips.
"Did you find the dog?" she asks.
"Shhh… please…" I whisper. "Yes, I found the dog."
She whispers back, "Well, I don't see him; where is he?"
"I ran him off."
"You… ran him off?"
"Of course…"
"But…"
"Shhh… please. Look," I say. "up there. It's a Hermit Thrush."

JUSTICE at OUR LEVEL

When my father worked for Universal Atlas Cement, at the Buffington plant, he would often have lunch, or have a drink after work, at a place in East Chicago (Indiana), called DeMar's. The owner was a man named Giovanni (Gianni) DeMartini (as I recall), who had changed his name to Johnnie DeMar, because he thought it sounded 'more American'.

When my mother's brother got married, my father found himself at some kind of gathering to celebrate the marriage, and one of the people he was introduced to was the bride's brother. He was a County Clerk or an assistant County Clerk or some position of authority, of which the guy was quite proud and extraordinarily self-impressed. Apparently, my father didn't seem appropriately impressed with the title, and the man took offense. To make things clear, the guy told him "I could have you arrested, for no reason, and thrown in jail, and kept there as long as I like!"

It's difficult not to imagine my father snorting derisively, turning his back, and walking away from a statement like that. But, as he tells it, he didn't.

However, a couple days later, while sitting at the bar at Johnnie DeMar's, my father was telling Johnnie about this—just a little casual conversation between a bar-keep and a regular customer —and Johnnie DeMar leaned over the bar, looked my father in the eye and said this: "He says somethin' like that to you again and—if you want me to—I'll send a couple of my goombas over there to tune him up."

DeMar leaned back against the back bar, shrugged and added, "… if you want me to. Just let me know." After additional thought he said, "We'll see if he gets the message."

He paused, thought some more, and said, "IF he DON'T get the message, we can break some bones… but that'll cost you."

Later, when my father had paid and was getting up to leave, Mr. DeMar reiterated, "We'll tune him up for free, but if we gotta break some bones, that'll cost you."

CONCLUSION

There are a wide variety of people and events in America, as I know it, which share a common thread—the presumption of Liberty. Succinctly, that is the bullheaded determination to make our own decisions and to handle things ourselves, without oversight, interference or unnecessary restraint.

This book portrays America before the madness; that is, before any orchestrated attempts were being made to purposefully replace the presumption of Liberty with a seemingly ever-emerging litany of almost inconceivable mindlessness.

But, here's hope: Americans have limited tolerance for idiocy.

R I M

Oh man, I can't believe I forgot to mention climate change, again!

Mansfield also writes under the names Henry Edward Fool and Darryl Mockridge (depending upon his mood, I suppose) Here is a list of some of his published work:

WHEN I WAS A LOW-LIFE: An American Education--by Henry Edward Fool
The culmination of nearly 50 years of writing—as well as occasional thought—concerning 4 college years in Richmond, Virginia, beginning 1967.

WORDS FOR THIS CAN NOT BE FOUND poetry of a sort by Henry Edward Fool

AN AMERICAN SAVAGE IN A FRENCH HOTEL: An Accurate Accounting of the Various Reasons I Should Be Hung -by Henry Edward Fool
Concerning 12 years working in a small privately owned French Hotel, in San Francisco.

EARWIG, includes "Jack Nicholson IS Santa Claus"- by Darryl Mockridge

AMERICAN RACONTEUR: Real American Writin' for Real American Readin'
by Henry Edward Fool
Concerning events 18 years prior to, and the nearly 40 years after the events recorded in When I Was A Low-Life

LOST IN THE DIN: Why Your Opinion on Politics and Religion Means NOTHING, and mine means **even less** - by Henry Edward Fool
Politics as seen from an honest POV

REFINEMENT: How a Good Marriage Can Nudge an Unwary Man in the Direction of Civility - by Henry Edward Fool
Concerning (yes, I'm as surprised as you are) marriage.

QUIT SMOKING in 17 DAYS, if you truly wish to- by Darryl Mockridge
(a booklet for smokers who are too intelligent to continue nursing that mindless habit.)

TWO WEEKS IN BLETANTE - by Darryl Mockridge
A visit to a non-existent island nation reveals the fact that law and common sense need not necessarily be, in every instance, mutually exclusive.

RETURN TO BLETANTE - by Darryl Mockridge
Previously expelled from Bletante–and set adrift at sea in a rubber raft—Mockridge finds himself invited back; this time as a Greatly Honored Guest of the Island Nation.

WHY GOD GAVE US GUNS, and other stories without meaning - by Darryl Mockridge
Mockridge explains Political/Social situations in the US—at a time when the madness had just begun… you know, **before** the big sneeze—through easily digestible stories.